Continuous Cables

Continuous Cables

AN EXPLORATION OF KNITTED CABLED KNOTS, RINGS, SWIRLS, AND CURLICUES

20 Designs plus an All-Original Stitch Dictionary

by Melissa Leapman

POTTER CRAFT

NEW YORK

For Frederikka, with love

The author and publisher would like to thank the Craft Yarn Council of America for providing the yarn weight standards and accompanying icons used in this book. For more information, please visit www.YarnStandards.com.

Copyright © 2008 by Melissa Leapman

Published in the United States by Potter Craft, an imprint of the Crown Publishing Group, a division of Random House, Inc., New York.
www.crownpublishing.com
www.pottercraft.com

POTTER CRAFT and colophon is a registered trademark of Random House, Inc.

Library of Congress Cataloging-in-Publication Data

Leapman, Melissa.
    Continuous cables : an exploration of knitted cabled knots, rings, swirls, and curlicues : 20 designs plus an all-original stitch dictionary / by Melissa Leapman—1st ed.
        p.   cm.
    Includes index.
    ISBN-13: 978-0-307-34687-2 (alk. paper)   1. Knitting—Patterns.   I. Title.
    TT825.L3855 2008
    746.43'2041—dc22   2008001089

ISBN 978-0-307-34687-2

Printed in China

Design by 3&Co. (www.threeandco.com)
Fashion photography by Alexandra Grablewski
Flat fabric photography by Jacob Hand
Technical illustrations by Judy Love
All charts and schematic illustrations by Melissa Leapman
Technical editor: Charlotte Quiggle

10 9 8 7 6 5 4 3 2 1

First Edition

Acknowledgments

I'd like to thank the following individuals for testing the patterns and creating the samples for this book: Gwen Gotsch, Cindy Grosch, Catherine Hollingsworth, Petra Horst, Tom Jensen, Cheryl Keeley, JoAnn Moss, Joan Murphy, Holly Neiding, Rachel Nissen, Dawn Penny, Laura Polley, Pam Porter, Judy Seip, Norma Jean Sternschein, and Angie Tzoumakas.

Once again, thanks go to Cascade Yarn Company for providing an unbelievably generous amount of yarn for the Stitch Dictionary of this book. Their Cascade 220 wool yarn shows off cables beautifully, comes in a gazillion colors (at least!), is nicely priced with nearly endless yardage, and is an absolute joy to knit with.

Special thanks go to the Orpheus Chamber Orchestra (www.orpheusnyc.com), a wonderful group of collaborative musicians, for inspiring Motif 19 on page 170—and so much more.

I am especially grateful to Charlotte Quiggle, whose expert tech editing improved this manuscript in many ways. It is always a pleasure to work with—and to play with <grin>—her on the team! Thank you.

Contents

Introduction

Mention the phrase "cable knitting," and most people—knitters and non-knitters alike—envision textured ropes, twists, and braids winding up knitted fabrics. Typically, these cable patterns are vertically arranged, beginning at the lower edge, meandering throughout a knitted piece, and ending at the upper edge.

If you've seen my previous cable knitting book, *Cables Untangled*, then you are already familiar with the wonderful variety of patterns that can be created simply by knitting stitches out of sequence.

Do you know, however, that knitters can also create circular, closed-ring shapes with cables? Just imagine: curlicues, rings, swirls, knots—even intricate Celtic-inspired motifs—all richly embossed on knits! Unlike vertical cables, these patterns suddenly appear in the middle of a plain fabric and just as dramatically disappear. Along the way, they twist and turn, seemingly at will, forming either simple or very intricate designs. Watching each row build on the one before is engaging, gratifying, and fun.

The knitting skills required for these beautiful closed-ring cables are the same as those used for traditional cables, with only a few additions: special increases and decreases are used to make these cables appear to begin from nothing and later, just as magically, disappear.

For thick, highly embossed cables, more stitches are added; fewer are required for daintier ones. Depending on the increase method used to introduce a cable (or the decrease method used to close the cable), these closed rings can be either round or angular in shape. The possibilities are nearly endless. I've included more than eighty closed-ring patterns in the Stitch Dictionary, starting on page 129. Most are completely new cables designed just for this collection!

I hope you will find closed-ring cabling as fascinating—and as exciting!—as I do.

First Things First: Cables Are Easier Than They Look!

Although cables may appear complicated and hard to knit, this time-honored technique is actually quite simple. No matter how intricate they appear, all cables are created using the same simple method: stitches are just worked out of order, exchanging places within a row. Holding the stitches to the front or back will result in different textured patterns.

TOOLS

When knitting a cable, you temporarily place a stitch or group of stitches onto a holder (called a *cable needle*) to keep it out of the way while you are working another stitch or group of stitches. Cable needles come in many shapes and sizes, from tiny wooden toothpicks to U-shaped hooks to short straight tools with ridges or a dip in the center to hold the stitches.

I prefer to use a regular 7" (18cm) double-pointed knitting needle as my cable needle. The longer length makes it easy to grasp, and since these needles come in packs of four or five, I don't get concerned about losing one!

Cable needles are commercially available in a variety of materials and sizes. Metal ones are smooth and slick, making them suitable for sliding stitches quickly and easily; beginners, however, might find them a

little too slippery. Wooden ones, on the other hand, have just enough texture to grab cabling stitches, and this small amount of friction will prevent unwanted slipping and sliding. If your yarn is especially slippery—such as rayon, bamboo, or mercerized cotton—these wooden needles are ideal.

Of course, in a pinch (like when you're aboard a plane), you can use whatever is handy: a bobby pin, an untwisted paper clip, a drinking straw—even a pen or pencil! Just be sure that your cabling tool has a smaller circumference than your main knitting needles; otherwise, you'll risk stretching the stitches as you transfer them.

Better yet, learn the technique of cabling without a cable needle described on pages 15 and 16. That way, you'll be good to go without any special cabling equipment at all!

BASIC CABLING HOW-TOS

Stitches in cables appear to travel toward the left or right, depending on where you hold the cable needle while knitting. If the cable needle is parked in front of the fabric, the cable moves to the left (see Left Cross); if it's placed in back, the cable moves to the right (see Right Cross).

CABLING UP CLOSE

Always slip stitches onto a cable needle purlwise (rather than knitwise), so that the stitches remain positioned on the needle correctly, ready to knit; this way they won't become twisted.

Sometimes, knit stitches move over other knit stitches to create beautiful textures (such as in the Cross Cables on pages 11 and 12).

Completely different patterns result when a combination of knit and purl stitches is worked while cabling. In the Traveling Cables described on pages 13 and 14, smooth knit stitches move across bumpy purl background stitches. Worked in pairs, these cables can create diamonds or zigzags.

CABLING UP CLOSE

For some knitters, the leftmost knit stitch on cables—and even on basic ribbings—tends to be oversized and wonky looking. It's easy to prevent this unevenness from occurring. Actually, the hardest part is remembering to do it! The fix involves the purl stitch to the left of the offending knit stitch. Here's what to do: on right-side rows, work the offending knit stitch the way you normally would. Then, when working the purl stitch immediately to its left, insert your right-hand needle into the stitch purlwise as you normally would, but wrap the yarn around the needle in the *opposite* direction—clockwise rather than counterclockwise—as you purl the stitch (see illustration below).

On the next row, this stitch will present itself to you as a twisted knit stitch. Knit it *through the back loop* to untwist it. As awkward as it seems at first, wrapping the yarn that other way uses up slightly less yarn and tightens up the knit stitch to the right.

Fortunately, most cabling is done on right-side rows, making it fun to watch the patterns develop—and rather easy to detect mistakes shortly after making them.

CABLING UP CLOSE

If you find you've crossed a cable in the wrong direction (even many, many rows later), relax. There's no need to rip out your precious knitting! Just unravel the cable down to the spot where the mistake occurred, and use a crochet hook to work the stitches back up, correctly recrossing the cable as you go.

Often, wrong-side rows are worked by simply knitting the knit stitches and purling the purl stitches as you see them on your needle. In many cases, you won't even need to refer to the chart while zipping through them. Some patterns, in fact, don't even include the wrong-side rows on the charts at all. Instead, only every other row is shown, with the tacit understanding that wrong-side rows are worked as the stitches present themselves.

To create different cable patterns, various combinations of stitches can be crossed, such as one stitch over two stitches, two stitches over two other stitches, or twelve stitches over another twelve stitches. With all these possibilities, the design variations are infinite! Be sure to check your pattern for the specifics for your particular project.

Cross Cables
Left Cross
(also known as Front Cross)

To cross a cable to the left, you'll hold the stitches on the cable needle to the front while working other stitches.

To cross two knit stitches to the left over two other knit stitches, for example, slip two stitches onto the cable needle purlwise (to avoid twisting them), and hold them in front of the fabric (see illustration 1).

Illustration 1

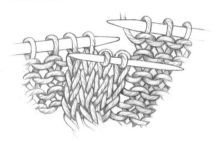

CABLING UP CLOSE

If you're using a double-pointed knitting needle as your cable needle, position it directly in front of the main left-hand knitting needle horizontally, and grasp both needles with your left hand as if they were one. Your cable tool will be out of your way as you work that first set of stitches, and you won't have to worry about it slipping out!

Now, working behind the stitches on the cable needle, knit two stitches from the main left-hand needle.

Finally, knit the two stitches that are being held on the cable needle (see illustration 2).

Illustration 2

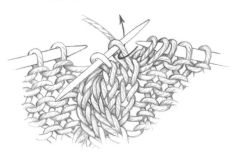

Take a look at what you've just done: the two stitches that used to be on the right-hand side have moved to the left, in front of the other two stitches.

Right Cross
(also known as Back Cross)
To create a cable that crosses to the right, you'll hold the stitches on the cable needle to the *back* while working other stitches.

For example, to cross two knit stitches to the right over two other knit stitches, slip two stitches onto a cable needle purlwise (to avoid twisting them) and hold them in back of the fabric.

With the cable needle behind the work, knit the next two stitches from the main left-hand knitting needle (see illustration 3).

Illustration 3

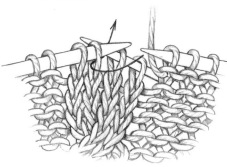

Now, knit the two stitches that are waiting on the cable needle (see illustration 4).

Illustration 4

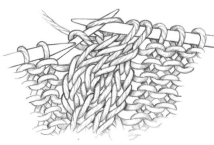

Examine your cable crossing: The two stitches that had been on the left-hand side have switched positions with the ones previously on the right; the ones on the right have crossed behind the ones on the left.

CABLING UP CLOSE
During your first few attempts at cabling, it might feel awkward to hold three different needles in your hands, and you might worry about dropping needles—or worse, stitches. Don't worry, your stitches won't unravel down to your cast-on edge! And remember, cabling, like any new skill, will seem easier and much more comfortable with practice. I'll bet you don't even remember how frustrated you were when you first learned to knit! Be patient with your needles—and yourself.

Twists
When a single knit stitch travels over another knit stitch, a little twist is formed. Like the Left and Right Cross, this maneuver can be performed using a cable needle, holding one stitch in front or behind the work as you knit.

Or, for faster knitting, use one of the following methods that don't require a cable needle at all!

Left Twist
Skip the first stitch on the left-hand needle, and with the right-hand needle behind the left, knit next stitch *through the back loop* (see illustration 5).

Illustration 5

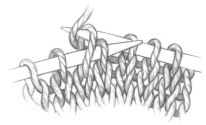

Knit the first stitch in its front loop the regular way, and then slip both stitches off the left-hand needle together (see illustration 6).

Illustration 6

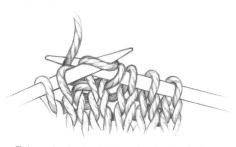

Take a look at what you've knitted: the two stitches have exchanged places, and the right-hand one has moved in front of the other stitch.

Right Twist
Knit two stitches together the regular way, but do not remove them from the left-hand needle (see illustration 7).

Illustration 7

Then, insert the point of the right-hand needle between these two stitches, and knit the first stitch again through its front loop (see illustration 8), and finally, slip both stitches off the left-hand needle together.

Illustration 8

Here, the two stitches have changed places, with the first one moving behind the second one.

Traveling Cables

Typically, stockinette stitch cables sit on a reverse stockinette stitch background. The contrasting background adds depth to the fabric, making the cabled sections "pop."

To move knit stitches to the left or to the right over purl stitches, simply place the stitches on the cable needle as before, but purl the background stitches instead of knitting them.

CABLING UP CLOSE

When you're knitting cables that contain both knit and purl stitches, be certain to bring the working yarn between the points of your main knitting needles when switching between knits and purls; if you wrap it around the right-hand needle instead, you'll inadvertently add a new stitch—not to mention a great big hole in your fabric.

Stitches Traveling to the Left

For two knit stitches traveling to the left over one purl stitch, for example, slip two stitches purlwise onto a cable needle, and hold them in front of the fabric.

Purl one stitch from the left-hand needle (see illustration 9).

Illustration 9

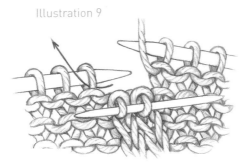

Then, knit the two stitches that are waiting on the cable needle (see illustration 10).

Illustration 10

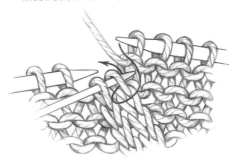

The two knit stitches have shifted one stitch to the left.

Stitches Traveling to the Right

To move two knit stitches to the right over one purl stitch, slip one stitch—the background stitch in this case—onto a cable needle purlwise, and hold it in back of the fabric.

Knit two stitches from the main left-hand needle (see illustration 11).

Illustration 11

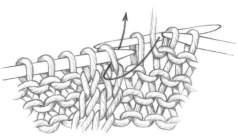

Then, purl the stitch that's waiting on the cable needle (see illustration 12).

Illustration 12

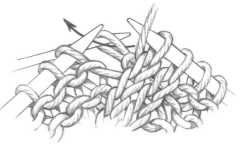

Here, the two knit stitches have moved one stitch to the right.

CABLING UP CLOSE

Whether you're a beginner or not, knowing whether to knit or purl a group of stitches when working these traveling cables can be confusing. To help keep things clear, keep in mind that when moving a stockinette stitch cable toward the left, purled background stitches will be worked first, with the traveling knitted stitches worked next; on the other hand, to move a cable toward the right, the knitted stitches must be worked first, with the purled background stitches worked second.

Of course, background fabrics other than reverse stockinette can be effective, too. Seed stitch is used in the woman's Quick-to-Knit Bulky Pullover on page 84, and a simple textured pattern is used in the Tweed Hoodie on page 93. These fabrics are not any more difficult to knit, although they might require a more vigilant reading of the charts.

Axis Cables

Axis cables are comprised of three groups of stitches: two outer sections are crossed in front of (or sometimes behind) a center group of stitches that remains stationary. In closed-ring cables, they are used when the stockinette "strands" cross over each other. Like other cables, they can cross to the left or to the right. To do this maneuver, two cable needles are used.

CABLING UP CLOSE

Hanging onto all those needles—let alone keeping track of where they go!—can definitely feel awkward. Using double-pointed needles instead of regular cable needles here can make the entire operation easier.

Left Axis Cable

In a Left Axis cable, stitches on the right-hand side cross over and exchange places with stitches on the left-hand side. To cross two knit stitches to the left over two knit stitches with a single purl stitch in the center as an axis, slip two stitches onto the first cable needle purlwise and hold them in front of the fabric, then slip the next stitch onto the second cable needle purlwise and hold it in back of the fabric, then knit the

next two stitches from the main left-hand needle (see illustration 13).

Illustration 13

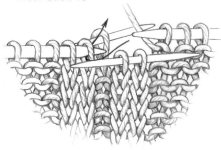

Purl the single stitch that's sitting on the second cable needle behind the work (see illustration 14).

Illustration 14

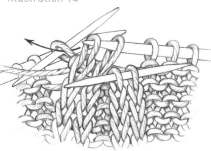

Finally, knit the two stitches from the first cable needle that is waiting in the front (see illustration 15).

Illustration 15

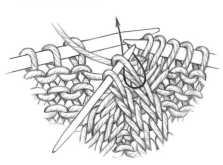

Two stitches have crossed over two other stitches toward the left, with a single purl stitch as the axis (see illustration 16).

Illustration 16

Right Axis Cable

Here, stitches on the left-hand side cross over and exchange places with stitches on the right-hand side. For example, to cross two sets of knit stitches over a single purl stitch toward the right, slip two stitches onto the first cable needle purlwise and hold them behind the fabric, then slip the middle axis stitch onto the second cable needle and hold it behind the work as well (see illustration 17).

Illustration 17

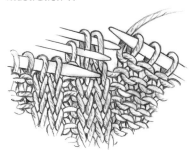

Knit two stitches from the main left-hand knitting needle (see illustration 18).

Illustration 18

For the central axis, purl the single stitch that is on the second cable needle (see illustration 19).

Illustration 19

Then, knit the two stitches from the remaining cable needle (see illustration 20).

Illustration 20

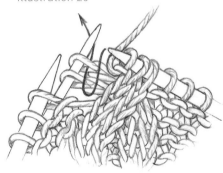

In this cable, two stitches have crossed over two other stitches toward the right, with a single purl stitch as the axis (see illustration 21).

Illustration 21

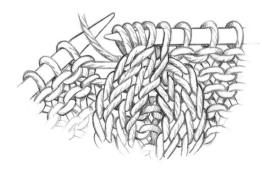

CABLING UP CLOSE
The first few times you try to knit axis cables, have someone read the text to you out loud as you knit. It'll be easier for you to manipulate the stitches and needles without also having to look down at a page!

CABLING WITHOUT A CABLE NEEDLE

Knitting isn't a race, but sometimes you'll want to speed things up. To make your cabling quicker, you can cross the stitches without a cable needle. This process involves setting up the stitches in their cabling position before knitting them.

For a Left Cross with two knit stitches over two other knit stitches, for example, slip all four stitches purlwise from the left-hand needle onto the right-hand needle (see illustration 22).

Illustration 22

Then, with the left-hand needle in front of the right-hand needle, skip the first two stitches on the right-hand needle, and insert the left-hand needle into the next two stitches on the right-hand needle from left to right (see illustration 23).

Illustration 23

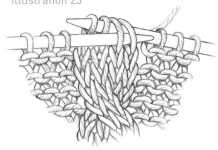

Now, slip all four stitches off the right-hand needle, allowing those first two stitches to hang in midair in the back of your work (see illustration 24). Don't forget to breathe here. And don't worry: those two stitches aren't going to go anywhere.

Illustration 24

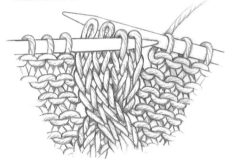

Rescue those two hanging stitches by placing them onto the right-hand needle from right to left (see illustration 25).

Illustration 25

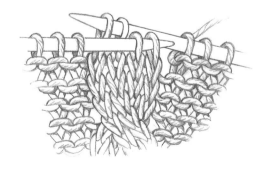

Slip the two stitches back onto the left-hand needle (see illustration 26).

Illustration 26

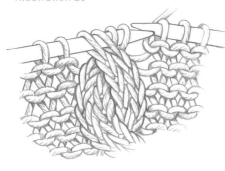

There! You've arranged the four stitches into their cabling position, so all you have to do is knit them in the order they present themselves to you on the left-hand needle.

To work a Right Cross with two stitches over two stitches without a cable needle, slip all four stitches onto the right-hand needle purlwise (see illustration 27).

Illustration 27

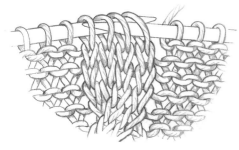

Working behind the right-hand needle, skip the first two stitches and insert the left-hand needle into the next two stitches from left to right (see illustration 28).

Illustration 28

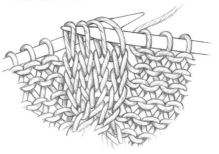

Slip all four stitches off the right-hand needle, allowing the first group of stitches to dangle in front of the work (see illustration 29). Don't forget to breathe!

Illustration 29

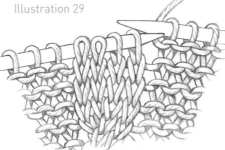

Working in front of the left-hand needle, replace those two hanging stitches back onto the right-hand needle (see illustration 30).

Illustration 30

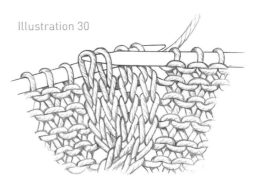

Finally, slip all four stitches back onto the left-hand needle (see illustration 31).

Illustration 31

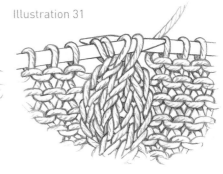

Knit these four stitches from the left-hand needle sequentially.

Knitting in Circles: Closed-Ring Cables

Using strategically placed increases and decreases, knitters can create circular cables that begin and end in the middle of the fabric. The bottoms and tops of these closed-rings can be either round or pointy, depending on the types of increases and decreases used.

CABLES AND GAUGE

Cables affect the gauge of knitted fabrics by drawing it in widthwise. Medium or worsted-weight yarn, for example, knits up to between 16 and 20 stitches over 4" (10cm). When worked in an allover cable pattern such as the Celtic Cables Pattern in the Fireside Afghan on page 44, however, worsted-weight yarn produces fabric with 22 stitches over 4" (10cm). Those extra 2–6 stitches might not seem like much, but they will certainly add up over a large area, such as a sweater or an afghan. Therefore, if a cable is started smack-dab in the middle of a stockinette or other non-cabled background, the fabric will gather just below and above the cabled section, creating an unwanted pleat or pucker.

In order to maintain the width of the fabric, new stitches must be added—quickly and dramatically—where the cabled sections start and then eliminated immediately when the cables are complete.

The number of increases (and subsequent decreases) required depends on the number of stitches that comprise the stockinette strands in the cables and on the shape of the closed rings.

CABLING UP CLOSE

Since the stitch count for these cables varies depending on which row of the cable you're on, it is important that you match the row gauge as well as the stitch gauge indicated in the project pattern in order for your garment to match the schematic.

The methods for increasing and decreasing described in this chapter are perfect for closed-ring cables: They're localized and will keep the knitted fabric uniform and without holes. Be sure to select the ones that will give you the rounded or pointy shape you want.

Let's explore round-shaped closed rings first and pointy ones second.

ROUND-SHAPED CLOSED-RING CABLES

Increases at the Base of Round-Shaped Closed-Ring Cables

To create a smooth, round bottom to a closed-ring cable, stitches are increased into a center stitch, with additional invisible increases worked on either side of this stitch.

If the stockinette portion of the cable is going to be two stitches across (such as in Panel 10 on page 136 or Motif 22 on page 173), then five stitches must be worked where there once was a single stitch.

If, however, the stockinette section of the cable will be three stitches wide instead of two stitches (such as in Panel 41 on page 156 or Motif 24 on page 175), then seven stitches must be worked where there once was a single stitch. This more dramatic increase is worked over two rows instead of one.

As knitters, we have many possible ways to add stitches. For example, we can knit into the front and back of a single stitch, creating two stitches where there used to be only one, but then there's a visible bump at the bottom of the increase. Or, we can work an alternating series of knit stitches and yarn overs all into a single stitch (as when making a bobble), but that causes a hole in the fabric, which isn't desirable at the bottom of a closed ring. For beautiful results, use the increase method described in this chapter that corresponds to the shape you would like for your closed ring.

Here's how to add stitches for the bottom of a rounded closed-ring cable:

First, do an invisible "**Make One Increase**" (abbreviated M1) by using the left-hand needle to scoop up the horizontal strand of yarn that's hanging between the knitting needles from front to back, and then knit this strand *through the back loop*, thereby twisting it to prevent a hole (see illustration 1). You've created one new stitch.

Illustration 1

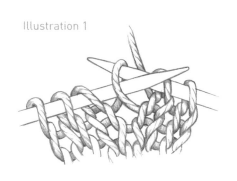

CABLING UP CLOSE

Sometimes, it might feel clumsy trying to get into the back loop. If it does, try inserting your right-hand needle into the front loop first, purlwise, and then bring it over and around the left-hand needle to the back. Sure, it'll take an extra second to do this little maneuver, but you'll get your needle into the desired position on the very first try!

Next, make an inconspicuous "**Three-in-One Increase**" (3-in-1 inc) into the next stitch by knitting into the back and then into the front of the indicated stitch, in that order, and then slip the two stitches off the left-hand needle and onto the right-hand needle (see illustration 2).

Illustration 2

To create the third stitch of this special increase, insert the left-hand needle from back to front into the little vertical strand that's beneath the two stitches just made (see illustration 3). Just pull up on it a little to create enough space for your needle to fit.

Illustration 3

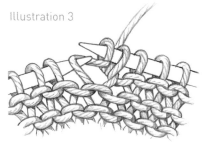

Now, knit into this vertical strand through its front loop (see illustration 4). This maneuver might seem awkward at first because of how tight it feels, but that's normal. After all, the main goal here is to add new stitches without creating holes below them!

Illustration 4

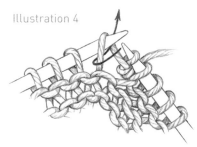

So far, you have worked four of the five stitches that are needed for the bottom of the closed-ring cable. For the final increased stitch, do another "Make One Increase." Be sure to scoop up that horizontal strand from front to back and then knit it *through the back loop*!

CABLING UP CLOSE

This last increase will likely feel extremely tight since five stitches are being worked where only one stitch existed in the previous row. If you become frustrated, consider using needles with very pointy tips, such as those currently marketed to lace knitters. The longer, narrow points will make it easier for you to get your needle into the desired spot.

Now, if the stockinette section of your cable consists of two stitches, you've already increased all the stitches required for a smooth, pucker-free start to the closed-ring design. But to create a thicker three-stitch cable, you still need to add two more stitches (one for each side of the cable). You will do this on the following row by working (purl, yarn over, purl) into the center stitch of that "Three-in-One Increase" from the previous row. This increase also creates three stitches out of one stitch.

Here's how to do the **"P1, Yarn Over, P1 Increase"**:

To begin, with the yarn in front, insert the right-hand needle purlwise into the indicated stitch and make a purl stitch, but don't remove the stitch from the left-hand needle (see illustration 5).

Illustration 5

Now, wrap the yarn around the needle from front to back to front to create a yarn over (see illustration 6). Still, do not remove the two stitches from the left-hand needle yet.

Illustration 6

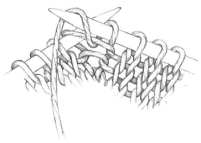

Next, to create the third stitch of this particular increase, reinsert the right-hand needle into that same stitch purlwise, and purl the stitch once more (see illustration 7).

Illustration 7

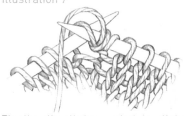

Finally, slip all three stitches off the left-hand needle and onto the right-hand needle.

CABLING UP CLOSE
Twisted Knit & Purl Stitches

Admittedly, those three new stitches will probably look just like a bunched-up mess on your right-hand needle. On the next row, however, everything will fall into place: the two outer stitches will each become part of the cabled stockinette section, and that yarn over in the center will be purled *through the back loop* to become part of the background for the middle of the closed ring. When purling *through the back loop*, be sure to insert the tip of the right-hand needle from back to front through the back leg of the yarn over (see illustration).

Now you have successfully added enough stitches for a rounded-bottom closed-ring cable.

Decreases at the Top of Round-Shaped Closed-Ring Cables

At the base of round-shaped closed rings, 5 or 7 stitches were worked where originally there was only one stitch. To create a nice, rounded shape at the top, those stitches must be decreased all at once in such a way that both sides of the ring come together in the center.

CABLING UP CLOSE

Of course, there are several decrease techniques, including simply knitting all the stitches together as one stitch, but that would create an unattractive bump on the fabric. For a smooth finish to a closed-ring cable, use one of the methods described in this chapter, choosing the one that corresponds to the shape you desire: round or pointy.

If you are working a cable that has 2-stitch stockinette sides with one purl stitch in between, you will combine all 5 of these stitches into a single stitch to close the cable. To do this, you will work a **"Five-to-One Decrease"** (5-to-1 dec) as follows. This technique involves manipulating stitches without knitting them, simply passing each stitch over a center stitch, one by one in alternate directions, until only the middle stitch remains.

Drop the working yarn to the back, and slip 3 stitches from the left-hand needle onto the right-hand needle.

*Pass the second stitch on the right-hand needle over the first stitch as if you were binding it off (see illustration 8).

◇◇◇

Illustration 8

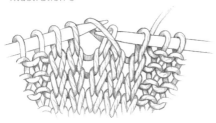

Slip the first stitch from the right-hand needle back onto the left-hand needle, and pass the second stitch on the left-hand needle over the first stitch (as if you were binding it off, except it will be in the opposite direction)* (see illustration 9).

Illustration 9

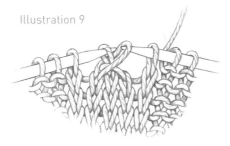

Now, slip the first stitch from the left-hand needle back onto the right-hand needle, and repeat from * to * once more.

Finally, knit the remaining stitch. Five stitches have been combined into one stitch.

CABLING UP CLOSE

On a first reading, this decrease technique might appear complicated, but it is really quite simple. Try having someone read it aloud to you as you actually do it with your needles and yarn. It'll be much easier to grasp when you aren't trying to knit and read at the same time.

If the stockinette sections of your cable are three stitches across (three knit stitches on each side with one purl stitch in the middle rather than two knit stitches on each side with one central purl stitch), just use a "Seven-to-One Decrease" (7-to-1 dec) instead of the "Five-to-One Decrease." It is worked the same way, except four stitches are slipped to begin with, and the steps from * to * are repeated twice more, instead of just once.

POINTY-SHAPED CLOSED-RING CABLES
Increases at the Base of Pointy-Shaped Closed-Ring Cables

To form closed-ring cables with more angular, pointy bottoms (such as Motif 28 on page 178 and Horizontal Band 9 on page 187), you will add stitches by making a pair of mirrored increases: a left-slanting increase in one stitch and a right-slanting increase into the following stitch. This technique looks different when worked into knit and purl stitches, so let's look at them separately.

To do a **"Left-Slanting Lifted Increase" into a purl stitch,** place the working yarn in the back, and insert the left-hand needle from front to back into the purl bump that is two rows below the first stitch on the right-hand needle (see illustration 10).

Illustration 10

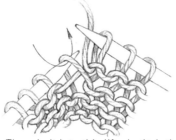

Then, knit into this lifted stitch the regular way to create an untwisted knit stitch (see illustration 11).

Illustration 11

For a **"Right-Slanting Lifted Increase" into a purl stitch,** with the yarn in the back of the work, insert the right-hand needle from front to back into the purl bump one row below the first stitch on the left-hand needle (see illustration 12).

Illustration 12

Now, place that lifted purl bump onto the left-hand needle, and knit it *through the back loop* (see illustration 13).

Illustration 13

After you've knitted into that purl bump in the row below, purl the stitch (which is still on the tip of your left-hand needle) as you normally would.

For a **"Left-Slanting Lifted Increase" into a knit stitch,** keep the working yarn in the back, and insert the left-hand needle from back to front into the left leg of the first stitch on the right-hand needle two rows below (see illustration 14).

◇◇◇

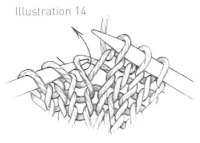

Illustration 14

Then, knit this loop *through the back loop* (see illustration 15).

Illustration 15

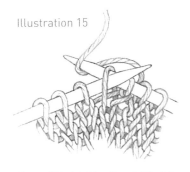

For a **"Right-Slanting Lifted Increase" into a knit stitch,** keep the working yarn in the back, and insert the right-hand needle from back to front into the right leg of the first stitch on the left-hand needle one row below (see illustration 16).

Illustration 16

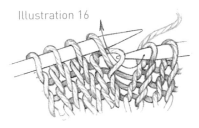

Place the lifted stitch onto the left-hand needle, then knit the lifted leg the regular way to create an untwisted knit stitch see illustration 17).

Illustration 17

After you've knitted into that lifted stitch, knit the stitch that's still on the tip of your left-hand needle as you normally would.

In each case, one stitch has been increased. By arranging increases in pairs—one slanting to the left and one slanting to the right—the base of the closed-ring cable appears seamless.

Decreases at the Top of Pointy-Shaped Closed-Ring Cables

At the base of pointy-shaped closed rings, four new stitches were added over two right-side rows—that's three rows total. At the top, those same four stitches will be quickly eliminated over two consecutive rows to create an angular shape.

Like the left- and right-slanting lifted increases at the base, the decreases will be worked in pairs, with one leaning to the left and the other leaning to the right: a left-slanting "SSK Decrease" and a right-slanting "K2tog Decrease."

For the **"SSK Decrease"** (also known as "Slip, Slip, Knit"), slip two stitches from the left-hand needle onto the right-hand needle one at a time knitwise (see illustration 18).

Illustration 18

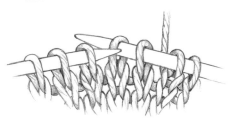

Then insert the point of the left-hand needle into the fronts of these two stitches, and knit them together from this position (see illustration 19).

Illustration 19

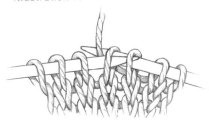

The resulting decrease stitch clearly slants toward the left.

For the **"K2tog Decrease"**—the simplest type of decrease in knitting—just insert the right-hand needle into two stitches on the left-hand needle instead of one stitch, and then knit them together as if they were one stitch.

Here, the resulting decrease stitch slants toward the right.

CABLING UP CLOSE

The second set of decreases for this pointy-shaped closed ring is worked on a wrong-side row. Knitters don't usually like performing exciting technical maneuvers on wrong-side rows, but here's one of those times it cannot be avoided. When the "SSK Decrease" and "K2tog Decrease" are done on the wrong side, they will appear as purl stitches on the right side of the fabric, gracefully "eating up" the stockinette strands that had created the closed rings!

The Foreign Language of Knitting Symbols and Charts

At first glance, knitting patterns seem to be written in a secret code of cryptic characters laid out mysteriously on a grid. Actually, the charts are wonderful visual tools that can make reading knitting patterns easier than those wordy instructions. Like foreign languages, knitting charts and their symbols are simple to translate once you're familiar with the "grammar" and "vocabulary."

A QUICK LESSON IN GRAMMAR

A knitting chart is a visual representation of the public side of knitted fabric.

Each square of the grid corresponds to one stitch, and each row of squares corresponds to one row of stitches.

Charts are read in the same way that the fabric is knit—from the lower edge up, with the first row at the bottom of the chart and the last row at the top.

Right-side rows are read from right to left, in the same order that stitches present themselves to you on the left-hand knitting needle. The following illustration shows the order that stitches will be worked for Row 1, a right-side row, in a chart:

6 5 4 3 2 1 ← 1 (RS)

Of course, at the end of this first row, you flip your knitting before starting the next row, and the wrong-side of the fabric faces you. Physically, the first stitch of this wrong-side row is the same stitch as the last stitch of the right-side row you just completed. Thus, wrong-side rows on charts are read in the opposite direction, from left to right, as shown below:

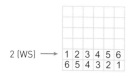

2 (WS) → 1 2 3 4 5 6
6 5 4 3 2 1

CABLING UP CLOSE

You might find it helpful to draw arrows on the left-hand side of wrong-side rows as a visual reminder that you'll be reading them from left to right. Some folks put arrows on the right-hand side of odd-numbered right-side rows, too.

Charts make it easy to see how many stitches are involved in a pattern. In some charts, bold vertical lines indicate the stitch repeat, and if extra stitches are required on each side to center the pattern on the fabric, they are shown to the left and right of the

CABLING UP CLOSE

Use sticky notes or a metal board with magnetic strips to keep track of where you are on the chart. Place the notes or strips immediately *above* the row you're on so you can see how that row relates to the rows you've already completed. Once you finish a row, just move the marker up!

Or, make a copy of the chart and use a highlighting marker to cross out the rows you've completed. This way, you can still see what's transpired on previous rows, and the row you're working on is still bright white.

repeat. In the woman's Swirl Pullover (page 74), the Lattice Pattern has a multiple of four plus six stitches; it is a four-stitch repeat with three "balancing" stitches on each side. To read the chart above, right, for example, you'd start at the lower right-hand corner, read from right to left, work the four stitches between the two bold lines as many times as is necessary to get across your fabric, and end the row with the stitch represented in this sample chart by the star. This stitch sits outside the stitch repeat and so is worked once per row. It is the last stitch of every right-side row, and since wrong-side rows are read from left to right, it is the first stitch of these rows.

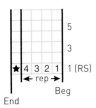

CABLING UP CLOSE
When working in the round rather than back and forth in rows, such as for the Simple Hat on page 39, the right side of the fabric is always facing you, so all rows of the chart are read from right to left.

As you glance through this book, you will notice that some of the charts (like Motif 9 on page 162, for instance) have irregular shapes rather than being rectangular as is usually the case. That's because the stitch count is not a constant for all rows in the pattern; remember, stitches are sometimes added just before cabled areas and are removed immediately after them in order to maintain the

CABLING UP CLOSE
Sometimes, individual pieces or sizes of the same garment will have different beginning and ending points within the stitch pattern. In the Traveling Diamonds Pattern for the woman's Sage Tunic on page 70, the sleeves and neckband begin at different spots in the chart. But don't worry! The tag lines underneath the chart tell you exactly what to do: when knitting the sleeves for this garment, you'll cast on a multiple of ten plus eleven stitches; when knitting the neckband, you'll cast on just the multiple of ten stitches. When reading the chart, begin and end where indicated for that particular piece of the garment.

width of the fabric. Even though the edges of the chart look uneven, the resulting fabric will have straight sides, unless the chart includes areas where actual shaping occurs (like for the top of a hat). Perfectly rectangular charts deal with the changing stitch count in a different way, by including gray-filled squares that "hold" the place where stitches either were or will eventually be. But more about that later. . . .

THE VOCABULARY LIST
Each symbol on a chart indicates the way a stitch or group of stitches will be worked, and the arrangement of symbols on the chart determines the stitch pattern.

Usually, the symbols visually resemble the way the resulting stitches will appear on the public side of the knitted fabric. The symbol for a knit stitch, for example, is a blank box,

mimicking the flat appearance of the knit stitch itself; the dot symbol for a purl stitch depicts the bumpy appearance of a purled stitch.

A symbol that occupies several squares of the grid indicates the number of stitches that will be involved in that particular knitting maneuver. Cables, obviously, are worked over more than one stitch, so cable symbols occupy several adjacent squares. In the charts in this book, each line or dot within every cable symbol represents one of the stitches being crossed, so you can quickly tell at a glance the number of stitches involved. For instance, three lines crossing three other lines would symbolize a six-stitch cable.

In many of these closed-ring cable charts, you will see gray squares. These symbols represent the places where stitches will eventually sit; until those stitches are increased into the fabric, the gray squares act as place holders for them. They are important because they allow all the cables and other stitches to visually line up correctly in the chart, but you will skip over them when you work a row containing them.

CABLING UP CLOSE
Those gray squares are called *No Stitch* in the Comprehensive Glossary of Symbols and in the Stitch Keys because you pay no attention to them when you see them in the chart. Don't slip a stitch on your needles but just skip over the gray square and move on to the next symbol.

At the top of the closed rings, it's easy to look at the symbols for the dramatic decreases and know how many stitches are involved: the numeral "five" underneath the little teepee signifies that you must decrease five stitches into one stitch, and the numeral "seven" lets you know that you will be decreasing seven stitches into one. It's rather intuitive, don't you think?

Even cable symbols look like the knitting maneuvers they represent. In a Left Cross, the dominant lines in the symbol cross toward the left, with the right-hand stitches moving in front of the others. When knitting the symbol, this is your clue to place the cable needle holding those stitches in front of your work.

On the other hand, Right Cross cable symbols show the left-hand stitches moving over the others toward the right. Since the right-hand stitches appear to be moving behind the left-hand ones, you will slip them onto your cable needle and hold them in back.

When knit stitches travel over other knit stitches in a cable, the symbol has diagonal lines representing the background stitches. However, if knit stitches travel over purl stitches instead, the cable symbol will have dots to represent the background stitches, as seen below.

All rows in charts are shown as they appear on the public side of the fabric. Consequently, the same symbol means different things on right-side and wrong-side rows. The blank box, for instance, represents a knit stitch on a right-side row, but if you're on a wrong-side row and want the stitch to appear as a knit stitch on the reverse side of the fabric, you must purl it.

CABLING UP CLOSE

Some knitters like to use a yellow highlighter to mark the wrong-side rows of charts. For them, it's a visual signal that symbols on those rows must be reversed—knit for purl and vice versa.

If a symbol is used on both right- and wrong-side rows of the chart, the stitch key will tell you which knitting maneuver to use where.

Usually, wrong-side rows are pretty simple: you just knit the knit stitches and purl the purl stitches as they present themselves to you on the knitting needle. Scan the entire chart before you begin knitting to confirm that this is the case. If so, you can zip along those wrong-side rows reading your knitting rather than the chart!

CABLING UP CLOSE

Some publications don't even include the wrong-side rows on the charts at all! Their rows are marked on the right-hand side with odd numbers only. This means that on wrong-side rows you'll just knit the knits and purl the purls when you get to them.

I'll bet that with some practice—and yes, a little bit of patience!—you'll find knitting from charts easy, fast, and maybe even fun!

CABLING UP CLOSE

- Enlarge your charts on a copier to make reading them easier.
- If you're an exceptionally visual person, use a color key to simplify reading the symbols: Choose a different color highlighter for each symbol (see illustration). Instead of deciphering each symbol individually, you'll have a useful color code!
- Place stitch markers on your knitting needles to separate each pattern repeat or panel.
- Use a row counter to keep track of where you are on the chart. If each cable panel across the width of your fabric has a different row repeat, use a separate row counter for each one.
- Study the stitch chart before working your pattern, especially if there are different cables in a panel that turn at different spots. Check to see whether the cables are related: Often cables

5

3

1 (RS)

KEY

☐ = K on RS; P on WS

• = P on RS; K on WS

 = Slip 2 sts onto cn and hold in front; P1; K2 from cn

 = Slip next st onto cn and hold in back; K2; P1 from cn

 = Slip 2 sts onto cn and hold in front; K2; K2 from cn

within a panel are balanced and turn on rows that are multiples of each other. For example, a narrow cable may turn every fourth row while a wider one turns evey eighth row. The cable

that turns at a faster rate can function as a handy "row counter" for determining when to work the cables whose turns occur at longer intervals.

- Use a length of waste yarn (thinner than and a different color from your main yarn) as a "row counter" to remind you when to turn a cable. For example, if you are working a cable that turns every eight rows, run the waste yarn up the side of the first 8-row cable in the row. Flip it forward on the first cabled row; after working four more rows, flip it toward the back of the fabric. Work four rows, flip it forward, and work your next cable row. The waste yarn will weave in and out of the fabric every four rows, and you'll never forget to turn that cable. If you have multiple cables that turn on different rows, use multiple pieces of waste yarn. When you are finished, just pull them out!

Abbreviations

ch chain

cn cable needle

g gram(s)

k knit

k3tog knit three stitches together in their front loops as one stitch

k2tog knit two stitches together in their front loops as one stitch

M1 insert LH needle under the horizontal strand between two stitches from front to back, and knit it *through the back loop*

M1P insert LH needle under the horizontal strand between two stitches from front to back, and purl it *through the back loop*

mm millimeter(s)

oz ounces

p purl

p2sso pass two slipped stitches over other stitch(es)

rnd(s) round(s)

sc single crochet

ssk slip the first and second stitches one at a time knitwise, then insert the point of the left-hand needle into the fronts of these stitches and knit them together from this position

ssp slip the first and second stitches one at a time knitwise, then slip them back to the left-hand needle; insert the point of the right-hand needle *through the back loops* of the two stitches (going into the second stitch first), and purl them together as one stitch

sssk slip the first, second, and third stitches one at a time knitwise, then insert the point of the left-hand needle into the fronts of these stitches and knit them together from this position

sssp slip the first, second, and third stitches one at a time knitwise, then slip them back to the left-hand needle; insert the point of the right-hand needle *through the back loops* of the three stitches (going into the third stitch first) and purl them together as one stitch

yd yard(s)

* repeat instructions after asterisk or between asterisks across row or for as many times as instructed

( ) repeat instructions within parentheses for as many times as instructed

[ ] repeat instructions within parentheses for as many times as instructed

Comprehensive Glossary to all Symbols Used in This Book

□ = K on RS; P on WS

• = P on RS; K on WS

■ = No stitch

Ω = K *through back loop* on RS; P *through back loop* on WS

Ω = P *through back loop* on RS; K *through back loop* on WS

K = Knot = K into (front, back, front) of next st, turn; P3, turn; slip 2 sts at once knitwise, K1, p2sso

B = Bobble = K into (front, back, front) of next st, turn; P1, (P1, yarn over, P1) all into next st, P1, turn; K5, turn; P2tog, P1, P2tog, turn; slip 2 sts at once knitwise, K1, P2sso

V = Increase 1 st = K into front and then into back of st

M = M1 Knitwise = Insert LH needle under the horizontal strand between two sts from front to back and K it *through back loop*

M = M1 Purlwise = Insert LH needle under the horizontal strand between two sts from front to back and P it *through back loop*

⋎ = Right-slanting lifted increase (see page 20)

⋏ = Left-slanting lifted increase (see pages 20–21)

Ⅴ = Central Double Increase = (Increases from 1 st to 3 sts) = K into back and then into front of indicated st and slip them off LH needle onto RH needle; insert point of LH needle behind the vertical strand that runs downward between the two sts just made and K *into the front of it*

⅋ = (Increases from 1 st to 3 sts) = (P1, yarn over, P1) into next st

⅋ = (Increases from 1 st to 3 sts) = (K1, yarn over, K1) into next st

⋋ = K2tog on RS; P2tog on WS

⋌ = SSK on RS; SSP on WS

⋌ = SSP on RS; SSK on WS

⋋ = P2tog on RS; K2tog on WS

⋌ = K3tog on RS; P3tog on WS

⋋ = SSSK on RS; SSSP on WS

⋏₃ = (Decreases from 3 sts to 1 st) = Slip next 2 sts with yarn in back, drop yarn; *pass the second st on RH needle over the first st on RH needle; slip first st from RH needle back to LH needle; pass the second st on LH needle over the first st on LH needle; pick up yarn and K remaining st

⋏₅ = (Decreases from 5 sts to 1 st) = Slip next 3 sts with yarn in back, drop yarn; *pass the second st on RH needle over the first st on RH needle; slip first st from RH needle back to LH needle; pass the second st on LH needle over the first st on LH needle; **slip first st from LH needle back to RH needle and repeat from * to ** once more; pick up yarn and K remaining st

⋏₇ = (Decreases from 7 sts to 1 st) = Slip next 4 sts with yarn in back, drop yarn; *pass the second st on RH needle over the first st on RH needle; slip first st from RH needle back to LH needle; pass the second st on LH needle over the first st on LH needle; **slip first st from LH needle back to RH needle and repeat from * to ** twice more; pick up yarn and K remaining st

⤫ = Right Twist = Slip next st onto cn and hold in back; K1; K1 from cn **OR** K2tog, leaving them on LH needle; insert point of RH needle between these 2 sts and K the first one again

⤬ = Left Twist = Slip next st onto cn and hold in front; K1; K1 from cn **OR** skip first st and K next st in back loop; then K the skipped st; slip both sts off LH needle together

⤫ = Slip next st onto cn and hold in back; K1; P1 from cn

⤬ = Slip next st onto cn and hold in front; P1; K1 from cn

◇◇

= Slip 2 sts onto cn and hold in back; K1; K2 from cn

= Slip next st onto cn and hold in back; K2; K1 from cn

= Slip 2 sts onto cn and hold in front; K1; K2 from cn

= Slip next st onto cn and hold in back; K2; P1 from cn

= Slip 2 sts onto cn and hold in front; P1; K2 from cn

= Slip 2 sts onto cn and hold in back; K2; K2 from cn

= Slip 2 sts onto cn and hold in front; K2; K2 from cn

= Slip 2 sts onto cn and hold in back; K2; P2 from cn

= Slip 2 sts onto cn and hold in front; P2; K2 from cn

= Slip next st onto cn and hold in back; K3; K1 from cn

= Slip 3 sts onto cn and hold in front; K1; K3 from cn

= Slip next st onto cn and hold in back; K3; P1 from cn

= Slip 3 sts onto cn and hold in front; P1; K3 from cn

= Slip 2 sts onto cn and hold in back; K3; P2 from cn

= Slip 3 sts onto cn and hold in front; P2; K3 from cn

= Slip 3 sts onto cn and hold in front; (P1, K1) from cn; K3 from cn

= Slip next st to cn and hold in back; K3; K st from cn through both back and front loops

= Slip next 3 sts onto cn and hold in front; K next st through both back and front loops

= Slip 2 sts onto cn and hold in back; K3; P2tog from cn

= Slip 3 sts onto cn and hold in front; P2tog; K3 from cn

= Slip 3 sts onto cn and hold in back; K3; K3 from cn

= Slip 3 sts onto cn and hold in front; K3; K3 from cn

= Slip 3 sts onto cn and hold in back; K3; P3 from cn

= Slip 3 sts onto cn and hold in front; P3; K3 from cn

= Slip next 2 sts to cn and hold in back; K3; K st from cn through both back and front loops; K second st from cn

= Slip next 3 sts to cn and hold in back; K3; P2tog the first 2 sts from cn; P1 the remaining st from cn

= Slip 2 sts onto cn #1 and hold in back; slip next st onto cn #2 and hold in back; K2; P1 from cn #2; K2 from cn #1

= Slip 2 sts onto cn #1 and hold in front; slip next st onto cn #2 and hold in back; K2; P1 from cn #2; K2 from cn #1

= Slip 3 sts onto cn #1 and hold in back; slip next st onto cn #2 and hold in back; K3; P1 from cn #2; K3 from cn #1

= Slip 3 sts onto cn #1 and hold in front; slip next st onto cn #2 and hold in back; K3; P1 from cn #2; K3 from cn #1

= Slip 3 sts onto cn and hold in front; (K1, P1) from cn; K3 from cn

= Slip 2 sts onto cn and hold in back; K3; (P1, K1) from cn

= Slip 2 sts onto cn and hold in back; K3; (K1, P1) from cn

= Slip 2 sts onto cn and hold in front; P2tog; K2 from cn

= Slip next 2 sts onto cn and hold in back; K2; P2tog from cn

= Slip next 3 sts onto cn and hold in front; K2; K3 from cn

◇◇

Designing with Closed-Ring Cables

One of my many goals in writing this book was to present garment patterns you'll enjoy knitting. But I hope that's just the jumping-off point! I've also designed many individual closed-ring cable patterns and have included them in a Stitch Dictionary (page 129). Play with them, choose your favorites, and design your own projects. Once you understand how these cables work, I hope you'll be inspired to be adventurous and create your own closed-ring cable patterns! Here are some basic guidelines and ideas to get you started.

THINKING LIKE A DESIGNER

As artists, knitwear designers use yarn and stitches "to draw with" and "to paint on" fabric. While Fair Isle and intarsia designers use colorwork to create pictures, cable designers work with traveling embossed stitches to create textured patterns on their knitted canvases.

Determining the Shape of Closed-Ring Cables

In Knitting in Circles (page 17), we explored the reasons why dramatic increases and decreases are necessary when knitting closed rings and explored two ways to "draw" them—pointy and round.

After the cabling section begins, the placement of the cables, the frequency with which the cables cross, and the direction and distance that they travel determine the way the fabric will look. If you vary any of these elements, you can change the shape that the cable is "drawing."

In the following illustration, for example, a Right Cross traveling cable is to the right of a Left Cross, and three stitches on each side are moving outward over one purl background stitch each side. Notice how the stockinette strands appear to separate, causing the bottom of the closed-ring cable to open up.

To force the bottom of the ring to open up faster to create a more rounded shape, substitute cables traveling over two purl stitches instead of one:

If, however, the arrangement of cable crossings is reversed, with the Left Cross to the right of the Right Cross, as follows, the cable seems to close rather than open, creating the upper section of a closed ring:

To make the top of the ring close up faster to "draw" a more rounded shape, just move the stockinette strands over two purl background stitches instead of one:

An interesting variation is to move only one side of a cable while keeping the other side stationary for several rows (see Panel 9 on page 135, for example). This technique causes the stockinette strands to move around at different angles.

The choice and placement of these cable crossings determine the shapes that appear on the knitted fabric.

Designing New Closed-Ring Motifs

Sometimes, staring at a blank sheet of paper when designing a new closed-ring cable can be quite intimidating! (Don't ask me how I know. . . .) Here are some ideas to get your creative juices flowing.

- Purchase an inexpensive cotton rope. Imagine it as the stockinette strands of your cable, and use your hands to twist it over and under itself to create shapes. Once you find a shape you like, chart it out, and get knitting!
- Research old Celtic art. The ornate illustrations in the *Book of Kells* are particularly inspiring.
- Study Celtic knotwork. Iain Bain's *Celtic Knotwork* (Sterling Publishing, 1997) is a classic.
- If Celtic isn't your thing, get a "How to Tie Knots" book or an art book about Chinese knots, and knit up some knots.

CABLING UP CLOSE
When designing, you can save knitting—not to mention ripping!—time by sketching your cable crossings on graph paper. Or, purchase some of the stitch charting software that's now available. Hold your chart an arm's length away to see if your arrangement of cables is creating the effect you want.

Using More Than One Knitting Technique in a Design
Closed-ring cables become even more striking when additional texture or color is introduced.

Typically, cables sit on top of reverse stockinette stitch backgrounds—smooth cable strands pop nicely on the bumpy reverse stockinette ground. However, other textured backgrounds can also be effective, such as those in the Tweed Hoodie on page 93 and the Quick-to-Knit Bulky Pullover on page 84. As you "play" with cables, be sure to experiment!

The Down Home Two-Color Throw Pillow on page 57 uses contrasting colors for the background and cable stitches and is knitted using the stranded Fair Isle technique (see page 31). Any of the projects or stitch patterns in this book can be worked this way.

CABLING UP CLOSE
Many beautiful handpainted and variegated yarns are available on the market these days. Try using one as your featured cabling yarn on top of a solid-colored background.

Placing Closed-Ring Cables Within Projects
The projects in this book suggest various ways to use closed-ring cables, including being showcased on the front or back of a garment, meandering along a throw rug or skirt, or patched together into an heirloom afghan. Here are some other suggestions for ways to incorporate your original closed-ring cables (or mine, found in the Stitch Dictionary on pages 129–189) into knitting projects!

- Combine several kinds of closed-ring designs into a single project. For example, work a horizontal band as a lower border for a sweater, then change to a vertical arrangement of cable panels for the body of the garment. It'll be a traditional Aran design with a difference!
- Place small closed-ring motifs on the backs of mittens or sock cuffs.
- Design your own "fisherman-style" sweater: flank a wide vertical cable panel with two alternating narrow ones on each side.

- Knit a scarf in a non-curling seed or moss stitch, and dress up each end with a pretty cable motif.
- Design a top-down skirt: choose a horizontal cable band (or two!) for the yoke, then work vertical cable panels for the rest of the length.

PRACTICAL USES FOR YOUR EXPLORATORY SWATCHES
Even if you never design your own original closed-ring cable on graph paper, I hope you'll enjoy playing with the designs in the Stitch Dictionary. Once you've knitted a bunch of swatches—even if they're different sizes and shapes—gather them up and use them. Here are some ideas.

- Lay out several swatches to see how their shapes work together, and find several that work in combination to create a large rectangular shape. Sew them together to create a unique patchwork afghan or wrap.
- Use a small closed-ring motif swatch as a patch pocket on a garment.
- If you have a serger, cut swatches all into the same size, say 4" (10cm) square, sew them together into a large rectangular piece of fabric, and then use a commercial sewing pattern to create a stunning jacket or coat.
- Rather than incorporate a motif swatch into the actual knitting of a garment, simply appliqué it on. Use whipstitch in a contrasting color for an old-fashioned, rustic look.
- Sew two large swatches together to make a beautiful pillow cover.

General Techniques

Since everyone knits at different technical levels, this section provides instructions for many of the specific techniques used in the project patterns. If a particular design excites you but some of the techniques used in it seem unfamiliar, please just go for it! Your knitter's curiosity will inspire you to build on your skills and grow.

For complete technical information on cable knitting, see the section entitled First Things First: Cables Are Easier Than They Look! That section begins on page 10.

KNITTING TECHNIQUES
Cable Cast On

This particular cast on is my favorite cast-on technique: It's beautiful, quick, and easy to do. Plus, it's perfect when the first row worked is a right-side row.

Begin by making a slipknot on your left-hand needle (see illustration 1).

Illustration 1

Insert the point of the right-hand needle knitwise into the loop that's sitting on the left-hand needle, and knit a stitch without removing the original stitch from the left-hand needle (see illustration 2); instead, transfer the new stitch from the right-hand needle to the left-hand one.

Illustration 2

One new stitch has been cast on.

For each successive stitch to be cast on, insert the point of the right-hand needle *between* the first two stitches on the left-hand needle to knit a stitch (see illustration 3). As before, do not remove the old stitch but slip the new one onto the left-hand needle; repeat until you have cast on the required number of stitches.

Illustration 3

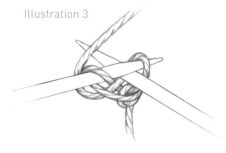

Twisted Knit Stitch

Knitting a stitch *through the back loop* will twist the bottom of the stitch and make it appear more pronounced on the background fabric.

To twist a knit stitch, insert the right-hand needle into the first stitch on the left-hand needle from front to back through its back loop, then wrap the yarn the usual way to complete the knit stitch (see illustration 4).

Illustration 4

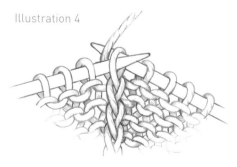

Twisted Purl Stitch (see page 19)

SSK Decrease (see page 21)

K2tog Decrease (see page 21)

SSP Decrease

This decrease method is used on wrong-side rows when you want the resulting stitch to slant to the left on the public side of the fabric.

Slip the first and second stitches from the left-hand needle to the right-hand needle one at a time knitwise, then slip them back to the left-hand needle, keeping them twisted (see illustration 5).

Illustration 5

Then, insert the point of the right-hand needle *through the back loops* of the two stitches (going into the second stitch first), and purl them together as one stitch (see illustration 6).

Illustration 6

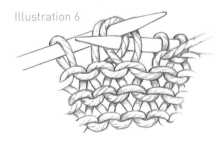

SSSP Decrease

This double decrease is used on wrong-side rows to slant the resulting stitch toward the left on the public side of the fabric. It is worked the same way as an SSP Decrease, but three stitches (instead of two) are slipped and then purled together to form a single stitch.

Bobbles

Knitted bobbles add unexpected texture to cabled fabrics. Multiple increases are worked into a single stitch, a few rows are worked over the increased stitches, then multiple decreases are worked to return to the original stitch count. There are several ways to knit a bobble, but here's my favorite:

Knit into the (front, back, front) of a single stitch, turn; working into these same three stitches, p1, (p1, yarn over, p1) all into the next stitch, then p1, turn; knit the five stitches, turn; decrease from five stitches down to three stitches as follows: P2tog, p1, p2tog, turn; finally, decrease from three stitches down to one stitch as follows: slip two stitches at once knitwise, knit the next stitch, then pass the two slipped stitches from the right-hand needle over the last knit stitch as if you were binding them off.

Note: The embossed knot in the Child's Cables and Knots Pullover on page 112 is simply a miniature bobble worked over three stitches and three rows instead of five.

Fair Isle Technique (also called stranded technique)

In this type of knitting, two colors are used in the same row, with the one not in use carried *loosely* behind the work on the wrong side until it's needed again. When using this method of two-color knitting, be especially careful not to pull these floats too taut or the fabric will pucker.

The Down Home Two-Color Throw Pillow on page 57 uses one color for the reverse stockinette background and a contrast color for the cabling yarn. Here's how to do it:

On right-side rows, purl across with the background yarn until you reach the stockinette cable stitches, then drop the background yarn to the back of your work, grab your cabling yarn from below the background yarn, and with the cabling yarn in back, knit the required number of stitches (see illustration 7).

Illustration 7

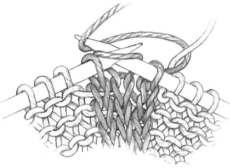

After the cable stitches are knit, drop the cabling yarn to the back of the work, pick up the background yarn, bring it to the front, and purl.

On wrong-side rows, knit across with the background yarn until you reach the cable stitches (which will appear as purl stitches on this side of the fabric), then drop the background yarn to the front of your work, pick up the cabling yarn from below the background yarn, and purl the required number of cable stitches (see illustration 8).

Illustration 8

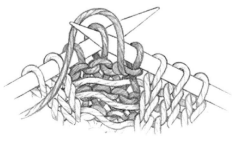

After the cable stitches have been purled, drop the cabling yarn to the front, pick up the background yarn again, and knit.

Three-Needle Bind Off

Some knitters use this technique to bind off and work their shoulder seams at the same time. If your sweater is particularly heavy, I don't recommend it. The resulting seam is quite stretchy, and your garment will surely grow—uncontrollably—in length. In this book, I use this type of seam to finish the hood of the Tweed Hoodie on page 97. It's practically invisible!

To knit this seam, hold the two pieces of fabric together with their right sides together in your left hand. Insert a third knitting needle knitwise into the first stitch on each left-hand needle, and knit the stitches together as if they were one stitch (see illustration 9).

Illustration 9

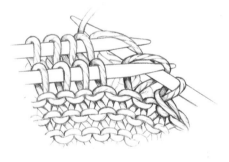

Slip the new stitch off onto the right-hand needle.

Insert the third needle knitwise into the next two stitches on the left-hand needles, and knit the stitches together, slipping the new stitch off onto the right-hand needle.

Pass the first stitch on the right-hand needle over the second stitch to bind it off.

Continue across the row, knitting together one stitch from each left-hand needle and binding off as you go.

EXTRA EMBELLISHMENTS
Basic Fringe

Fringe can stabilize the edge of a piece of knitting and is a simple decorative addition to any project!

Hold several strands of yarn together and fold in half. With the right side of your project facing you, use a crochet hook to draw the folded end from the right side to the wrong side on the edge of your project.

Pull the loose ends through the folded loop (see illustration 10), then tighten the knot.

Illustration 10

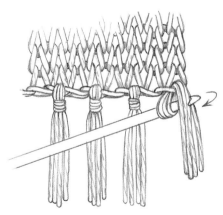

Trim the fringe evenly after all tufts are attached.

Two-Color Twisted Cord

Interlock two lengths of yarn, each in a different color, and tie a knot in each end to secure (see illustration 11).

Illustration 11

With someone holding one end, or with one end tied to a doorknob, twist the strands clockwise until the yarn is taut and begins to curl (see illustration 12).

Illustration 12

Fold in half, allow the cords to twist back on each other, and secure the two ends together to prevent unraveling (see illustration 13).

Illustration 13

FINISHING TECHNIQUES
Blocking

Prior to seaming your knitted pieces, take the time to block them into shape. You'll be surprised how this simple process can improve the appearance of your projects and even out your most unruly stitches! To block, follow the laundering instructions on the yarn label, then use rustless pins to shape the damp fabric to your desired measurements and allow it to dry. Or, gently steam each piece into shape by placing a damp cloth over it, and then carefully waft a hot steam iron just above the fabric. Don't actually touch the iron to the fabric or you'll risk flattening it.

Hiding Yarn Tails

Use a pointed-end yarn needle to make short running stitches on the wrong side of your fabric in a diagonal line for about one inch (2.5cm) or so, piercing the yarn strands that comprise the stitches of your fabric. Then, work back again to where you began, working alongside your previous running stitches. Finally, to secure the tail, work a stitch or two and actually pierce the stitches you just created. Be sure to work each tail individually, in opposite diagonal directions, and you will secure your yarn ends while keeping the public side of your fabric beautiful.

Mattress Stitch Seam (also called Invisible Weaving)

First, lay your pieces flat, with the public sides of the fabric facing you, matching patterns and stripes, if applicable.

Thread a blunt-end yarn needle with your sewing yarn, then bring the needle up from back to front through the left-hand piece of fabric, going in one stitch from the edge, leaving a 6" (15cm) tail.

Bring the yarn up and through the corresponding spot on the right-hand piece to secure the lower edges.

Insert the needle from front to back into the same spot on the left-hand piece where the needle emerged last time, and bring it up through the corresponding place of the next row of knitting.

Insert the needle from front to back into the same spot on the right-hand piece where the needle emerged last time, and bring it up through the corresponding place of the next row of knitting.

Repeat the last two steps until you've sewn a couple of inches, then pull firmly on the sewing yarn to bring the pieces of fabric together, allowing the two stitches on the edges of each pieces to roll to the wrong side.

Continue this way until your seam is complete (see illustration 14).

Illustration 14

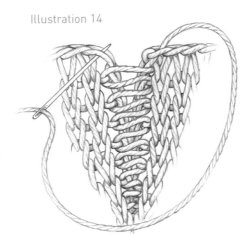

Sweater Assembly

Sweater pieces fit together like a jigsaw puzzle, with the type of armhole determining how the front, back, and sleeves interlock.

Refer to the illustrations below when assembling sweaters.

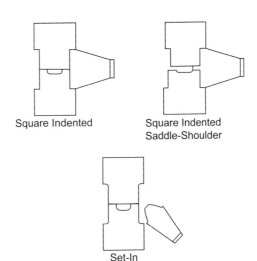

Square Indented

Square Indented Saddle-Shoulder

Set-In

You Can Do It!

SIMPLE STARTER PROJECTS

◇◇◇◇◇◇◇◇◇◇◇◇◇◇◇◇◇◇◇◇◇◇◇◇◇◇◇◇◇◇◇◇◇◇◇

If you've never tried a closed-ring cable before, here's where to start. In these first two projects, shaping is kept to a minimum so you can focus on learning and practicing the cable techniques.

If reading cable charts has you nervous, don't worry! Each cable stitch pattern in this section is offered in both text and chart form. Before you know it, you'll be reading knitting charts like a pro!

Simple Pillow

Practice making increases at the bottom of the cables and decreases at the top of them while knitting this cute pillow.

SKILL LEVEL Easy

SIZE
One size

FINISHED MEASUREMENTS
7¾" x 12¾" (19.5cm x 32.5cm), excluding border

MATERIALS
- Classic Elite Yarns *Montera* (50% llama/50% wool; each approximately 3½ oz/100g and 127 yd/116m), 2 hanks in #3823 Spring Leaf, (4) medium/worsted
- One pair of size 9 (5.5mm) knitting needles or size needed to obtain gauge
- Two stitch markers
- One size 8 (5mm) 36" (90cm) circular knitting needle
- Two cable needles
- Blunt-end yarn needle
- Upholstery foam, cut to size

GAUGE
16 stitches and 24 rows = 4" (10cm) in Reverse Stockinette Stitch Pattern. **To save time, take time to check gauge.**

STITCH PATTERNS
Reverse Stockinette Stitch Pattern
(any number of stitches)
Row 1 (RS): Purl across.
Row 2: Knit across.
Repeat Rows 1 and 2 for pattern.
Center Cable Motif Pattern
See chart, page 38, or refer to the written-out translation to the right.

◇◇◇◇◇ TRANSLATION OF THE CABLE CHART ◇◇◇◇◇

Center Cable Motif Pattern (17 stitches, increasing to 35 stitches)
Row 1 (RS): P2, [M1, 3-in-1 inc, M1, p5] twice, M1, 3-in-1 inc, M1, p2.
Row 2: K2, *p2, [(p1, yarn over, p1) into next stitch, p2, p5] twice, p2, (p1, yarn over, p1) into next stitch, p2, k2.
Row 3: Slip 2 stitches onto cn and hold in back, k3, p2 from cn, [purl next stitch *through the back loop*, slip 3 stitches onto cn and hold in front, p1, k3 from cn, p3, slip next stitch onto cn and hold in back, k3, purl stitch from cn] twice, purl next stitch *through the back loop*, slip 3 stitches onto cn and hold in front, p2, k3 from cn.
Rows 4, 6, 8, 10, 12, 14, 16, 18, 20, 22, 24, and 26: Knit the knit stitches and purl the purl stitches as you come to them on your needles.

Row 5: K3, p4, slip 3 stitches onto cn and hold in front, p2, k3 from cn, slip next stitch onto cn and hold in back, k3, purl stitch from cn, p3, slip 3 stitches onto cn and hold in front, p1, k3 from cn, slip 2 stitches onto cn and hold in back, k3, p2 from cn, p4, k3.

Row 7: Slip 3 stitches onto cn and hold in front, p1, k3 from cn, [p5, slip 3 stitches onto cn and hold in front, k3, k3 from cn] twice, p5, slip next stitch onto cn and hold in back, k3, purl stitch from cn.

Row 9: P1, [slip 3 stitches onto cn and hold in front, p2, k3 from cn, p1, slip 2 stitches onto cn and hold in back, k3, p2 from cn] three times, p1.

Row 11: P3, [slip 3 stitches onto cn #1 and hold in back, slip next stitch onto cn #2 and hold in back, k3, p1 from cn #2, k3 from cn #1, p4] twice, slip 3 stitches onto cn #1 and hold in back, slip next stitch onto cn #2 and hold in back, k3, p1 from cn #2, k3 from cn #1, p3.

Row 13: P1, slip 2 stitches onto cn and hold in back, k3, p2 from cn, [p1, slip 3 stitches onto cn and hold in front, p2, k3 from cn, slip 2 stitches onto cn and hold in back, k3, p2 from cn] twice, p1, slip 3 stitches onto cn and hold in front, p2, k3 from cn, p1.

Row 15: P1, k3, [p5, slip 3 stitches onto cn and hold in front, k3, k3 from cn] twice, p5, k3, p1.

Row 17: Same as Row 9.

Row 19: Same as Row 11.

Row 21: Same as Row 13.

Row 23: Slip next stitch onto cn and hold in back, k3, purl stitch from cn, [p5, slip 3 stitches onto cn and hold in front, k3, k3 from cn] twice, p5, slip 3 stitches onto cn and hold in front, p1, k3 from cn.

Row 25: K3, p4, slip 2 stitches onto cn and hold in back, k3, p2 from cn, slip 3 stitches onto cn and hold in front, p1, k3 from cn, p3, slip next stitch onto cn and hold in back, k3, purl stitch from cn, slip 3 stitches onto cn and hold in front, p2, k3 from cn, p4, k3.

Row 27: Slip 3 stitches onto cn and hold in front, p2, k3 from cn, [p1, slip next stitch onto cn and hold in back, k3, purl stitch from cn, p3, slip 3 stitches onto cn and hold in front, p1, k3 from cn] twice, p1, slip 2 stitches onto cn and hold in back, k3, p2 from cn.

Row 28: K2, [7-to-1 dec, k5] twice, 7-to-1 dec, k2.

For the pillow, keep 8 stitches on each side in Reverse Stockinette Stitch Pattern, and work Rows 1–18 of Center Cable Motif Pattern once, then repeat Rows 11–18 three more times, then work Rows 19–28 once.

BACK OF PILLOW
Cast on 31 stitches.

Begin Reverse Stockinette Stitch Pattern, and work even until the piece measures approximately 2" (5cm) from the beginning, ending after a wrong-side row.

Set Up Patterns
Work Row 1 of Reverse Stockinette Stitch Pattern over the the first 7 stitches, place marker, work Row 1 of Center Cable Motif Pattern over the middle 17 stitches, place marker, work Row 1 of Reverse Stockinette Stitch Pattern across to end of row.

Continue as established until Row 18 of Center Cable Motif Pattern is completed, then repeat Rows 11–18 three more times, then work Rows 19–28 once, keeping stitches on both sides of markers in Reverse Stockinette Stitch Pattern.

Continue in Reverse Stockinette Stitch Pattern for 2" (5cm), ending after a wrong-side row.

Bind off.

FRONT
Work as for the Back.

FINISHING
Block the pieces to finished measurements.

Applied I-Cord Edging
With circular needle, pick up 50 stitches evenly spaced around each long side of the pillow front, 3 stitches into each corner, and 28 stitches evenly spaced along each short side of the pillow front—168 stitches total.

Using cable cast on, cast on 3 stitches onto the left-hand needle. Working across one side of the pillow, *k2, slip next stitch, k1 stitch from pillow edge, pass the slipped stitch over the last knitted stitch, then slip these 3 stitches back onto the left-hand needle; repeat from * until all picked up stitches are worked—3 stitches remain.

Bind off.

Sew bound-off and cast-on ends of I-Cord Edging together.

With wrong sides together, sew three sides of the pillow together.

Insert foam inside pillow and sew the last side.

CENTER CABLE MOTIF PATTERN

17 sts (inc to 35 sts)

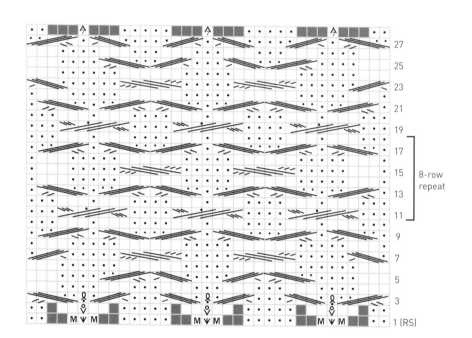

8-row repeat

27
25
23
21
19
17
15
13
11
9
7
5
3
1 (RS)

• = P on RS; K on WS

▪ = No stitch

M = M1 Knitwise = Insert LH needle under the horizontal strand between two sts from front to back and K it *through back loop*

V = Central Double Increase = (Increases from 1 st to 3 sts) = K into back and then into front of indicated st and slip them off LH needle onto RH needle; insert point of LH needle behind the vertical strand that runs downward between the two sts just made and K *into the front of it*

☐ = K on RS; P on WS

⬖ = (Increases from 1 st to 3 sts) = (P1, yarn over, P1) into next st

= Slip 2 sts onto cn and hold in back; K3; P2 from cn

⬧ = P *through back loop*

= Slip 3 sts onto cn and hold in front; P1; K3 from cn

= Slip next st onto cn and hold in back; K3; P1 from cn

= Slip 3 sts onto cn and hold in front; P2; K3 from cn

= Slip 3 sts onto cn and hold in front; K3; K3 from cn

= Slip 3 sts onto cn #1 and hold in back; slip next st onto cn #2 and hold in back; K3; P1 from cn #2; K3 from cn #1

⋏ = (Decreases from 7 sts to 1 st) = Slip next 4 sts with yarn in back, drop yarn; *pass the second st on RH needle over the first st on RH needle; slip first st from RH needle back to LH needle; pass the second st on LH needle over the first st on LH needle; **slip first st from LH needle back to RH needle and repeat from * to ** twice more; pick up yarn and K remaining st

Simple Hat

This hat is a great beginner's cabling project. It's fun—and fast!—to knit.

SKILL LEVEL Easy

SIZES
Average Woman's (Man's) Size. Instructions are for the woman's size, with changes for the man's size noted in parentheses as necessary.

FINISHED MEASUREMENTS
Hat Circumference: 19¼ (22)" [48 (56)cm]

MATERIALS
- JCA/Reynolds *Andean Alpaca Regal* (90% alpaca/10% wool; each approximately 3½ oz/100g and 110 yd/106m), 1 ball in #127 for the woman's version (2 balls in #967 for the man's version), ④ medium/worsted
- One size 10 (6mm) circular knitting needle, 16" (40cm) long or size needed to obtain gauge
- Set of size 10 (6mm) double-pointed knitting needles or size needed to obtain gauge
- One cable needle
- One stitch marker
- Blunt-end yarn needle

GAUGE
16 stitches and 22 rnds = 4" (10cm) in Cable Rib Pattern.
To save time, take time to check gauge.

STITCH PATTERNS
K2 P3 Rib Pattern (multiple of 5 stitches)
Pattern Rnd (RS): *K2, p3; repeat from * around.
Repeat Pattern Rnd for pattern.
Cable Rib Pattern
See chart, page 41, or refer to the written out translation on page 40.

◇◇◇◇ TRANSLATION OF THE CABLE CHART ◇◇◇◇

Hat Cable and Rib Pattern (multiple 10 stitches, increases to 17 stitches)

Rnd 1 (RS): *K2, p8, M1P; repeat from * around.

Rnd 2: *K2, p9; repeat from * around.

Rnds 3 and 4: Same as Round 2.

Rnd 5: *K2, p4, M1, 3-in-1 inc, M1, p4; repeat from * around.

Rnd 6: *K2, p4, k2, (p1, yarn over, p1) into next stitch, k2, p4; repeat from * around.

Rnd 7: *K2, p3, slip next stitch onto cn and hold in back, k3, p1 from cn, purl next stitch *through the back loop*, slip the next 3 stitches onto cn and hold in front, p1, k3 from cn, p3; repeat from * around.

Rnd 8: *K2, p3, (k3, p3) twice; repeat from * around.

Rnd 9: *K2, p2, slip next stitch onto cn and hold in back, k3, p1 from cn, p3, slip the next 3 stitches onto cn and hold in front, p1, k3 from cn, p2; repeat from * around.

Rnd 10: *K2, p2, k3, p5, k3, p2; repeat from * around.

Rnd 11: *K2, p2, k3, p2, make bobble (see Notes), p2, k3, p2; repeat from * around.

Rnd 12: Same as Round 10.

Rnd 13: *K2, p2, slip the next 3 stitches onto cn and hold in front, p1, k3 from cn, p3, slip next stitch onto cn and hold in back, k3, p1 from cn, p2; repeat from * around.

Rnd 14: Same as Round 8.

Rnd 15: *K2, p3, slip the next 3 stitches onto cn and hold in front, p1, k3 from cn, p1, slip next stitch onto cn and hold in back, k3, p1 from cn, p3; repeat from * around.

Rnd 16: *K2, p4, 7-to-1 dec, p4; repeat from * around.

Rnds 17–24: *K2, p9; repeat from * around.

Rnd 25: *K1, ssk, p8; repeat from * around.

Rnd 26: *K1, ssk, p7; repeat from * around.

Rnd 27: *K1, ssk, p6; repeat from * around.

Rnd 28: *K1, sssk, p4; repeat from * around.

Rnd 29: *K1, sssk, p2; repeat from * around.

Rnd 30: *K1, sssk; repeat from * around.

NOTES

- This hat is made in the round.
- When making the hat, change to double-pointed needles when there are no longer enough stitches remaining to knit comfortably with the circular needle.
- When making the man's version, omit the bobbles and work purl stitches instead.
- To make a bobble, knit into (front, back, front) of the next stitch, turn; p1, (p1, yarn over, p1) all into next stitch, p1, turn; k5, turn; p2tog, p1, p2tog, turn; slip 2 stitches at once knitwise, k1, p2sso.

HAT

With circular needle, cast on 70 (80) stitches. Join, being careful not to twist stitches. Place marker to indicate beginning of round.

Begin K2 P3 Rib Pattern, and work even until the piece measures approximately 4 (5½)" [10 (14)cm] from the beginning.

Begin Cable Rib Pattern, following chart or refer to written instructions at left.

When Round 30 of Cable Rib Pattern has been completed, remove marker.

Next Rnd: K1, *ssk; repeat from * until 7 (8) stitches remain.

Cut yarn, leaving a long tail.

Using a blunt-end yarn needle, thread the tail through the remaining stitches, draw up tightly, and fasten securely.

Block.

CABLE RIB PATTERN
mult 10 sts (inc to mult 17 sts, dec to mult 2 sts)

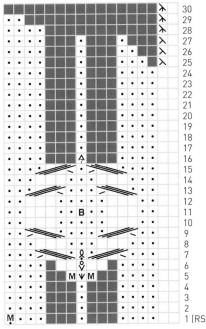

KEY

- • = P on RS; K on WS

- ▨ = No stitch

- **M** (with dot) = M1 Purlwise = Insert LH needle under the horizontal strand between two sts from front to back and P it *through back loop*

- **M** = M1 Knitwise = Insert LH needle under the horizontal strand between two sts from front to back and K it *through back loop*

- **Ψ** = Central Double Increase = (Increases from 1 st to 3 sts) = K into back and then into front of indicated st and slip them off LH needle onto RH needle; insert point of LH needle behind the vertical strand that runs downward between the two sts just made and K *into the front of it*

- ☐ = K on RS

- ᥅ = (Increases from 1 st to 3 sts) = (P1, yarn over, P1) into next st

- ⟋⟋⟋ • = Slip next st onto cn and hold in back; K3; P1 from cn

- Ƽ = P *through back loop*

- • ⟍⟍⟍ = Slip 3 sts onto cn and hold in front; P1; K3 from cn

- **B** = Bobble = K into (front, back, front) of next st, turn; P1, (P1, yarn over, P1) all into next st, P1, turn; K5, turn; P2tog, P1, P2tog, turn; slip 2 sts at once knitwise, K1, p2sso

- ⋏ = (Decreases from 7 sts to 1 st) = Slip next 4 sts with yarn in back, drop yarn; *pass the second st on RH needle over the first st on RH needle; slip first st from RH needle back to LH needle; pass the second st on LH needle over the first st on LH needle; **slip first st from LH needle back to RH needle and repeat from * to ** twice more; pick up yarn and K remaining st

- ⅄ = SSK

- ⋏ = SSSK

Comfy Cables

ACCENTS FOR THE HOME

◇◇◇◇◇◇◇◇◇◇◇◇◇◇◇◇◇◇◇◇◇◇◇◇◇◇◇◇◇◇◇◇◇◇◇◇

Here are several projects for your home that
feature closed-ring cables. With this collection of
patterns—afghans, a throw pillow, even a place
mat—you can showcase your skills in nearly
every room!

Fireside Afghan

Graceful cables travel across this toasty afghan. Plus, it looks more complicated than it is: once you've completed a couple of pattern repeats, I bet you won't even have to look at the chart anymore!

SKILL LEVEL   Intermediate

SIZE
One size

FINISHED MEASUREMENTS
Approximately 46" x 72" (117cm x 183cm), excluding fringe

MATERIALS
- Malabrigo *Handpainted Worsted Merino* (100% merino wool; each approximately 3½ oz/100g and 216 yd/198m), 17 hanks in #194 Cinnabar, ④ medium/worsted
- One size 10 (6mm) circular knitting needle, 29" (74cm) long or longer or size needed to obtain gauge
- Two stitch markers
- Two cable needles
- One blunt-end yarn needle
- One large crochet hook for attaching fringe

GAUGE
One repeat of Celtic Cables Pattern (70 stitches, increases to 82 stitches) = 12¾" (32.5cm) and 26 rows = 4" (10cm). **To save time, take time to check gauge.**

STITCH PATTERNS
Right Side Celtic Cables Pattern
See chart, page 46.
Center Celtic Cables Pattern
See chart, pages 46 and 47.
Left Side Celtic Cables Pattern
See chart, page 47.

NOTE
For even color distribution, alternate between two balls of yarn, working two rows from one ball, then two rows from the second ball, carrying the unused yarn *loosely* along the side of the work.

AFGHAN
Cast on 271 stitches.

Set Up Patterns
Row 1 (RS): Work Row 1 of Right Side Celtic Cables Pattern over the first 20 stitches, place marker, work Row 1 of Center Celtic Cables Pattern over the next 210 stitches (repeating the chart three times), place marker, work Row 1 of Left Side Celtic Cables Pattern to end of row.

Continue even in patterns as established until the piece measures approximately 72" (183cm) from the beginning, ending after Row 15 of patterns.

Next Row: Bind off while working Row 16 of patterns.

FINISHING
Block as necessary.

Fringe
For each tuft of fringe, cut four 9" (23cm) lengths of yarn.

With crochet hook, attach fringe evenly across both short ends of afghan as desired.

Trim fringe evenly.

RIGHT SIDE CELTIC CABLES PATTERN
20 sts (dec to 17 sts)

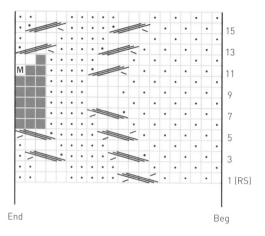

15

13

11

9

7

5

3

1 (RS)

End

Beg

CENTER CELTIC CABLES PATTERN
mult 70 sts (inc to mult 82 sts)

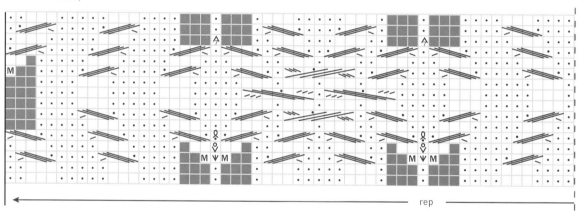

rep

Note: Right-hand side of this chart appears on opposite page on other side of dotted line.

LEFT SIDE CELTIC CABLES PATTERN
41 sts (dec to 32 sts)

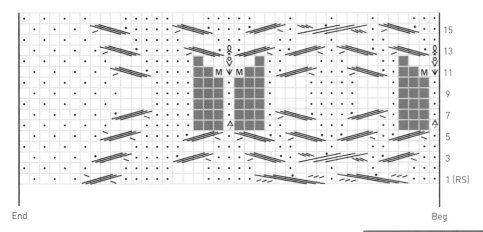

End   Beg

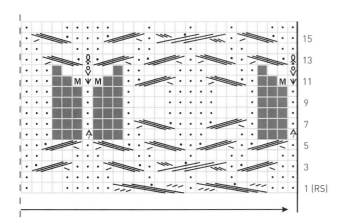

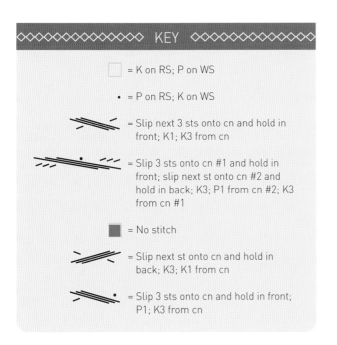

KEY

   = K on RS; P on WS

• = P on RS; K on WS

 = Slip next 3 sts onto cn and hold in front; K1; K3 from cn

 = Slip 3 sts onto cn #1 and hold in front; slip next st onto cn #2 and hold in back; K3; P1 from cn #2; K3 from cn #1

= No stitch

= Slip next st onto cn and hold in back; K3; K1 from cn

= Slip 3 sts onto cn and hold in front; P1; K3 from cn

= Slip next st onto cn and hold in back; K3; P1 from cn

= Slip 3 sts onto cn #1 and hold in back; slip next st onto cn #2 and hold in back; K3; P1 from cn #2; K3 from cn #1

M = M1 Knitwise = Insert LH needle under the horizontal strand between two sts from front to back and K it *through back loop*

Ⅴ = Central Double Increase = (Increases from 1 st to 3 sts) = K into back and then into front of indicated st and slip them off LH needle onto RH needle; insert point of LH needle behind the vertical strand that runs downward between the two sts just made and K *into the front of it*

= (Increases from 1 st to 3 sts) = (P1, yarn over, P1) into next st

= P *through back loop*

= (Decreases from 7 sts to 1 st) = Slip next 4 sts with yarn in back, drop yarn; *pass the second st on RH needle over the first st on RH needle; slip first st from RH needle back to LH needle; pass the second st on LH needle over the first st on LH needle; **slip first st from LH needle back to RH needle and repeat from * to ** twice more; pick up yarn and K remaining st

Stowe Cabin Throw Rug

The side borders of this rug are made in an unusual way: Before binding off, you will unravel several stitches all the way down to their cast-on edges to begin the fringe. Try it. It's very cool!

SKILL LEVEL Intermediate

SIZE
One size

FINISHED MEASUREMENTS
Approximately 35" x 57" (89cm x 145cm), excluding fringe

MATERIALS
- Plymouth Yarn Company *Encore Worsted* (75% acrylic/25% wool; each approximately 3½ oz/100g and 200 yd/180m), 10 balls in #6002 Rimouski, ④ medium/worsted
- One size 6 (4mm) circular knitting needle, 29" (74cm) long or longer
- One size 8 (5mm) circular knitting needle, 29" (74cm) long or longer or size needed to obtain gauge
- One cable needle
- One blunt-end yarn needle
- One medium-sized crochet hook for attaching fringe

GAUGE
With larger needle, one repeat of Intertwined Cables Pattern (40 stitches, increases to 52 stitches) = 7¾" (19.5cm) and 30 rows = 4" (10cm). **To save time, take time to check gauge.**

STITCH PATTERNS
Stockinette Stitch Pattern (any number of stitches)
Row 1 (RS): Knit across.
Row 2: Purl across.
Repeat Rows 1 and 2 for pattern.
Border Pattern
See chart, page 50.
Intertwined Cables Pattern
See chart, pages 50 and 51.

NOTE
Five stitches on each side are unraveled at the end of knitting to create part of fringe.

RUG
With smaller needle, using cable cast-on technique, cast on 302 stitches.

Set Up Patterns
Row 1 (RS): Work Row 1 of Stockinette Stitch Pattern over the first 5 stitches, place marker, work Row 1 of Border Pattern over the next 292 stitches, place marker, work Row 1 of Stockinette Stitch Pattern to end of row.

Continue even in patterns as established until the piece measures approximately 2" (5cm) from the beginning, ending after Row 4 of Border Pattern.

Change to larger needle.

Next Row (RS): Work Row 1 of Stockinette Stitch Pattern over the first 5 stitches, place marker, work Row 1 of Intertwined Cables Pattern over the next 292 stitches, place marker, work Row 1 of Stockinette Stitch Pattern to end of row.

Continue even in patterns as established until the piece measures approximately 33" (84cm) from the beginning, ending after Row 4 of Intertwined Cables Pattern.

Next Row (RS): Work Row 1 of Stockinette Stitch Pattern over the first 5 stitches, place marker, work Row 1 of Border Pattern over the next 292 stitches, place marker, work Row 1 of Stockinette Stitch Pattern to end of row.

Continue even in patterns as established for approximately 2" (5cm), ending after Row 4 of Border Pattern.

Next Row: P5, bind off the middle 292 stitches in pattern, p5.

FINISHING
Remove knitting needle, and unravel remaining 5 stitches on each side down to the cast-on edge.

Block to measurements, removing the kinks from the loops you've unraveled.

Fringe
For each tuft of fringe, cut one 10" (25.5cm) length of yarn.

Fold one length in half and, using crochet hook, pull through the edge at the base of one unraveled "fringe loop." Tie an overhand knot close to the edge of the fabric, using both the loop and the additional length of yarn.

Repeat for each loop across.

Trim fringe evenly, cutting loops.

Repeat on the opposite side of the rug.

Block to finished measurements.

INTERTWINED CABLES PATTERN
mult 40 + 12 sts (inc to mult 52 + 12 sts)

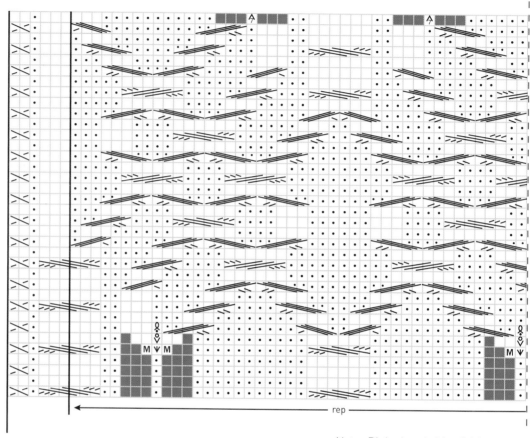

End

rep

Note: Right-hand side of this chart appears on opposite page on other side of dotted line.

BORDER PATTERN
mult 20 + 12 sts

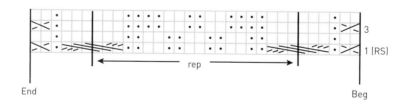

End

rep

3

1 (RS)

Beg

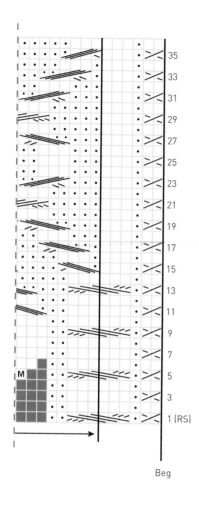

Beg

= Right Twist = Slip next st onto cn and hold in back; K1; K1 from cn **OR** K2tog, leaving them on LH needle; insert point of RH needle between these 2 sts and K the first one again

• = P on RS; K on WS

= Slip 3 sts onto cn and hold in front; K3; K3 from cn

= No stitch

M = M1 Knitwise = Insert LH needle under the horizontal strand between two sts from front to back and K it *through back loop*

V = Central Double Increase = (Increases from 1 st to 3 sts) = K into back and then into front of indicated st and slip them off LH needle onto RH needle; insert point of LH needle behind the vertical strand that runs downward between the two sts just made and K *into the front of it*

= Left Twist = Slip next st onto cn and hold in front; K1; K1 from cn **OR** skip first st and K next st in back loop; then K the skipped st; slip both sts off LH needle together

= K on RS; P on WS

= (Increases from 1 st to 3 sts) = (P1, yarn over, P1) into next st

= P *through back loop*

= Slip 3 sts onto cn and hold in front; P2; K3 from cn\

= Slip next st onto cn and hold in back; K3; P1 from cn

= Slip 3 sts onto cn and hold in front; P1; K3 from cn

= Slip 2 sts onto cn and hold in back; K3; P2 from cn

= Slip 3 sts onto cn and hold in back; K3; K3 from cn

= (Decreases from 7 sts to 1 st) = Slip next 4 sts with yarn in back, drop yarn; *pass the second st on RH needle over the first st on RH needle; slip first st from RH needle back to LH needle; pass the second st on LH needle over the first st on LH needle; **slip first st from LH needle back to RH needle and repeat from * to ** twice more; pick up yarn and K remaining st

Tweed Sampler Afghan

Here's a project that's great fun to knit. Three different cable patterns provide tons of texture. And the long rectangular strips are easy enough that you can pop one in your bag and add to it during otherwise wasted moments while running errands.

SKILL LEVEL   Intermediate

SIZE
One size

FINISHED MEASUREMENTS
Approximately 52" x 66" (132cm x 167.5cm)

MATERIALS
- Aurora Yarn's/Ornaghi Filati's *Tibet* (55% wool/40% acrylic/5% viscose; each approximately 3½ oz/100g and 132 yd/120m), 32 balls in #210 Banana Tweed, **(5)** bulky
- One pair of size 10 (6mm) knitting needles or size needed to obtain gauge
- Two stitch markers
- Two cable needles
- Blunt-end yarn needle

GAUGE
16 stitches and 20 rows = 4" (10cm) in Reverse Stockinette Stitch Pattern. **To save time, take time to check gauge.**

STITCH PATTERNS
Reverse Stockinette Stitch Pattern
(any number of stitches)
Row 1 (RS): Purl across.
Row 2: Knit across.
Repeat Rows 1 and 2 for pattern.
Cable Pattern A
See chart, page 55.
Cable Pattern B
See chart, page 55.
Cable Pattern C
See chart, page 56.

ASSEMBLY ILLUSTRATION

C	B	C
B	C	B
C	B	C
B	C	B
C	B	C
B	C	B

A · A · A · A

NOTES

- For assembly, see illustration above.
- Right Twist = Slip next stitch onto cn and hold in back; k1; k1 from cn **OR** k2tog, leaving stitches on the left-hand needle; insert point of the right-hand needle between these 2 stitches, and knit the first one again.
- To move 1 stitch to the right, slip next stitch onto cn and hold in back; k1; p1 from cn.
- To move 1 stitch to the left, slip next stitch onto cn and hold in front; p1; k1 from cn.
- To M1 knitwise slanting to the left: On right-side rows, insert the left-hand needle under the horizontal strand between two stitches from front to back, and knit it *through the back loop*.
- To M1 knitwise slanting to the right: On right-side rows, insert the left-hand needle under the horizontal strand between two stitches from back to front, and knit it *through the front loop*.
- To M1 purlwise slanting to the left: On right-side rows, insert the left-hand needle under the horizontal strand between two stitches from front to back and purl it *through the back loop*.
- To M1 purlwise slanting to the right: On right-side rows, insert the left-hand needle under the horizontal strand from back to front and purl it *through the front loop*.

AFGHAN PIECE A (MAKE 4. FINISHED MEASUREMENTS: 4½" x 66" [11.5cm x 167.5cm])

Cast on 34 stitches.

Begin Cable Pattern A Chart, and repeat Rows 1–8 until the piece measures approximately 66" (167.5cm) from the beginning, ending after Row 1 of pattern.

Bind off in pattern.

AFGHAN PIECE B (MAKE 9. FINISHED MEASUREMENTS: 11¼" x 11" [28.5cm x 28cm])

Cast on 51 stitches.

Work Reverse Stockinette Stitch Pattern for 6 rows.

Set Up Patterns

Next Row (RS): Work Row 1 of Reverse Stockinette Stitch Pattern over the first 11 stitches, place marker, work Row 1 of Cable Pattern B Chart over the middle 29 stitches, place marker, work Row 1 of Reverse Stockinette Stitch Pattern across to end of row.

Work patterns as established until Row 44 of Cable Pattern B Chart is completed.

Work 6 rows Reverse Stockinette Stitch Pattern.

Bind off.

AFGHAN PIECE C (MAKE 9. FINISHED MEASUREMENTS: 11¼" x 11" [28.5cm x 28cm])

Cast on 51 stitches.

Work Reverse Stockinette Stitch Pattern for 6 rows.

Set Up Patterns

Next Row (RS): Work Row 1 of Reverse Stockinette Stitch Pattern over the first 15 stitches, place marker, work Row 1 of Cable Pattern C Chart over the middle 21 stitches, place marker, work Row 1 of Reverse Stockinette Stitch Pattern across to end of row.

Work patterns as established until Row 44 of Cable Pattern C Chart is completed.

Work 6 rows Reverse Stockinette Stitch Pattern.

Bind off.

FINISHING

Block Afghan Pieces to finished measurements.

◇◇

With the right sides facing, sew the pieces together following the assembly illustration on page 53.

Border

With the right side facing, pick up and knit 266 stitches along one long side of the afghan.

Row 1 (WS): P2, *k2, p2; repeat from * across.

Row 2: K2, M1 knitwise slanting to the right, *p2, right twist, p2, k2; repeat from * across to the last 8 stitches, ending row with p2, right twist, p2, M1 knitwise slanting to the left, k2.

Row 3: P3, *k2, p2; repeat from * across to last stitch, ending row with p1.

Row 4: K2, M1 knitwise slanting to the right, k1, p1, *move 1 stitch to the right, move 1 stitch to the left, p1, k2, p1; repeat from * across to the last 8 stitches, ending row with move 1 stitch to the right, move 1 stitch to the left, p1, k1, M1 knitwise slanting to the left, k2.

Row 5: P4, k1, *p1, k2, p1, k1, p2, k1; repeat from * across to the last 9 stitches, ending row with p1, k2, p1, k1, p4.

Row 6: K2, M1 purlwise slanting to the right, k2, p1, *move 1 stitch to the left, move 1 stitch to the right, p1, k2, p1; repeat from * across to the last 9 stitches, ending row with move 1 stitch to the left, move 1 stitch to the right, p1, k2, M1 purlwise slanting to the left, k2.

Row 7: P2, k1, *p2, k2; repeat from * across to the last 5 stitches, ending row with p2, k1, p2.

Row 8: K2, M1 purlwise slanting to the right, p1, *k2, p2, right twist, p2; repeat from * across to the last 5 stitches, ending row with k2, p1, M1 purlwise slanting to the left, k2.

Row 9: P2, *k2, p2; repeat from * across.

Row 10: K2, M1 knitwise slanting to the right, p2, *k2, p1, move 1 stitch to the right, move 1 stitch to the left, p1; repeat from * across to the last 6 stitches, ending row with k2, p2, M1 knitwise slanting to the left, k2.

Row 11: P3, k2, *p2, k1, p1, k2, p1, k1; repeat from * across to the last 7 stitches, ending row with p2, k2, p3.

Row 12: K2, M1 knitwise slanting to the right, k1, p2, *k2, p1, move 1 stitch to the left, move 1 stitch to the right, p1; repeat from * across to the last 7 stitches, ending row with k2, p2, k1, M1 knitwise slanting to the left, k2.

Row 13: P4, *k2, p2; repeat from * across to the last 2 stitches, ending row with p2.

Row 14: K2, M1 purlwise slanting to the right, *right twist, p2, k2, p2; repeat from * across to the last 4 stitches, ending row with right twist, M1 purlwise slanting to the left, k2.

Row 15: P2, k1, *p2, k2; repeat from * across to the last 5 stitches, ending row with p2, k1, p2.

Row 16: K2, M1 purlwise slanting to the right, *move 1 stitch to the right, move 1 stitch to the left, p1, k2, p1; repeat from * across to the last 6 stitches, ending row with move 1 stitch to the right, move 1 stitch to the left, M1 purlwise slanting to the left, k2.

Row 17: Bind off *loosely* in pattern.

Repeat for the other long side.

With the right side facing, pick up and knit 202 stitches along one short side of afghan.

Work same as for long side of edging.

Bind off *loosely* in pattern.

Repeat for the other short side.

Using mattress stitch (see page 33), sew the corners together.

◇◇◇◇◇◇◇◇◇◇◇◇◇◇◇ KEY ◇◇◇◇◇◇◇◇◇◇◇◇◇◇◇

• = P on RS; K on WS

■ = No stitch

M = M1 Knitwise = Insert LH needle under the horizontal strand between two sts from front to back and K it *through back loop*

Ⱳ = Central Double Increase = (Increases from 1 st to 3 sts) = K into back and then into front of indicated st and slip them off LH needle onto RH needle; insert point of LH needle behind the vertical strand that runs downward between the two sts just made and K *into the front of it*

☐ = K on RS; P on WS

Ỿ = (Increases from 1 st to 3 sts) = (P1, yarn over, P1) into next st

ᛉ = P *through back loop*

= Slip 2 sts onto cn and hold in back; K3; P2 from cn

= Slip 3 sts onto cn and hold in front; P2; K3 from cn

◇◇

CABLE PATTERN A
(34 sts)

CABLE PATTERN B
29 sts (inc to 42 sts)

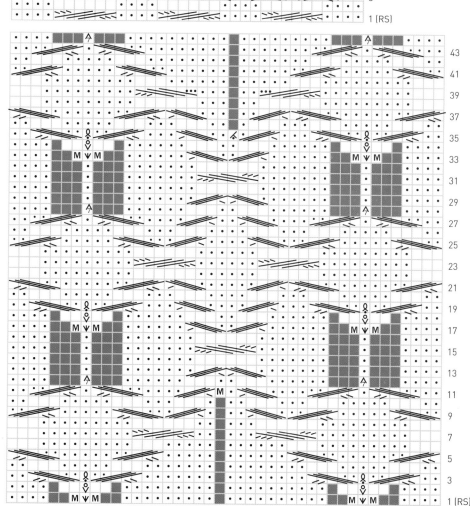

 = Slip 3 sts onto cn and hold in front; K3;
K3 from cn

 = Slip 3 sts onto cn and hold in back; K3;
K3 from cn

 = Slip 3 sts onto cn and hold in front; P1;
K3 from cn

 = Slip next st onto cn and hold in back; K3;
P1 from cn

= (Decreases from 7 sts to 1 st) = Slip next 4
sts with yarn in back, drop yarn; *pass the
second st on RH needle over the first st on

RH needle; slip first st from RH needle back
to LH needle; pass the second st on LH
needle over the first st on LH needle; **slip
first st from LH needle back to RH needle
and repeat from * to ** twice more; pick up
yarn and K remaining st

= P2tog

 = Slip 3 sts onto cn and hold in back; K3;
P3 from cn

 = Slip 3 sts onto cn and hold in front; P3;
K3 from cn

CABLE PATTERN C
21 sts (inc to 39 sts)

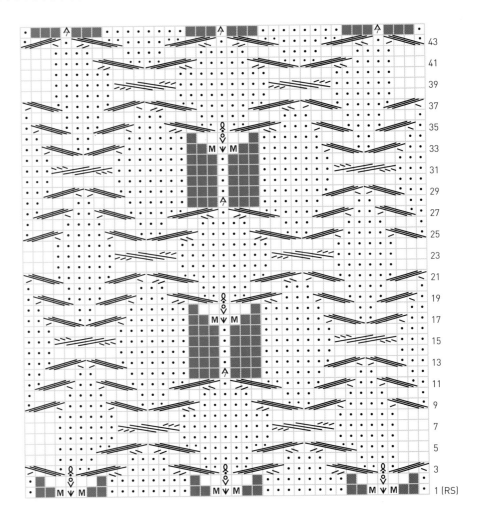

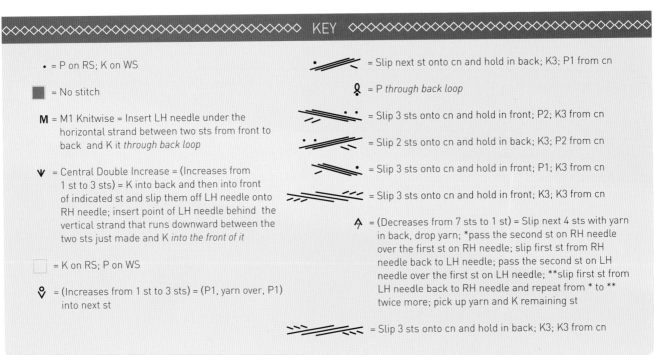

KEY

• = P on RS; K on WS

■ = No stitch

M = M1 Knitwise = Insert LH needle under the horizontal strand between two sts from front to back and K it *through back loop*

Ⅴ = Central Double Increase = (Increases from 1 st to 3 sts) = K into back and then into front of indicated st and slip them off LH needle onto RH needle; insert point of LH needle behind the vertical strand that runs downward between the two sts just made and K *into the front of it*

□ = K on RS; P on WS

Ⅴ = (Increases from 1 st to 3 sts) = (P1, yarn over, P1) into next st

= Slip next st onto cn and hold in back; K3; P1 from cn

Ⴝ = P *through back loop*

= Slip 3 sts onto cn and hold in front; P2; K3 from cn

= Slip 2 sts onto cn and hold in back; K3; P2 from cn

= Slip 3 sts onto cn and hold in front; P1; K3 from cn

= Slip 3 sts onto cn and hold in front; K3; K3 from cn

ⴷ = (Decreases from 7 sts to 1 st) = Slip next 4 sts with yarn in back, drop yarn; *pass the second st on RH needle over the first st on RH needle; slip first st from RH needle back to LH needle; pass the second st on LH needle over the first st on LH needle; **slip first st from LH needle back to RH needle and repeat from * to ** twice more; pick up yarn and K remaining st

= Slip 3 sts onto cn and hold in back; K3; K3 from cn

Down Home Two-Color Throw Pillow

Your closed-ring cables will really be "stand-outs" when they are worked a color different from the background. Knit this pillow in colors to match your décor!

SKILL LEVEL   Experienced

SIZE
One size

FINISHED MEASUREMENTS
Approximately 20" x 20" (51cm x 51cm)

MATERIALS
- Cascade Yarn *Cascade 128* (100% wool; each approximately 3½ oz/100g and 128 yd/117m), 4 hanks each in #8686 Chocolate (A) and #7803 Fuchsia (B), ⑤ bulky
- One pair of size 10 (6mm) knitting needles or size needed to obtain gauge
- Two cable needles
- Blunt-end yarn needle
- One 20" (51cm) pillow form

GAUGE
14 stitches and 20 rows = 4" (10cm) in Reverse Stockinette Stitch Pattern. **To save time, take time to check gauge.**

STITCH PATTERNS
Reverse Stockinette Stitch Pattern
(any number of stitches)
Row 1 (RS): Purl across.
Row 2: Knit across.
Repeat Rows 1 and 2 for pattern.
Two-Color Cable Motif Pattern
See chart, page 59.

◇◇

NOTE

When working with two colors in pattern, use the stranded knitting technique, carrying the yarn *loosely* across the wrong side of the fabric to prevent puckering (see page 31).

SQUARE A (MAKE 4)

With A, cast on 35 stitches.

Work Reverse Stockinette Stitch Pattern for 7 rows.

Set Up Patterns

Next Row (WS): K17, bring the yarn to the front, join B, p1, change to A and bring it to the back, k17.

Next Row (RS): With A, p9, work Row 1 of Two-Color Cable Motif Pattern over the middle 17 stitches; p9 with A.

Work Two-Color Cable Motif Pattern over the middle 17 stitches (increases to 35 stitches) with 9 stitches each side in Reverse Stockinette Stitch Pattern until Row 36 of Two-Color Motif Pattern is completed.

Working with A only, work 8 rows Reverse Stockinette Stitch Pattern.

Bind off.

SQUARE B (MAKE 4)

Same as Square A *except* reverse colors.

FINISHING

Back of Pillow Assembly

With the right sides facing, sew the squares together, alternating Squares A and B as shown in assembly illustration at right.

Front of Pillow Assembly

Work as for the back of the pillow.

Block the pieces to measurements.

Sew three side seams.

Insert the pillow form.

Sew the remaining side seam.

Twisted Cord

Cut ten 7-yd (6.5m) strands each of A and B.

Make a twisted cord using both colors (see page 32).

Sew the cord around the edges of the pillow to cover the side seams, adjusting length if necessary.

ASSEMBLY ILLUSTRATION

Square A	Square B
Square B	Square A

◇◇

TWO-COLOR CABLE MOTIF PATTERN
17 sts (inc to 35 sts)

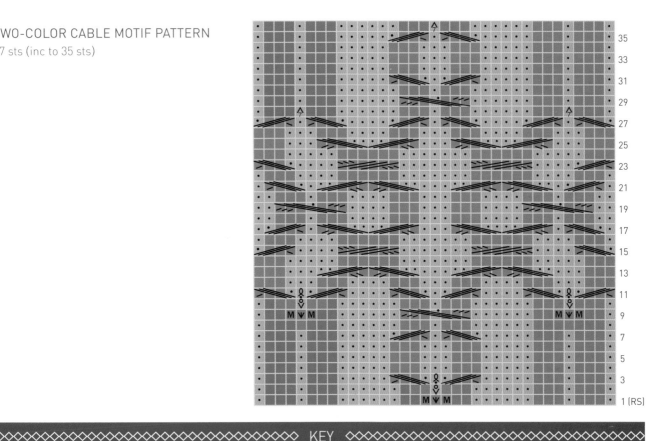

KEY

NOTE: Chart shows Fuchsia-colored background with Chocolate-colored cabled contrast, as worked for Square A; for Square B, reverse colors. When working chart, on RS rows, work all purl sts with the background color, and work all knit sts with the contrast color; on WS rows, work all knit sts with the background color, and work all purl sts with the contrast color

• = P on RS; K on WS

■ = No stitch

M = M1 Knitwise = Insert LH needle under the horizontal strand between two sts from front to back and K it *through back loop*

∨ = Central Double Increase = (Increases from 1 st to 3 sts) = K into back and then into front of indicated st and slip them off LH needle onto RH needle; insert point of LH needle behind the vertical strand that runs downward between the two sts just made and K *into the front of it*

☐ = K on RS; P on WS

⚥ = (With cabled contrast color, P1; bring background color from under cabled contrast color, and yarn over; bring cabled contrast color over background color, and P1) all in next st

= Slip next st onto cn and hold in back; K3; P1 from cn

⚢ = P *through back loop*

= Slip next 3 sts onto cn and hold in front; P1; K3 from cn

= Slip 3 sts onto cn #1 and hold in front; slip next st onto cn #2 and hold in back; with cabled contrast color, K3 ; with background color, P1 from cn #2; with cabled contrast color, K3 from cn #1

= Slip next 3 sts onto cn and hold in front; P2; K3 from cn

= Slip next 2 sts onto cn and hold in back; K3; P2 from cn

= Slip next 3 sts onto cn and hold in back; K3; K3 from cn

↑ = (Decreases from 7 sts to 1 st) = Slip next 4 sts with yarn in back, drop yarn; *pass the second st on RH needle over the first st on RH needle; slip first st from RH needle back to LH needle; pass the second st on LH needle over the first st on LH needle; **slip first st from LH needle back to RH needle and repeat from * to ** twice more; pick up yarn and K remaining st

Celtic Motif Throw

Seed stitch borders and solid reverse stockinette ground are the perfect setting for this Celtic-inspired motif.

SKILL LEVEL   Intermediate

SIZE
One size

FINISHED MEASUREMENTS
Approximately 39½" x 57" (100.5cm x 145cm)

MATERIALS
- Dale of Norway *Freestyle* (100% wool; each approximately 1¾ oz/50g and 88 yd/80m), 31 balls in #5533 Periwinkle, (4) medium/worsted
- One pair of size 7 (4.5mm) knitting needles or size needed to obtain gauge
- Two stitch markers
- Two cable needles
- Blunt-end yarn needle

GAUGE
20 stitches and 28 rows = 4" (10cm) in Reverse Stockinette Stitch Pattern. Each finished afghan block measures approximately 8¾" x 9¾" (22cm x 25cm).
To save time, take time to check gauge.

STITCH PATTERNS
Seed Stitch Pattern (multiple of 2 + 1 stitches)
Pattern Row: *K1, p1; repeat from * across, ending row with k1.
Repeat Pattern Row for pattern.
Reverse Stockinette Stitch Pattern (any number of stitches)
Row 1 (RS): Purl across.
Row 2: Knit across.
Repeat Rows 1 and 2 for pattern.
Motif Pattern
See chart, page 62.

AFGHAN BLOCK (MAKE 30)
Cast on 41 stitches.

Begin Seed Stitch Pattern, and work even for 7 rows.

Set Up Patterns
Next Row (RS): Work Seed Stitch Pattern over the first 5 stitches, place marker, work Row 1 of Reverse Stockinette Stitch Pattern over the middle 31 stitches, place marker, work Seed Stitch Pattern to end of row.

Continue even in patterns as established for 5 more rows.

Next Row (RS): Work Seed Stitch Pattern over the first 5 stitches, place marker, work Row 1 of Cable Motif Pattern over the middle 31 stitches, place marker, work Seed Stitch Pattern to end of row.

Continue patterns as established until Row 44 of Cable Motif Pattern is completed.

Next Row (RS): Work Seed Stitch Pattern over the first 5 stitches, place marker, work Row 1 of Reverse Stockinette Stitch Pattern over the middle 31 stitches, place marker, work Seed Stitch Pattern to end of row.

Continue even in patterns as established for 5 more rows.

Work even in Seed Stitch Pattern for 7 rows.

Bind off.

FINISHING
Block all pieces to finished measurements.

With the right side facing, sew the afghan blocks together into 5 strips of 6 Afghan Blocks each.

Sew the strips together.

CABLE MOTIF PATTERN
31 sts (inc to 59 sts)

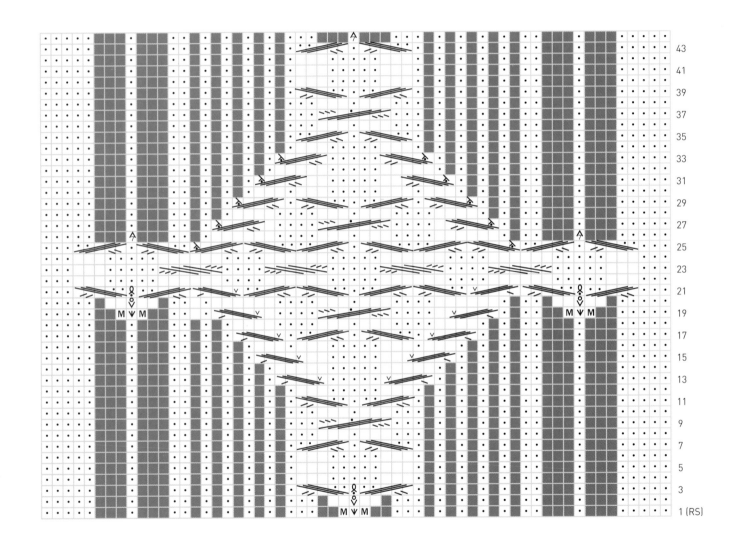

KEY

• = P on RS; K on WS

█ = No stitch

M = M1 Knitwise = Insert LH needle under the horizontal strand between two sts from front to back and K it *through back loop*

Ⅴ = Central Double Increase = (Increases from 1 st to 3 sts) = K into back and then into front of indicated st and slip them off LH needle onto RH needle; insert point of LH needle behind the vertical strand that runs downward between the two sts just made and K *into the front of it*

☐ = K on RS; P on WS

⏾ = (P1, yarn over, P1) into next st

 = Slip next 2 sts onto cn and hold in back; K3; P2 from cn

႙ = P *through back loop*

 = Slip next 3 sts onto cn and hold in front; P2; K3 from cn

 = Slip next 3 sts onto cn #1 and hold in back; slip next st onto cn #2 and hold in back; K3; P1 from cn #2; K3 from cn #1

 = Slip next st to cn and hold in back; K3; K st from cn through both back and front loops

 = Slip next 3 sts onto cn and hold in front; K next st through both back and front loops

 = Slip next 3 sts onto cn and hold in front; K3; K3 from cn

Ⱥ = (Decreases from 7 sts to 1 st) = Slip next 4 sts with yarn in back, drop yarn; *pass the second st on RH needle over the first st on RH needle; slip first st from RH needle back to LH needle; pass the second st on LH needle over the first st on LH needle; **slip first st from LH needle back to RH needle and repeat from * to ** twice more; pick up yarn and K remaining st

 = Slip next 3 sts onto cn and hold in front; P2tog; K3 from cn

= Slip next 2 sts onto cn and hold in back; K3; P2tog from cn

Sunday Brunch Place Mat

A textured border in a contrasting color makes this table topper special. And the mitered corners are not only beautiful, they're easy to knit and a breeze to sew together! Knit a set to give as a unique house gift.

SKILL LEVEL   Intermediate

SIZE
One size

FINISHED MEASUREMENTS
Approximately 18" x 14" (45.5cm x 35.5cm)

MATERIALS
- Muench Yarns/GGH *Samoa* (50% cotton/50% acrylic; each approximately 1¾ oz/50g and 104 yd/95m), 1 ball in Dark Peach #82 (A) and 2 balls in Light Peach #43 (B) for each place mat, (**4**) medium/worsted
- One pair of size 7 (4.5mm) knitting needles or size needed to obtain gauge
- Two stitch markers
- One cable needle
- Blunt-end yarn needle

GAUGE
17 stitches and 24 rows = 4" (10cm) in stockinette stitch.
To save time, take time to check gauge.

STITCH PATTERNS
Stockinette Stitch Pattern (any number of stitches)
Row 1 (RS): Knit across.
Row 2: Purl across.
Repeat Rows 1 and 2 for pattern.
Left-Hand Border Pattern
See chart, page 66.
Center Border Pattern
See chart, page 67.
Right-Hand Border Pattern
See chart, page 67.

NOTE
Row 1 of each chart in this pattern is a wrong-side row; begin knitting at the left-hand side of the charts.

PLACE MAT
With A, cast on 52 stitches.

Begin Stockinette Stitch Pattern, and work even until the piece measures approximately 8" (20.5cm).

Bind off.

FINISHING
Block to measurements.

Lower Edging
With the right side facing and B, pick up and knit 52 stitches along the cast-on edge of the Place Mat.

Set Up Patterns
Next Row (WS): Beginning at the left-hand side of the chart, work Row 1 of Left-Hand Border Pattern over the first 9 stitches, place marker, repeat Row 1 of Center Border Pattern twice over the next 32 stitches, place marker, work Row 1 of Right-Hand Border Pattern over the next 11 stitches to end of row.

Continue patterns as established, increasing as indicated in the charts, until Row 20 is complete.

Bind off in pattern.

Upper Edging
With the right side facing and B, pick up and knit 52 stitches along the bound-off edge of the Place Mat.

Complete same as for lower edging.

Side Edging
With the right side facing and B, pick up and knit 36 stitches along one side of the Place Mat.

Set Up Patterns

Next Row (WS): Beginning at the left-hand side of the chart, work Row 1 of Left-Hand Border Pattern over the first 9 stitches, place marker, work Row 1 of Center Border Pattern over the next 16 stitches, place marker, work Row 1 of Right-Hand Border Pattern over the next 11 stitches to end of row.

Continue patterns as established, increasing as indicated in the charts, until Row 20 is complete.

Bind off in pattern.

Repeat along the other side of the Place Mat.

Sew the corners of the borders together.

Block again, if necessary.

LEFT-HAND BORDER PATTERN

9 sts (inc to 21 sts, dec to 19 sts)

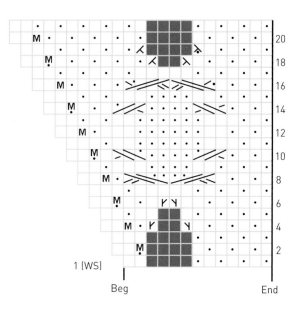

1 (WS)

Beg   End

CENTER BORDER PATTERN
16 sts (inc to 20 sts)

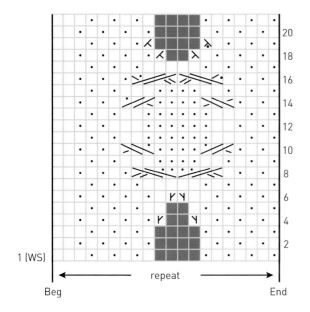

RIGHT-HAND BORDER PATTERN
11 sts (inc to 23 sts, dec to 21 sts)

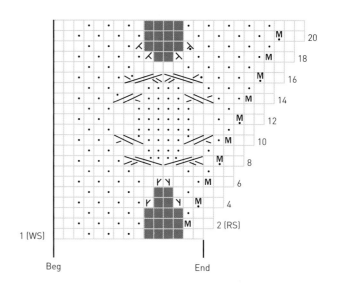

KEY

☐ = K on RS; P on WS

M = M1 Knitwise = Insert LH needle under the horizontal strand between two sts from front to back and K it *through back loop*

■ = No stitch

• = P on RS; K on WS

M̥ = M1 Purlwise = Insert LH needle under the horizontal strand between two sts from front to back and P it *through back loop*

Y = Left-slanting lifted increase

Y = Right-slanting lifted increase

= Slip 2 sts onto cn and hold in back; K2; P2 from cn

= Slip 2 sts onto cn and hold in front; P2; K2 from cn

= Slip next st onto cn and hold in back; K2; P1 from cn

= Slip 2 sts onto cn and hold in front; P1; K2 from cn

= Slip 2 sts onto cn and hold in front; K1; K2 from cn

= Slip 2 sts onto cn and hold in front; P1, K1; K2 from cn

= Slip 2 sts onto cn and hold in back; K2; (P1, K1) from cn

= P2tog on RS; K2tog on WS

= K2tog on RS; P2tog on WS

= SSK on RS; SSP on WS

Cable Style

CLOTHING FOR WOMEN

◇◇◇◇◇◇◇◇◇◇◇◇◇◇◇◇◇◇◇◇◇◇◇◇◇◇◇◇◇◇◇◇◇◇◇◇◇

Here are several projects that are sure to become favorites to both knit and wear, and closed-ring cables make each of them special.

If you're looking for (almost) immediate gratification, whip up the Quick-to-Knit Bulky Pullover or Sleeveless Shell. For a real show-stopper, knit the sporty Hoodie. The cable motif isolated on its back will surely attract attention— and compliments!

Sage Tunic

This design looks much more complicated than it really is. Entwined cables form horizontal bands that encircle the body, and a deceptively simple traveling stitch pattern is used on the sleeves. As a bonus, those tiny knots add lots of eye movement, breaking up the horizontal lines to make this a flattering sweater for most figure types!

SKILL LEVEL   Intermediate

SIZES

Small (Medium, Large, 1X, 2X). Instructions are for the smallest size, with changes for the other sizes noted in parentheses as necessary.

FINISHED MEASUREMENTS

Bust: 36 (40, 44, 48, 52)" [91 (101.5, 112, 122, 132)cm]
Total length: 28" (71cm)

MATERIALS

- Naturally *Sensation* (70% merino wool/30% angora; each approximately 1¾ oz/50g and 131 yd/120m), 13 (14, 15, 16, 17) hanks in Green #302, (4) medium/worsted
- One pair of size 7 (4.5mm) knitting needles or size needed to obtain gauge
- One size 7 (4.5mm) circular knitting needle, 16" (40cm) long
- Two cable needles
- One stitch marker
- Blunt-end yarn needle

GAUGE

20 stitches and 28 rows = 4" (10cm) in Main Cable Pattern. **To save time, take time to check gauge.**

STITCH PATTERNS

Traveling Diamonds Pattern
See chart, page 73.
Main Cable Pattern
See chart, page 73.
Reverse Stockinette Stitch Pattern (any number of stitches)
Row 1 (RS): Purl across.
Row 2: Knit across.
Repeat Rows 1 and 2 for pattern.

NOTES

- For sweater assembly, refer to the illustration for square indented construction on page 33.
- When increasing stitches within the pattern, use the M1 method.

BACK

Cast on 91 (101, 111, 121, 131) stitches.

Begin Traveling Diamonds Pattern, and work Rows 1–10 once.

Begin Main Cable Pattern, and repeat Rows 1–36 until the piece measures approximately 19½ (19½, 19, 18½, 18½)" [49.5 (49.5, 48.5, 47, 47)cm] from the beginning, ending after Row 18 (18, 14, 10, 10) of Main Cable Pattern.

Shape Armholes

Bind off 14 stitches at the beginning of the next 2 rows.

Continue even until the piece measures approximately 26½" (67.5cm) from the beginning, ending after Row 30 of Main Cable Pattern.

Shape Neck

Next Row (RS): Work across the first 24 (29, 34, 39, 44) stitches; join second ball of yarn and bind off the middle 15 stitches, work to end of row.

Work both sides at once with separate balls of yarn, and bind off 4 stitches at each neck edge once, bind off 3 stitches at each neck edge once.

Continue even in Reverse Stockinette Stitch Pattern until the piece measures approximately 28" (71cm) from the beginning.

Bind off.

FRONT
Work as for the Back.

SLEEVES
Cast on 51 stitches.

Work Rows 1 and 2 of Traveling Diamonds Pattern.

Continue with Traveling Diamonds Pattern, repeating Rows 3–10 only, and *at the same time*, increase 1 stitch at each side every 4th row 0 (0, 2, 12, 14) times, every 6th row 4 (8, 18, 10, 8) times, then every 8th row 13 (9, 0, 0, 0) times, working new stitches into pattern as they accumulate—85 (85, 91, 95, 95) stitches.

Continue even until the Sleeve measures approximately 22¼ (21¼, 20½, 19½, 19)" [56.5 (54, 52, 49.5, 48.5)cm] from the beginning.

Bind off.

Repeat for the second Sleeve.

FINISHING
Block pieces to finished measurements.

Sew shoulder seams.

Neck Edging
With the right side facing and circular needle, pick up and knit 81 stitches around neckline; place marker for beginning of round, and join.

Beginning and ending where indicated, work Rows 1–10 of Traveling Diamonds Pattern.

Bind off in pattern.

Set in the Sleeves.

Sew sleeve and side seams.

KEY

- ☐ = K on RS; P on WS

- • = P on RS; K on WS

- = Slip next st onto cn and hold in front; P1; K1 from cn

- = Slip next st onto cn and hold in back; K1; P1 from cn

- = Right Twist = Slip next st onto cn and hold in back; K1; K1 from cn **OR** K2tog, leaving them on LH needle; insert point of RH needle between these 2 sts and K the first one again

- = Left Twist = Slip next st onto cn and hold in front; K1; K1 from cn **OR** skip first st and K next st in back loop; then K the skipped st; slip both sts off LH needle together

- ■ = No stitch

- **M** = M1 Knitwise = Insert LH needle under the horizontal strand between two sts from front to back and K it *through back loop*

- **V** = Central Double Increase = (Increases from 1 st to 3 sts) = K into back and then into front of indicated st and slip them off LH needle onto RH needle; insert point of LH needle behind the vertical strand that runs downward between the two sts just made and K into the front of it

- = Slip 2 sts onto cn and hold in back; K2; P2 from cn

- = Slip 2 sts onto cn and hold in front; P2; K2 from cn

- = Slip 2 sts onto cn #1 and hold in back; slip next st onto cn #2 and hold in back; K2; P1 from cn #2; K2 from cn #1

- = Slip 2 sts onto cn #1 and hold in front; slip next st onto cn #2 and hold in back; K2; P1 from cn #2; K2 from cn #1

- ⚲ = (Decreases from 5 sts to 1 st) = Slip next 3 sts with yarn in back, drop yarn; *pass the second st on RH needle over the first st on RH needle; slip first st from RH needle back to LH needle; pass the second st on LH needle over the first st on LH needle; **slip first st from LH needle back to RH needle and repeat from * to ** once more; pick up yarn and K remaining st

TRAVELING DIAMONDS PATTERN
mult 10 + 11 sts

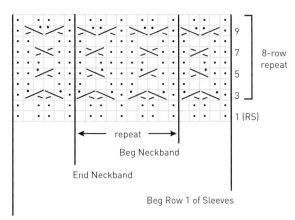

8-row repeat

1 (RS)
3
5
7
9

repeat

Beg Neckband

End Neckband

Beg Row 1 of Sleeves

End Row 1 of Sleeves

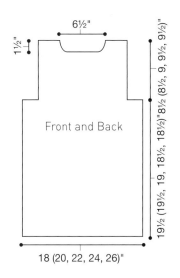

6½"

1½"

Front and Back

19½ (19½, 19, 18½, 18½)" 8½ (8½, 9, 9½, 9½)"

18 (20, 22, 24, 26)"

17 (17, 18, 19, 19)"

Sleeve

22¼ (21¼, 20½, 19½, 19)"

10"

MAIN CABLE PATTERN
mult 10 + 11 sts (inc to mult 14 + 15 sts)

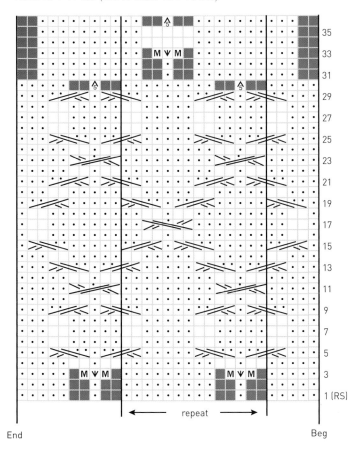

1 (RS)
3
5
7
9
11
13
15
17
19
21
23
25
27
29
31
33
35

repeat

End

Beg

Swirl Pullover

An unusual cable flows up the center of this design and is set off perfectly by the side cables and lattice filler pattern.

SKILL LEVEL   Intermediate

SIZES
Small (Medium, Large, 1X, 2X). Instructions are for the smallest size, with changes for the other sizes noted in parentheses as necessary.

FINISHED MEASUREMENTS
Bust: 36 (40, 44, 48, 52)" [91 (101.5, 112, 122, 132)cm]
Total length: 23¼ (23¼, 23¼, 23¾, 23¾)" [59 (59, 59, 60.5, 60.5)cm]

MATERIALS
- Classic Elite *Skye Tweed* (100% lambswool; each approximately 1¾ oz/50g and 112 yd/102m), 17 (18, 19, 20, 21) balls in #1229 Island Foam, (4) medium/worsted
- One pair size 5 (3.75mm) knitting needles
- One pair size 7 (4.5mm) knitting needles or size needed to obtain gauge
- Six stitch markers
- Two cable needles
- Blunt-end yarn needle

GAUGE
29 stitches and 28 rows = 4" (10cm) in Lattice Pattern with larger needles. **To save time, take time to check gauge.**

STITCH PATTERNS
P3 K3 Rib Pattern (multiple of 6 + 3 stitches)
Row 1 (RS): *P3, k3; repeat from * across, ending with p3.
Row 2: *K3, p3; repeat from * across, ending with k3.
Repeat Rows 1 and 2 for pattern.
Axis Cable Pattern
See chart, page 78.
Lattice Pattern
See chart, page 78.
Braided Cable Pattern
See chart, page 78.
Swirl Pattern
See chart, page 79.

NOTES
- For sweater assembly, refer to the illustration for the square indented saddle-shoulder construction on page 33.
- When decreasing stitches within the pattern, work k2tog or p2tog depending on the stitch pattern.
- When increasing stitches within the pattern, use the M1 method.

BACK
With smaller needles, cast on 121 (133, 145, 169, 181) stitches.

Set Up Patterns
Work Row 1 of P3 K3 Rib Pattern over the first 57 (63, 69, 81, 87) stitches, place marker, work Row 1 of Axis Cable Pattern over the middle 7 stitches, place marker, work Row 1 of P3 K3 Rib Pattern across to end of row.

Continue even in patterns as established until the piece measures approximately 2¾" (7cm) from the beginning, ending after Row 3 of Axis Cable Pattern.

Next Row (WS): Work patterns as established, and *at the same time*, increase 4 (6, 8, 4, 6) stitches evenly spaced before first marker and 4 (6, 8, 4, 6) stitches evenly spaced following second marker—129 (145, 161, 177, 193) stitches.

Set Up Patterns
Next Row (RS): Change to larger needles, and work Row 1 of Lattice Pattern over the first 14 (22, 30, 30, 38) stitches, place marker, work Row 1 of Braided Cable Pattern over the next 9 stitches, place marker, work Row 1 of Lattice Pattern over the next 22 (22, 22, 30, 30) stitches, place marker, work Row 1 of Swirl Pattern over the next 39 stitches, place marker, work Row 1 of Lattice Pattern over the next 22 (22, 22, 30, 30) stitches, place marker, work Row 1 of Braided Cable Pattern over the next 9 stitches, place marker, work Row 1 of Lattice Pattern over the next 14 (22, 30, 30, 38) stitches.

Continue even in patterns as established until the piece measures approximately 13½ (13½, 13, 13, 13)" [34.5 (34.5, 33, 33, 33)cm] from the beginning, ending after a wrong-side row.

Shape Armholes
Bind off 13 (21, 29, 29, 37) stitches at the beginning of the next 2 rows.

Continue even until the piece measures approximately 20¾" (52.5cm) from the beginning, ending after a wrong-side row.

Shape Shoulders
Bind off 8 (8, 8, 10, 10) stitches at the beginning of the next 8 rows.

Bind off the remaining 45 stitches.

FRONT
Work as for the Back until the piece measures approximately 20" (51cm) from the beginning, ending after Row 2 of Swirl Cable Pattern.

Shape Neck and Shoulders
Next Row (RS): Continuing patterns as established, work across the first 43 (43, 43, 51, 51) stitches, join second ball of yarn and bind off the middle 17 stitches, work across to end of row.

Working both sides at once with separate balls of yarn, continue patterns as established, and bind off 3 stitches at each neck edge once, bind off 2 stitches at each neck edge once, then decrease 1 stitch at each neck edge every row 6 times, and *at the same time*, when front measures same as back to shoulders, shape shoulders as for the Back.

SLEEVES
With smaller needles, cast on 63 (63, 63, 69, 69) stitches.

Begin P3 K3 Rib Pattern, and work even until the piece measures approximately 2¾" (7cm) from the beginning, increasing 5 (5, 5, 7, 7) stitches evenly spaced using M1 method along last row, ending after a wrong-side row—68 (68, 68, 76, 76) stitches.

Set Up Patterns
Next Row (RS): Change to larger needles, work Row 1 of Lattice Pattern over the first 14 stitches, place marker, work Row 1 of Braided Cable Pattern over the next 9 stitches, place marker, work Row 1 of Lattice Pattern over the next 22 (22, 22, 30, 30) stitches, place marker, work Row 1 of Braided Cable Pattern over the next 9 stitches, place marker, work Row 1 of Lattice Pattern over the next 14 stitches to end of row.

Continue patterns as established, and increase 1 stitch each side every other row 6 (8, 22, 22, 24) times, then every 4th row 26 (24, 14, 14, 12) times, working new stitches in Lattice Pattern as they accumulate—132 (132, 140, 148, 148) stitches.

Continue even until the Sleeve measures approximately 21½ (22, 21, 21, 21½)" [54.5 (56, 53.5, 53.5, 54.5)cm] from the beginning.

Shape Saddle

Bind off 55 (55, 59, 59, 59) stitches at the beginning of the next 2 rows—22 (22, 22, 30, 30) stitches remain.

Continue even in pattern as established until the saddle fits along the shoulder of the Front and Back.

Bind off.

Repeat for the second sleeve.

FINISHING

Block the pieces to finished measurements.

Sew the right saddle between the Front and Back shoulders.

Sew the left saddle to the Front.

Neckband

With the right side facing and smaller needles, pick up and knit 90 stitches along the neckline.

Next Row (WS): P1, work (p3, k3) 9 times, place marker, work Row 2 of Axis Cable Pattern over 7 stitches at center front neck opening, place marker, work (k3, p3) 4 times, ending row with k3, p1.

Next Row: K1, work pattern as established across the next 27 stitches, slip marker, work Row 3 of Axis Cable Pattern over the next 7 stitches, slip marker, work pattern as established across the next 54 stitches, ending row with k1.

Continue even in patterns as established until the band measures approximately 4" (10cm) from the beginning, ending after Row 6 of Axis Cable Pattern.

Bind off *loosely* in pattern.

Sew the left saddle to the Back.

Sew the side of the neckband.

Set in the Sleeves.

Sew the sleeve and side seams.

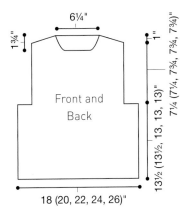

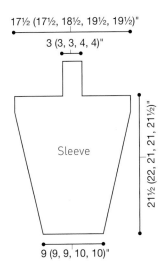

AXIS CABLE PATTERN 7sts

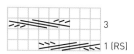

LATTICE PATTERN mult 4 + 6 sts

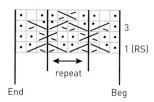

BRAIDED CABLE PATTERN 9 sts

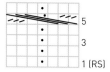

KEY

• = P on RS; K on WS

= Slip 3 sts onto cn and hold in front; P1; K3 from cn

= Slip 3 sts onto cn #1 and hold in front; slip next st onto cn #2 and hold in back; K3; P1 from cn #2; K3 from cn #1

= Slip next st onto cn and hold in back; K3; P1 from cn

☐ = K on RS; P on WS

= Slip 2 sts onto cn and hold in back; K3; P2 from cn

= Slip 3 sts onto cn and hold in front; P2; K3 from cn

= Slip 3 sts onto cn #1 and hold in back; slip next st onto cn #2 and hold in back; K3; P1 from cn #2; K3 from cn #1

M = M1 Knitwise = Insert LH needle under the horizontal strand between two sts from front to back and K it *through back loop*

Ѵ = Central Double Increase = (Increases from 1 st to 3 sts) = K into back and then into front of indicated st and slip them off LH needle onto RH needle; insert point of LH needle behind the vertical strand that runs downward between the two sts just made and K *into the front of it*

� = (P1, yarn over, P1) into next st

ᛘ = P *through back loop*

ᛮ = (Decreases from 7 sts to 1 st) = Slip next 4 sts with yarn in back, drop yarn; *pass the second st on RH needle over the first st on RH needle; slip first st from RH needle back to LH needle; pass the second st on LH needle over the first st on LH needle; **slip first st from LH needle back to RH needle and repeat from * to ** twice more; pick up yarn and K remaining st

= Slip next st onto cn and hold in front; P1; K1 from cn

= Slip next st onto cn and hold in back; K1; P1 from cn

= Right Twist = On WS rows, slip next st onto cn and hold in back; P1; P1 from cn

= Left Twist = On WS rows, slip next st onto cn and hold in front; P1; P1 from cn

= Slip 3 sts onto cn and hold in back; K3; K3 from cn

= Slip 3 sts onto cn and hold in front; K3; K3 from cn

SWIRL PATTERN
39 sts (inc to 45 sts)

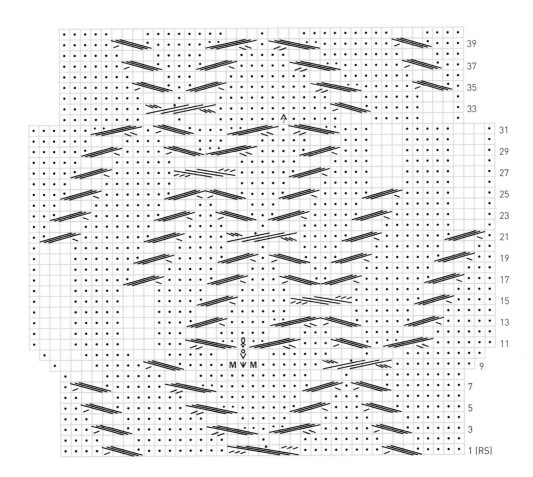

Honeysuckle Sleeveless Shell

I'll bet this sweater won't languish at the bottom of your knitting bag waiting to be sewn together: its armbands and neckbands are integrated into the knitting of the pieces for quick and easy finishing.

SKILL LEVEL   Experienced

SIZES
Extra-Small (Small, Medium, Large, 1X, 2X). Instructions are for the smallest size, with changes for the other sizes noted in parentheses as necessary.

FINISHED MEASUREMENTS
Bust: 32 (34½, 37, 39½, 43½, 47½)" [81 (87.5, 94, 100.5, 110.5, 120.5)cm]
Total length: 22" (56cm)

MATERIALS
- Kolláge Yarns *Cornucopia* (100% corn; each approximately 1 oz/34g and 100 yd/101m), 10 (11, 12, 13, 14, 15) hanks in Torchlight, ③ light/DK
- One pair size 5 (3.75mm) knitting needles
- One pair size 7 (4.5mm) knitting needles or size needed to obtain gauge
- Two stitch markers
- Two cable needles
- Blunt-end yarn needle

GAUGE
24 stitches and 37 rows = 4" (10cm) in Reverse Stockinette Stitch Pattern with larger needles. **To save time, take time to check gauge.**

STITCH PATTERNS
K1 P1 Rib Pattern (multiple of 2 + 1 stitches)
Row 1 (RS): *K1, p1; repeat from * across, ending row with k1.
Row 2: *P1, k1; repeat from * across, ending row with p1.
Repeat Rows 1 and 2 for pattern.

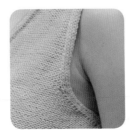

◇◇◇

Reverse Stockinette Stitch Pattern (any number of stitches)
Row 1 (RS): Purl across.
Row 2: Knit across.
Repeat Rows 1 and 2 for pattern.
Center Cable Panel
See chart, page 83.

NOTES

- **For Body Decrease Row:** On right-side rows, p6, p2tog, work across in patterns as established until 8 stitches remain, ending row with ssp, p6.
- **For Body Increase Row:** On right-side rows, p6, M1P, work across in patterns as established until 6 stitches remain, ending row with M1P, p6.
- **For Armhole Double Decrease Row:** On right-side rows, k5, sssk, work across in patterns as established until 8 stitches remain, ending row with k3tog, k5. On wrong-side rows, p5, p3tog, work across in patterns as established until 8 stitches remain, ending row with sssp, p5.
- **For Armhole Decrease Row:** On right-side rows, k5, ssk, work across in patterns as established until 7 stitches remain, ending row with k2tog, k5. On wrong-side rows, p5, p2tog, work across in patterns as established until 7 stitches remain, ending row with ssp, p5.
- **For Neck Decrease Row:** On right-side rows, work across first side of front until 7 stitches remain this side of neck, k2tog, k5. On second side of neck, with second ball of yarn, k5, ssk, work across to end of row.

BACK

With smaller needles, cast on 101 (109, 117, 125, 137, 149) stitches.

Begin K1 P1 Rib Pattern, and work even until the piece measures approximately 3" (7.5cm) from the beginning, ending after a wrong-side row.

Change to larger needles.

Next Row (RS): Work Row 1 of Reverse Stockinette Stitch Pattern over the first 39 (43, 47, 51, 57, 63) stitches, place marker, work Row 1 of Center Cable Panel over the next 23 stitches, place marker, work Row 1 of Reverse Stockinette Stitch Pattern over 39 (43, 47, 51, 57, 63) stitches to end of row.

Work one row even in patterns as established.

Waist Shaping
Next Row (RS): Work Body Decrease Row (see Notes).

Continue patterns as established, and repeat Body Decrease Row every 10th row 2 more times, then every 8th row twice.

Work even until the piece measures approximately 9¼ (9¼, 9½, 9½, 9½, 9½)" [23.5 (23.5, 24, 24, 24, 24)cm] from the beginning, ending after a wrong-side row.

Next Row (RS): Work Body Increase Row (see Notes).

Continue patterns as established, and repeat Body Increase Row every 6th row once, then every 8th row 3 more times.

Work even until the piece measures approximately 13½ (13, 12½, 12½, 12, 12)" [34.5 (33, 32, 32, 30.5, 30.5)cm] from the beginning, ending after a wrong-side row.

Shape Armholes
Next Row (RS): Use cable cast on to cast on 3 stitches, then knit each of the 3 cast-on stitches, k2, ssk, work across in patterns as established until 4 stitches remain, ending row with k2tog, k2.

Next Row: Use cable cast on to cast on 3 stitches, then purl each of the 3 cast-on stitches, p3, work across in patterns as established until 6 stitches remain, ending row with p6.

Continue patterns as established, and work Armhole Double Decrease Row every row 0 (0, 0, 3, 6, 11) times, Armhole Decrease Row every row 10 (14, 16, 14, 14, 9) times, then every other row 2 (1, 1, 0, 0, 0) times.

Continue even in patterns as established until the piece measures approximately 20¼" (51.5cm) from the beginning, ending after Row 9 of Center Cable Panel—81 (83, 87, 89, 89, 91) stitches.

Shape Neck
Next Row (WS): Work pattern as established across the first 17 (18, 20, 21, 21, 22) stitches; join second ball of yarn and bind off the middle 47 stitches, work patterns as established to end of row.

◇◇◇

Next Row: Work both sides at once with separate balls of yarn and work Neck Decrease Row—16 (17, 19, 20, 20, 21) stitches remain on each side.

Work even until the piece measures approximately 20½" (52cm) from the beginning, ending after a wrong-side row.

Shape Shoulders

Bind off 5 stitches at the beginning of the next 2 rows, bind off 2 (2, 2, 2, 2, 3) stitches at the beginning of the next 6 rows, bind off 2 (2, 2, 3, 3, 3) stitches at the beginning of the next 2 rows, bind off 2 (2, 3, 3, 3, 2) stitches at the beginning of the next 2 rows, then bind off 1 (2, 3, 3, 3, 2) stitches at the beginning of the next 2 rows.

FRONT

Work as for the Back until the piece measures approximately 16" (40.5cm) from the beginning, ending after Row 30 of Center Cable Panel. Place marker on center purl stitch.

Shape Neck

Next Row (RS): Work patterns as established to 3 stitches before center marked stitch, slip the next 3 stitches onto cn #1 and hold in front of work, slip the next stitch onto cn #2 and hold in back of work, k3 stitches from main left-hand needle; for second side of neck, join second ball of yarn, use cable cast on to cast on 2 stitches onto the left-hand needle, knit the 2 new cast-on stitches, k1 from cn #2, k3 stitches from cn #1, work patterns as established across to end of row.

Next Row: Work both sides at once with separate balls of yarn, and work patterns as established across first side; on second side of neck, use cable cast on to cast on 3 stitches, purl the 3 cast-on stitches, work across patterns as established to end of row.

Work both sides at once with separate balls of yarn, and work Neck Decrease Row (see Notes) on the next row and then every other row 15 times, then every 4th row 5 times, and *at the same time,* when piece measures same as back to shoulders, shape shoulders same as for Back—6 stitches remain on each side.

Continue even on 6 stitches at each side until bands, when slightly stretched, meet at the center back of neck.

Bind off.

FINISHING

Block the pieces to finished measurements.

Fold 3 cast-on stitches at each armhole edge to the wrong side and whipstitch into place.

Sew the shoulder seams.

Fold 3 cast-on stitches on each neck edge to the wrong side and whipstitch into place.

Sew the inner edge of the neckbands to the back neck.

Sew the bound-off edges of the neckbands together at the back of neck.

Sew the side seams.

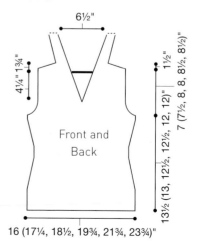

6½"

4¼" 1¾"

1½"

7 (7½, 8, 8, 8½, 8½)"

13½ (13, 12½, 12½, 12, 12)"

Front and Back

16 (17¼, 18½, 19¾, 21¾, 23¾)"

CENTRAL CABLE PATTERN
23 sts (inc to 35 sts)

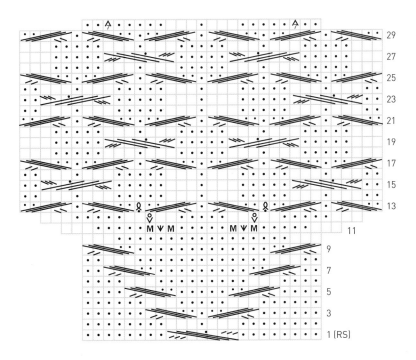

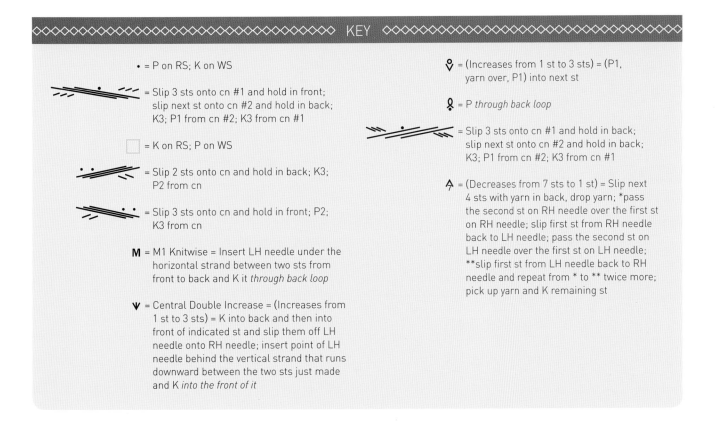

KEY

• = P on RS; K on WS

= Slip 3 sts onto cn #1 and hold in front; slip next st onto cn #2 and hold in back; K3; P1 from cn #2; K3 from cn #1

☐ = K on RS; P on WS

= Slip 2 sts onto cn and hold in back; K3; P2 from cn

= Slip 3 sts onto cn and hold in front; P2; K3 from cn

M = M1 Knitwise = Insert LH needle under the horizontal strand between two sts from front to back and K it *through back loop*

ⱴ = Central Double Increase = (Increases from 1 st to 3 sts) = K into back and then into front of indicated st and slip them off LH needle onto RH needle; insert point of LH needle behind the vertical strand that runs downward between the two sts just made and K into the front of it

= (Increases from 1 st to 3 sts) = (P1, yarn over, P1) into next st

= P *through back loop*

= Slip 3 sts onto cn #1 and hold in back; slip next st onto cn #2 and hold in back; K3; P1 from cn #2; K3 from cn #1

= (Decreases from 7 sts to 1 st) = Slip next 4 sts with yarn in back, drop yarn; *pass the second st on RH needle over the first st on RH needle; slip first st from RH needle back to LH needle; pass the second st on LH needle over the first st on LH needle; **slip first st from LH needle back to RH needle and repeat from * to ** twice more; pick up yarn and K remaining st

Quick-to-Knit Bulky Pullover

In this sweater design, an intricate cable motif sits smack-dab in a field of textured seed stitch. For me, it's the perfect knitting project: the chart on the front offers a fun technical workout, but the back and sleeves are simple, mindless knitting.

SKILL LEVEL   Experienced

SIZES
Small (Medium, Large, 1X, 2X). Instructions are for the smallest size, with changes for the other sizes noted in parentheses as necessary.

FINISHED MEASUREMENTS
Bust: 34 (38, 43, 47½, 52)" [86 (96.5, 109, 120.5, 132)cm]
Total length: 22 (22½, 23, 23½, 24)" [56 (57, 58.5, 59.5, 61)cm]

MATERIALS
- Plymouth Yarn Company *Baby Alpaca Grande* (100% baby alpaca; each approximately 3½ oz/100g and 110 yd/101m), 10 (11, 12, 13, 14) hanks in #1310 Soft Lime, ⑤ bulky
- One pair size 9 (5.5mm) knitting needles
- One pair size 10 (6mm) knitting needles or size needed to obtain gauge
- Two cable needles
- One blunt-end yarn needle

GAUGE
14 stitches and 24 rows = 4" (10cm) in Seed Stitch Pattern with larger needles; with larger needles, the Cable Medallion Pattern measures 9" x 11½" (23cm x 29cm). **To save time, take time to check gauge.**

STITCH PATTERNS
Seed Stitch Pattern (multiple of 2 + 1 stitches)
Patt Row (RS): *K1, p1; repeat from * across, ending row with k1.
Repeat Patt Row for pattern.

Lower Cable Medallion Pattern
See chart, page 87.
Upper Cable Medallion Pattern
See chart, page 88.
K1 P1 Rib Pattern (multiple of 2 stitches)
Patt Row (RS): *K1, p1; repeat from * across.
Repeat Patt Row for pattern.

NOTES
- For ease in finishing, instructions include one selvedge stitch on each side; these stitches are not reflected in final measurements.
- For sweater assembly, refer to the illustration for set-in sleeve construction on page 33.
- When decreasing stitches within the pattern, work k2tog or p2tog depending on the stitch pattern.
- When increasing stitches within the pattern, use the M1 method.

BACK

With larger needles, cast on 61 (69, 77, 85, 93) stitches.

Begin Seed Stitch Pattern, and continue even until the piece measures approximately 3" (7.5cm) from the beginning, ending after a wrong-side row.

Decrease for Waist

Continue pattern as established, and decrease 1 stitch at each side on the next row, then every 10th row once, then every 8th row twice—53 (61, 69, 77, 85) stitches remain.

Continue even in pattern as established until the piece measures approximately 9½ (9½, 9½, 9½, 9¾)" [24 (24, 24, 24, 25)cm] from the beginning, ending after a wrong-side row.

Increase for Bust

Continue pattern as established, and increase 1 stitch at each side on the next row, then every 6th row 3 times—61 (69, 77, 85, 93) stitches.

Continue even in patterns as established until the piece measures approximately 14 (14, 14, 14, 14½)" [35.5 (35.5, 35.5, 35.5, 37)cm] from the beginning, ending after a wrong-side row.

Shape Armholes

Bind off 3 (4, 5, 6, 7) stitches at the beginning of the next 2 rows, then bind off 2 (2, 2, 2, 4) stitches at the beginning of the next 2 rows—51 (57, 63, 69, 71) stitches remain.

Decrease 1 stitch at each side every row 0 (2, 2, 4, 4) times, every other row 1 (3, 6, 6, 6) times, then every 4th row 2 (1, 0, 0, 0) times—45 (45, 47, 49, 51) stitches remain.

Continue even in patterns as established until the piece measures approximately 21 (21½, 22, 22½, 23)" [53.5 (54.5, 56, 57, 58.5)cm] from the beginning, ending after a wrong-side row.

Shape Shoulders

Bind off 3 (3, 3, 4, 4) stitches at the beginning of the next 4 rows, then bind off 4 (4, 5, 4, 5) stitches at the beginning of the next 2 rows—25 stitches remain.

Bind off.

FRONT

Work as for the Back until the piece measures approximately 4 (4½, 4½, 5, 5)" [10 (11.5, 11.5, 12.5, 12.5)cm] from the beginning, ending after a wrong-side row.

Set Up Patterns

Continue shaping the same as for the Back, and *at the same time*, work Cable Medallion Pattern over the middle 31 stitches (increases to 55 stitches), and continue Seed Stitch Pattern as established on stitches on both sides.

When Row 34 of Lower Cable Medallion Pattern is complete, work Rows 1–34 of Upper Cable Medallion Pattern, keeping Seed Stitch Pattern as established on both sides.

When Row 68 of Upper Cable Medallion Pattern is completed, work Seed Stitch Pattern over all stitches until the piece measures approximately 19 (19½, 20, 20½, 21)" [48.5 (49.5, 51, 52, 53.5)cm] from the beginning, ending after a wrong-side row.

Shape Neck

Next Row (RS): Work across the first 18 (18, 19, 20, 21) stitches; join second ball of yarn and bind off the middle 9 stitches, work to end of row.

Work both sides at once with separate balls of yarn, and bind off 2 stitches at each neck edge twice—14 (14, 15, 16, 17) stitches remain on each side. Next, decrease 1 stitch at each neck edge every row twice, then decrease 1 stitch at each neck edge every other row twice—10 (10, 11, 12, 13) stitches remain on each side.

Continue even, if necessary, until the piece measures same as Back to shoulders, ending after a wrong-side row.

Shape Shoulders

Work as for the Back.

SLEEVES

With larger needles, cast on 35 stitches.

Begin Seed Stitch Pattern, and increase 1 stitch at each side on the next row, every 8th row 0 (0, 5, 10, 10) times, every 10th row 4 (9, 5, 1, 1) times, then every 12th row 4 (0, 0, 0, 0) times—53 (55, 57, 59, 59) stitches.

◇◇

Continue even until the piece measures approximately 17¾" (45cm) from the beginning, ending after a wrong-side row.

Shape Cap

Bind off 3 (4, 5, 6, 7) stitches at the beginning of the next 2 rows—47 (47, 47, 47, 45) stitches remain.

Decrease 1 stitch at each side every row 7 (1, 0, 0, 0) times, every other row 8 (14, 14, 13, 11) times, then every 4th row 0 (0, 1, 2, 3) times—17 stitches remain.

Work even for 0 (0, 0, 1, 1) row.

Bind off 2 stitches at the beginning of the next 4 rows—9 stitches remain.

Bind off.

Repeat for the second sleeve.

FINISHING

Block the pieces to finished measurements.

Sew the right shoulder seam.

Neckband

With the right side facing and smaller needles, pick up and knit 72 stitches along the neckline.

Begin K1 P1 Rib Pattern, and work even until neckband measures approximately 4" (10cm) from the beginning.

Bind off *loosely* in pattern.

Sew the left shoulder seam, including the side of the neckband.

Set in the Sleeves.

Sew the sleeve and side seams.

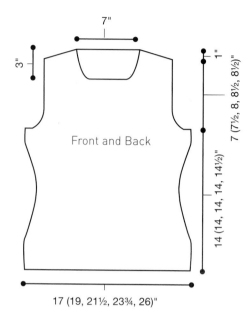

Front and Back

7"

3"

1"

7 (7½, 8, 8½, 8½)"

14 (14, 14, 14, 14½)"

17 (19, 21½, 23¾, 26)"

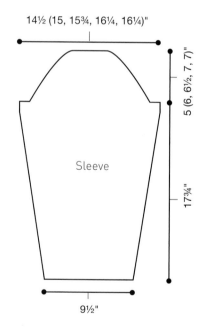

14½ (15, 15¾, 16¼, 16¼)"

5 (6, 6½, 7, 7)"

Sleeve

17¾"

9½"

LOWER CABLE MEDALLION PATTERN
31 sts (inc to 55 sts)

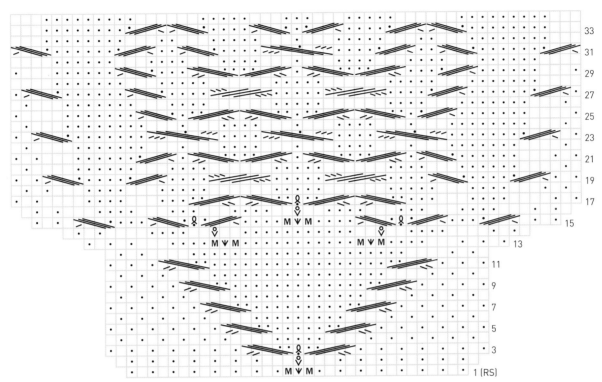

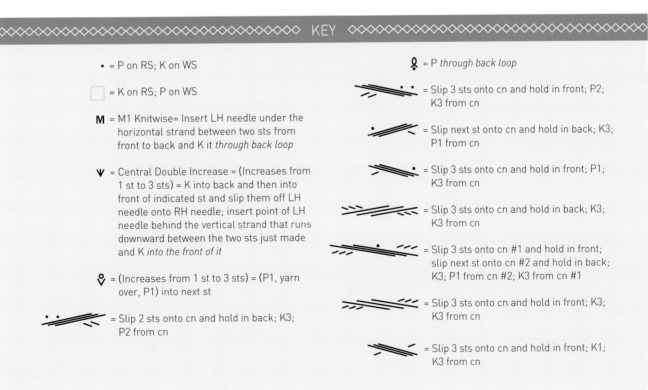

- • = P on RS; K on WS

- ☐ = K on RS; P on WS

- **M** = M1 Knitwise= Insert LH needle under the horizontal strand between two sts from front to back and K it *through back loop*

- **Ѵ** = Central Double Increase = (Increases from 1 st to 3 sts) = K into back and then into front of indicated st and slip them off LH needle onto RH needle; insert point of LH needle behind the vertical strand that runs downward between the two sts just made and K *into the front of it*

- ♀ = (Increases from 1 st to 3 sts) = (P1, yarn over, P1) into next st

- = Slip 2 sts onto cn and hold in back; K3; P2 from cn

- ♀ = P *through back loop*

- = Slip 3 sts onto cn and hold in front; P2; K3 from cn

- = Slip next st onto cn and hold in back; K3; P1 from cn

- = Slip 3 sts onto cn and hold in front; P1; K3 from cn

- = Slip 3 sts onto cn and hold in back; K3; K3 from cn

- = Slip 3 sts onto cn #1 and hold in front; slip next st onto cn #2 and hold in back; K3; P1 from cn #2; K3 from cn #1

- = Slip 3 sts onto cn and hold in front; K3; K3 from cn

- = Slip 3 sts onto cn and hold in front; K1; K3 from cn

UPPER CABLE MEDALLION PATTERN
55 sts (inc to 31 sts)

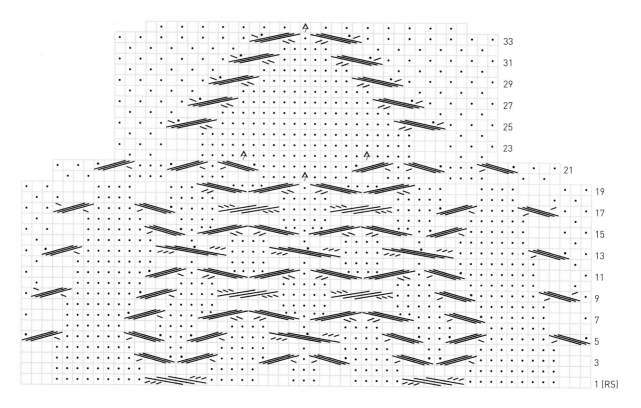

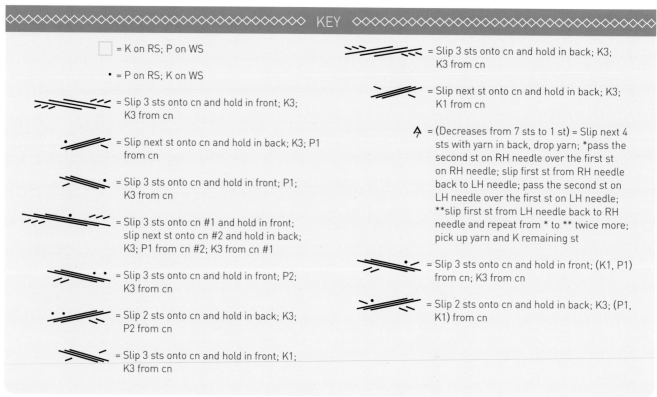

KEY

☐ = K on RS; P on WS

• = P on RS; K on WS

= Slip 3 sts onto cn and hold in front; K3; K3 from cn

= Slip next st onto cn and hold in back; K3; P1 from cn

= Slip 3 sts onto cn and hold in front; P1; K3 from cn

= Slip 3 sts onto cn #1 and hold in front; slip next st onto cn #2 and hold in back; K3; P1 from cn #2; K3 from cn #1

= Slip 3 sts onto cn and hold in front; P2; K3 from cn

= Slip 2 sts onto cn and hold in back; K3; P2 from cn

= Slip 3 sts onto cn and hold in front; K1; K3 from cn

= Slip 3 sts onto cn and hold in back; K3; K3 from cn

= Slip next st onto cn and hold in back; K3; K1 from cn

Ⱥ = (Decreases from 7 sts to 1 st) = Slip next 4 sts with yarn in back, drop yarn; *pass the second st on RH needle over the first st on RH needle; slip first st from RH needle back to LH needle; pass the second st on LH needle over the first st on LH needle; **slip first st from LH needle back to RH needle and repeat from * to ** twice more; pick up yarn and K remaining st

= Slip 3 sts onto cn and hold in front; (K1, P1) from cn; K3 from cn

= Slip 2 sts onto cn and hold in back; K3; (P1, K1) from cn

Interlocked Cables Skirt

Anxious to knit yourself something other than a sweater? Make this skirt instead! The interlocked cables will encircle you without adding inches, and the side seams will help prevent stretch lengthwise.

SKILL LEVEL   Intermediate

SIZES
Small (Medium, Large, 1X). Instructions are for the smallest size, with changes for the other sizes noted in parentheses as necessary.

FINISHED MEASUREMENTS
Hip: 35 (42, 49, 56)" [89 (106.5, 124.5, 142)cm]
Total length: 20" (51cm)

MATERIALS
- Skacel Collection/Zitron *Ecco* (100% merino wool; each approximately 1¾ oz/50g and 120 yd/110m), 8 (9, 10, 11) balls in #144 Grape, **3** light/DK
- One pair of size 5 (3.75 mm) knitting needles or size needed to obtain gauge
- Two cable needles
- Blunt-end yarn needle
- Elastic, ¾" (2cm) wide, cut to fit waist

GAUGE
25 stitches and 36 rows = 4" (10cm) in Main Cable Pattern. **To save time, take time to check gauge.**

STITCH PATTERNS
Stockinette Stitch Pattern (any number of stitches)
Row 1 (RS): Knit across.
Row 2: Purl across.
Repeat Rows 1 and 2 for pattern.
Lower Cable Pattern
See chart, page 90.
Main Cable Pattern
See chart, page 91.
Upper Cable Pattern
See chart, page 91.

LOWER CABLE PATTERN
mult 22 + 21 sts (inc to mult 30 + 25 sts, dec to mult 26 + 21sts)

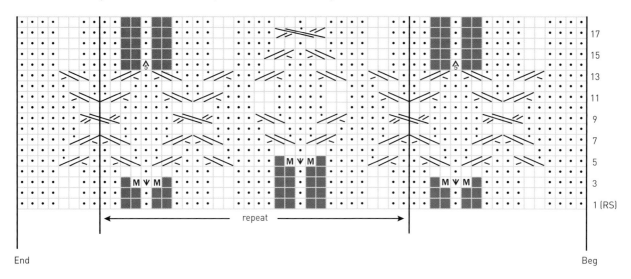

End   repeat   Beg

17
15
13
11
9
7
5
3
1 (RS)

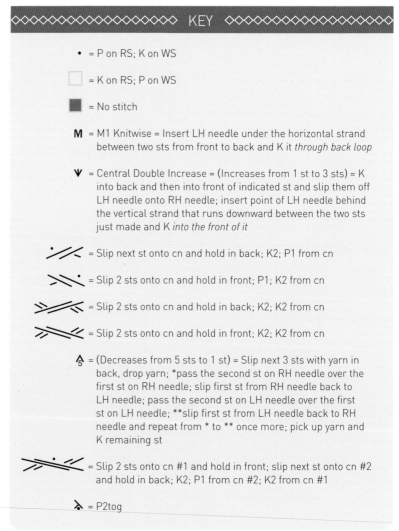

KEY

• = P on RS; K on WS

☐ = K on RS; P on WS

■ = No stitch

M = M1 Knitwise = Insert LH needle under the horizontal strand between two sts from front to back and K it *through back loop*

Ψ = Central Double Increase = (Increases from 1 st to 3 sts) = K into back and then into front of indicated st and slip them off LH needle onto RH needle; insert point of LH needle behind the vertical strand that runs downward between the two sts just made and K *into the front of it*

= Slip next st onto cn and hold in back; K2; P1 from cn

= Slip 2 sts onto cn and hold in front; P1; K2 from cn

= Slip 2 sts onto cn and hold in back; K2; K2 from cn

= Slip 2 sts onto cn and hold in front; K2; K2 from cn

= (Decreases from 5 sts to 1 st) = Slip next 3 sts with yarn in back, drop yarn; *pass the second st on RH needle over the first st on RH needle; slip first st from RH needle back to LH needle; pass the second st on LH needle over the first st on LH needle; **slip first st from LH needle back to RH needle and repeat from * to ** once more; pick up yarn and K remaining st

= Slip 2 sts onto cn #1 and hold in front; slip next st onto cn #2 and hold in back; K2; P1 from cn #2; K2 from cn #1

= P2tog

MAIN CABLE PATTERN
mult 26 + 21 sts (dec to mult 22 + 21 sts, inc to mult 26 + 25 sts)

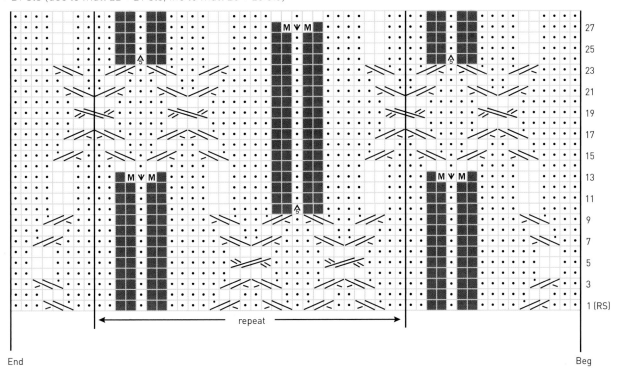

End

repeat

Beg

UPPER CABLE PATTERN
mult 22 + 21 sts (inc to mult 25 + 24 sts, dec to mult 20 + 20 sts)

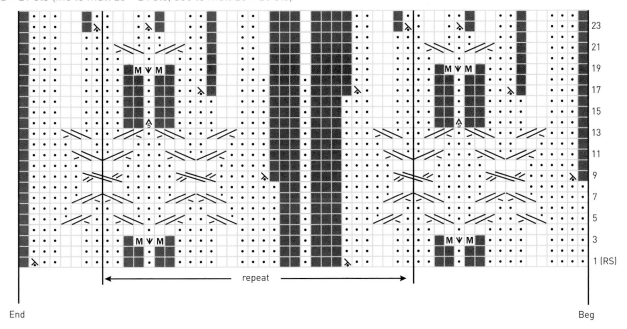

End

repeat

Beg

BACK

Cast on 93 (111, 129, 147) stitches.

Begin Stockinette Stitch Pattern, and work even for 5 rows, allowing lower edge to curl.

Next Row (WS): Purl, increasing 16 (20, 24, 28) stitches using M1P method evenly across—109 (131, 153, 175) stitches.

Work Rows 1–18 of Lower Cable Pattern.

Begin Main Cable Pattern, repeating Rows 1–28 of chart four times total.

Work Rows 1–10 of Main Cable Pattern once. Piece should measure approximately 16½" (42cm) from the beginning.

Work Rows 1–24 of Upper Cable Pattern—100 (120, 140, 160) stitches remain.

Waistband

Next Row (RS): P3, *k2, p2; repeat from * to last stitch, ending row with p1.

Next Row: K3, *p2, k2; repeat from * to last stitch, ending row with k1.

Repeat last 2 rows until the waistband measures approximately 2" (5cm).

Bind off *loosely* in pattern.

FRONT

Work as for the Back.

FINISHING

Block pieces to measurements.

Sew side seams.

Fold waistband in half to the wrong side, insert elastic, and *loosely* whipstitch into place.

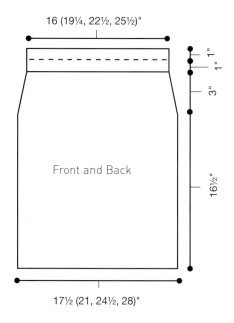

16 (19¼, 22½, 25½)"

1"

1"

3"

Front and Back

16½"

17½ (21, 24½, 28)"

Tweed Hoodie

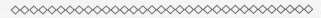

An intricate Celtic knot decorates the back of this sporty design. Sure, it'll require a tad more concentration than the rest of the sweater, but it's only 56 rows!

SKILL LEVEL   Experienced

SIZES
Small (Medium, Large, 1X, 2X). Instructions are for the smallest size, with changes for the other sizes noted in parentheses as necessary.

FINISHED MEASUREMENTS
Bust (Zipped): 35½ (38, 42, 46, 50)" [90 (96.5, 106.5, 117, 127)cm]
Length: 20½ (20½, 22½, 22½, 22½)" [52 (52, 57, 57, 57)cm]

MATERIALS
- Tahki-Stacy Charles *Donegal Tweed* (100% wool; each approximately 3½ oz/100g and 183 yd/167m), 7 (8, 8, 9, 9) Hanks in #847 Scarlet, 🔢4 medium/worsted
- One pair of size 8 (5mm) knitting needles or size needed to obtain gauge
- Two size 8 (5mm) double-pointed needles or size needed to obtain gauge
- Two stitch markers
- Two cable needles
- Three stitch holders
- Blunt-end yarn needle
- 18 (18, 20, 20, 20)" [45.5 (45.5, 51, 51, 51)cm] separating zipper to match yarn
- Sewing thread to match yarn
- Pointed-end sewing needle

GAUGE
20 stitches and 26 rows = 4" (10cm) in Textured Stitch Pattern. **To save time, take time to check gauge.**

STITCH PATTERNS
Textured Stitch Pattern (multiple of 2 + 1 stitches)
Row 1 (RS): K1, *p1, k1; repeat from * across.
Row 2: Knit across.
Repeat Rows 1 and 2 for pattern.

Cable Medallion Pattern
See chart, page 98.
Stockinette Stitch Pattern (any number of stitches)
Row 1 (RS): Knit across.
Row 2: Purl across.
Repeat Rows 1 and 2 for pattern.
Front Cable Panel
See chart, page 98.

NOTES
- For ease in finishing, instructions include one selvage stitch on each side; these stitches are not reflected in the final measurements.
- For fully fashioned decreases, on right-side rows: K2, ssk, work across in pattern as established until 4 stitches remain in row, ending row with k2tog, k2. On wrong-side rows: P2, p2tog, work across in pattern as established until 4 stitches remain in row, ending row with ssp, p2.
- When increasing stitches within the pattern, use the M1 method.
- For sweater assembly, refer to the illustration for set-in construction on page 33.

BACK
Cast on 89 (97, 107, 117, 127) stitches. Work Textured Stitch Pattern even until the piece measures approximately 7¾ (7¾, 9¾, 9¾, 9¾)" [19.5 (19.5, 25, 25, 25)cm] from the beginning, ending after a wrong-side row.

Place Medallion
Next Row (RS): Continue Textured Stitch Pattern across the first 26 (30, 35, 40, 45) stitches, place marker, work Row 1 of Cable Medallion Pattern over the middle 37 stitches, place marker, continue pattern across to end of row.

Continue even in patterns as established until the piece measures approximately 12 (11¾, 13½, 13, 12½)" [30.5 (30, 34.5, 33, 32)cm] from the beginning, ending after a wrong-side row.

Shape Armholes

Bind off 2 (3, 4, 5, 6) stitches at the beginning of the next 2 rows.

Continue patterns as established, and work fully fashioned decreases (see Notes) each side of every row 3 (5, 11, 15, 19) times, then every other row 6 (6, 4, 3, 3) times. **At the same time**, when Row 56 of Cable Medallion is completed, maintain 3 stitches at each side in Stockinette Stitch Pattern, and work Textured Stitch Pattern over all other stitches—67 (69, 69, 71, 71) stitches remain.

Continue even in pattern as established until the piece measures approximately 19½ (19½, 21½, 21½, 21½)" [49.5 (49.5, 54.5, 54.5, 54.5)cm] from the beginning, ending after a wrong-side row.

Shape Shoulders

Bind off 6 stitches at the beginning of the next 4 rows, then bind off 5 (6, 6, 7, 7) stitches at the beginning of the next 2 rows—33 stitches remain.

Slip stitches onto a stitch holder.

LEFT FRONT

Cast on 45 (49, 53, 59, 63) stitches.

Begin Textured Stitch Pattern, and work even for 6 rows.

Set Up Patterns

Next Row (RS): Work Textured Stitch Pattern over the first 33 (37, 41, 47, 51) stitches, place marker, work Set-Up Row 1 of Front Cable Panel (on page 98) over the next 9 stitches, place marker, work Textured Stitch Pattern over 3 stitches to end of row.

Continue even in patterns as established until Set-Up Row 4 of Front Cable Panel is completed—51 (55, 59, 65, 69) stitches.

Continue even in patterns as established, working Rows 1–12 of Front Cable Panel over 15 Cable Panel stitches, with Textured Stitch Pattern over all other stitches, until the piece measures approximately 12 (11¾, 13½, 13, 12½)" [30.5 (30, 34.5, 33, 32)cm] from the beginning, ending after a wrong-side row.

Shape Armhole

Next Row (RS): Bind off 2 (3, 4, 5, 6) stitches, then continue in pattern across to end of row—49 (52, 55, 60, 63) stitches remain.

Continue patterns as established, working fully fashioned decreases at armhole edge every row 3 (5, 11, 15, 19) times, then every other row 6 (6, 4, 3, 3) times—40 (41, 40, 42, 41) stitches remain.

Continue even in patterns as established, maintaining 3 stitches at armhole edge in Stockinette Stitch Pattern, until the piece measures approximately 18 (18, 20, 20, 20)" [45.5 (45.5, 51, 51, 51)cm] from the beginning, ending after a right-side row.

Shape Neck

Next Row (WS): Slip 18 stitches at neck edge onto holder, then continue in pattern across to end of row.

Bind off 3 (3, 2, 3, 2) stitches at the neck edge once, then decrease 1 stitch using k2tog or p2tog, depending on stitch pattern, at neck edge every other row twice.

Continue even in pattern as established until the piece measures the same as the Back to the shoulder, ending after a wrong-side row.

Shape Shoulder

Bind off 6 stitches at the shoulder edge every other row twice.

Work one row even.

Bind off remaining 5 (6, 6, 7, 7) stitches.

RIGHT FRONT

Cast on 45 (49, 53, 59, 63) stitches.

Begin Textured Stitch Pattern, and work even for 6 rows.

◇◇◇

Set Up Patterns

Next Row (**RS**): Work Textured Stitch Pattern over the first 3 stitches, place marker, work Set-Up Row 1 of Front Cable Panel over the next 9 stitches, place marker, work Textured Stitch Pattern over 33 (37, 41, 47, 51) stitches to end of row.

Continue even in patterns as established until Set-Up Row 4 is completed—51 (55, 59, 65, 69) stitches.

Continue even in patterns as established, working Rows 1–12 of Front Cable Panel over 15 Cable Panel stitches, with Textured Stitch Pattern over all other stitches, until the piece measures approximately 12 (11¾, 13½, 13, 12½)" [30.5 (30, 34.5, 33, 32)cm] from the beginning, ending after a right-side row.

Shape Armhole

Next Row (**WS**): Bind off 2 (3, 4, 5, 6) stitches, then continue in pattern across to end of row—49 (52, 55, 60, 63) stitches remain.

Continue patterns as established, working fully fashioned decreases at armhole edge every row 3 (5, 11, 15, 19) times, then every other row 6 (6, 4, 3, 3) times—40 (41, 40, 42, 41) stitches remain.

Continue even in patterns as established, maintaining 3 stitches at armhole edge in Stockinette Stitch Pattern, until the piece measures approximately 18 (18, 20, 20, 20)" [45.5 (45.5, 51, 51, 51)cm] from the beginning, ending after a wrong-side row.

Shape Neck

Next Row (**RS**): Slip 18 stitches at neck edge onto holder, then continue in pattern across to end of row.

Bind off 3 (3, 2, 3, 2) stitches at the neck edge once, then decrease 1 stitch using k2tog or p2tog, depending on stitch pattern, at neck edge every other row twice.

Continue even in pattern as established until the piece measures the same as the Back to the shoulder, ending after a right-side row.

Shape Shoulder

Bind off 6 stitches at the shoulder edge every other row twice.

Work one row even.

Bind off remaining 5 (6, 6, 7, 7) stitches.

SLEEVES

Cast on 47 (47, 49, 49, 49) stitches.

Begin Textured Stitch Pattern, and increase 1 stitch at each side every 6th row 0 (9, 9, 11, 19) times, every 8th row 10 (7, 7, 6, 0) times, then every 10th row 3 (0, 0, 0, 0) times—73 (79, 81, 83, 87) stitches.

Work even until the piece measures approximately 17½ (17½, 18, 18, 18)" [44.5 (44.5, 45.5, 45.5, 45.5)cm] from the beginning, ending after a wrong-side row.

Shape Cap

Bind off 2 (3, 4, 5, 6) stitches at the beginning of the next 2 rows—69 (73, 73, 73, 75) stitches remain.

Work fully fashioned decreases at each side every other row 4 (5, 8, 11, 12) times, then every row 18 (19, 16, 13, 13) times—25 stitches remain.

Bind off 3 stitches at the beginning of the next four rows—13 stitches remain.

Bind off.

Repeat for the second sleeve.

FINISHING

Block pieces to measurements.

Sew shoulder seams.

Hood

With right side facing, pick up and knit 18 stitches from right front neck holder, 14 stitches along right front neck, 33 stitches from back neck holder, 14 stitches along left front neck, and 18 stitches from left front neck holder—97 stitches total.

Next Row (**WS**): Work the first 18 stitches in pattern as established, k29, place marker, p3, place marker, k29, work pattern as established to end of row.

Continue to work the first and last 18 stitches in patterns as established, work the remaining stitches in Textured

◇◇◇

Stitch Pattern, with Stockinette Stitch Pattern over the 3 stitches between markers, and work even for 6 rows.

Next Row (RS): Continue patterns as established across the first 47 stitches, M1, slip marker, k3, slip marker, M1, work patterns as established to end of row—99 stitches.

Work even in patterns as established for 9 rows, working 3 stitches between markers in Stockinette Stitch Pattern.

Next Row (RS): Continue patterns as established across the first 48 stitches, M1, k3, M1, work patterns as established to end of row—101 stitches.

Work even in patterns as established for 9 rows.

Next Row (RS): Continue patterns as established across the first 49 stitches, M1, k3, M1, work patterns as established to end of row—103 stitches.

Work even in patterns as established until the Hood measures approximately 12" (30.5cm) from the beginning, ending after Row 6 of Front Cable Panel.

Next Row (RS): Continue patterns as established across the first 48 stitches, ssk, k3, k2tog, work patterns as established to end of row—101 stitches.

Work even in patterns as established for 1 row.

Next Row (RS): Continue patterns as established across the first 47 stitches, ssk, k3, k2tog, work patterns as established to end of row—99 stitches.

Work even in patterns as established for 1 row.

Next Row (RS): Continue patterns as established across the first 46 stitches, ssk, k3, k2tog, work patterns as established to end of row—97 stitches.

Work even in patterns as established for 1 row.

Next Row (RS): Continue patterns as established across the first 45 stitches, ssk, k1, (k2tog) twice, removing markers, work patterns as established to end of row—94 stitches.

Work 1 row even.

Divide remaining stitches onto two double-pointed needles, putting 47 stitches onto each needle, and, holding right sides of the work facing each other, seam the top of the hood together using the three-needle bind off (see page 32).

Set in the Sleeves.

Sew the sleeve and side seams.

Sew in zipper.

FRONT CABLE PANEL
9 sts (inc to 15 sts)

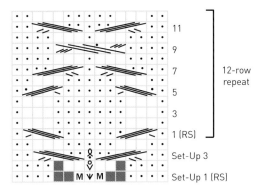

12-row repeat

11
9
7
5
3
1 (RS)
Set-Up 3
Set-Up 1 (RS)

CABLE MEDALLION PATTERN
37 sts (inc to 61 sts)

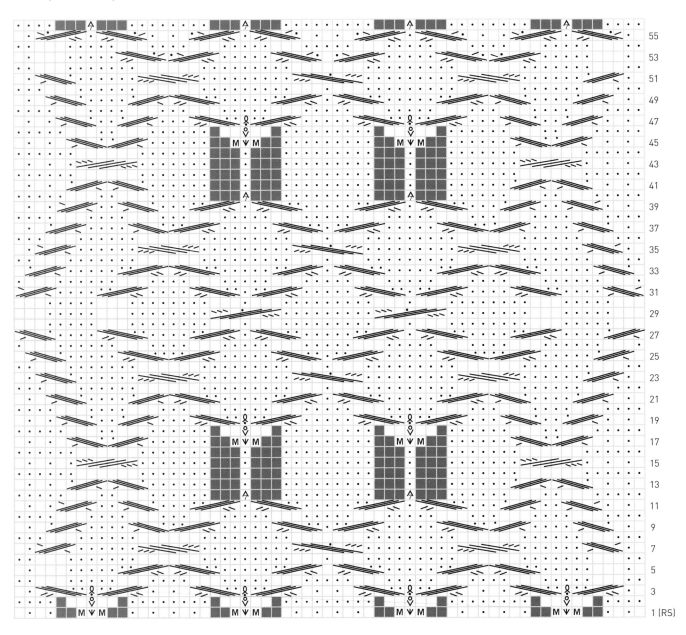

◇◇

◇◇◇◇◇◇◇◇◇◇◇◇◇◇◇◇◇◇◇◇ KEY ◇◇◇◇◇◇◇◇◇◇◇◇◇◇◇◇◇◇◇◇

□ = K on RS; P on WS

• = P on RS; K on WS

■ = No stitch

M = M1 Knitwise = Insert LH needle under the horizontal strand between two sts from front to back and K it *through back loop*

Ѡ = Central Double Increase = (Increases from 1 st to 3 sts) = K into back and then into front of indicated st and slip them off LH needle onto RH needle; insert point of LH needle behind the vertical strand that runs downward between the two sts just made and K *into the front of it*

ᵛ = (Increases from 1 st to 3 sts) = (P1, yarn over, P1) into next st

= Slip 2 sts onto cn and hold in back; K3; P2 from cn

ꝑ = P *through back loop*

= Slip 3 sts onto cn and hold in front; P2; K3 from cn

= Slip 3 sts onto cn and hold in front; K1; K3 from cn

= Slip 3 sts onto cn and hold in front; K3; K3 from cn

= Slip 3 sts onto cn #1 and hold in front; slip next st onto cn #2 and hold in back; K3; P1 from cn #2; K3 from cn #1

= Slip next st onto cn and hold in back; K3; K1 from cn

= Slip 3 sts onto cn and hold in front; P1; K3 from cn

= Slip next st onto cn and hold in back; K3; P1 from cn

ʌ = (Decreases from 7 sts to 1 st) = Slip next 4 sts with yarn in back, drop yarn; *pass the second st on RH needle over the first st on RH needle; slip first st from RH needle back to LH needle; pass the second st on LH needle over the first st on LH needle; **slip first st from LH needle back to RH needle and repeat from * to ** twice more; pick up yarn and K remaining st

= Slip 3 sts onto cn and hold in back; K3; K3 from cn

= Slip 3 sts onto cn #1 and hold in back; slip next st onto cn #2 and hold in back; K3; P1 from cn #2; K3 from cn #1

= Slip 2 sts onto cn and hold in back; K3; (P1, K1) from cn

= Slip 3 sts onto cn and hold in front; (P1, K1) from cn; K3 from cn

= Slip 2 sts onto cn and hold in back; K3; (K1, P1) from cn

= Slip 3 sts onto cn and hold in front; (K1, P1) from cn; K3 from cn

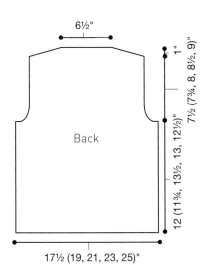

6½"

1"

7½ (7¾, 8, 8½, 9)"

12 (11¾, 13½, 13, 12½)"

Back

17½ (19, 21, 23, 25)"

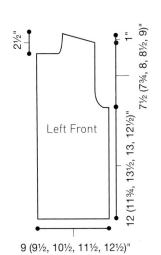

2½"

1"

7½ (7¾, 8, 8½, 9)"

12 (11¾, 13½, 13, 12½)"

Left Front

9 (9½, 10½, 11½, 12½)"

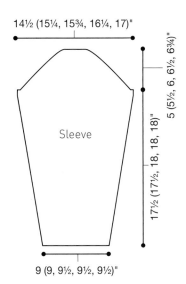

14½ (15¼, 15¾, 16¼, 17)"

5 (5½, 6, 6½, 6¾)"

17½ (17½, 18, 18, 18)"

Sleeve

9 (9, 9½, 9½, 9½)"

◇◇

Cables to Give

GIFTS FOR FRIENDS
AND FAMILY

◇◇◇◇◇◇◇◇◇◇◇◇◇◇◇◇◇◇◇◇◇◇◇◇◇◇◇◇◇◇◇◇◇

Handmade gifts are always special. Here are
some projects with closed-ring cables that will
"wow" everyone on your list. They are fun to
knit—not to mention to receive.

Baby Blocks

Practice your cabling technique while knitting up these bite-size charts. For variety—and to use up scrap yarn!—why not make the face of each block in a different color?

SKILL LEVEL   Intermediate

SIZES
One size

FINISHED MEASUREMENTS
4" x 4" x 4" (10cm x 10cm x 10cm)

MATERIALS
- Plymouth Yarn Company *Encore DK* (75% acrylic/25% wool; each approximately 1¾ oz/50g and 150 yd/137m), 1 ball for each baby block (sample projects were made in #1201 Pale Green, #793 Light Blue, and #896 Petal Yellow), (3) light/DK
- One pair of size 6 (4mm) knitting needles or size needed to obtain gauge
- Two stitch markers
- Two cable needles
- Blunt-end yarn needle
- Upholstery foam, cut to size

GAUGE
22 stitches and 31 rows = 4" (10cm) in Reverse Stockinette Stitch Pattern. Each square measures 4" (10cm) square. **To save time, take time to check gauge.**

STITCH PATTERNS
Reverse Stockinette Stitch Pattern
(any number of stitches)
Row 1 (RS): Purl across.
Row 2: Knit across.
Repeat Rows 1 and 2 for pattern.
Motif A
See chart, page 104.
Motif B
See chart, page 105.
Motif C
See chart, page 105.

SQUARE A (MAKE 2)
Cast on 23 stitches.

Begin Reverse Stockinette Stitch Pattern, and work even until the piece measures approximately ½" (13mm) from the beginning, ending after a wrong-side row.

Set Up Patterns
Next Row (RS): Work Row 1 of Reverse Stockinette Stitch Pattern over the first 7 stitches, place marker, work Row 1 of Motif A over the next 9 stitches, place marker, work Row 1 of Reverse Stockinette Stitch Pattern over the next 7 stitches.

Continue even in patterns as established until Row 23 of Motif A chart has been completed.

Beginning with a wrong-side row, continue even in Reverse Stockinette Stitch Pattern until the piece measures approximately 4" (10cm) from the beginning.

Bind off.

SQUARE B (MAKE 2)
Cast on 23 stitches.

Begin Reverse Stockinette Stitch Pattern, and work even until the piece measures approximately ¾" (2cm) from the beginning, ending after a wrong-side row.

Set Up Patterns

Next Row (RS): Work Row 1 of Reverse Stockinette Stitch Pattern over the first 5 stitches, place marker, work Row 1 of Motif B over the next 13 stitches, place marker, work Row 1 of Reverse Stockinette Stitch Pattern over the next 5 stitches.

Continue even in patterns as established until Row 20 of Motif B chart has been completed.

Beginning with a right-side row, continue even in Reverse Stockinette Stitch Pattern until the piece measures approximately 4" (10cm) from the beginning.

Bind off.

SQUARE C (MAKE 2)

Cast on 23 stitches.

Begin Reverse Stockinette Stitch Pattern, and work even until the piece measures approximately ¾" (2cm) from the beginning, ending after a wrong-side row.

Set Up Pattern

Next Row (RS): Work Row 1 of Reverse Stockinette Stitch Pattern over the first 5 stitches, place marker, work Row 1 of Motif C over the next 13 stitches, place marker, work Row 1 of Reverse Stockinette Stitch Pattern over the next 5 stitches.

Continue even in patterns as established until Row 18 of Motif C chart has been completed.

Beginning with a right-side row, continue even in Reverse Stockinette Stitch Pattern until the piece measures approximately 4" (10cm) from the beginning.

Bind off.

FINISHING

With the right sides facing, sew 5 faces of block together, placing matching squares on opposite sides of the block. Insert the foam block, position the last face of block, and sew the last four seams.

MOTIF A
9 sts (inc to 15 sts)

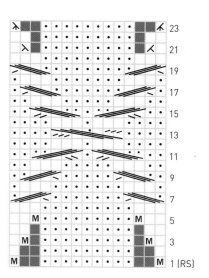

KEY

M = M1 Knitwise = Insert LH needle under the horizontal strand between two sts from front to back and K it *through back loop*

= No stitch

• = P on RS; K on WS

= K on RS; P on WS

= Slip next 3 sts onto cn and hold in front; P1; K3 from cn

= Slip next st onto cn and hold in back; K3; P1 from cn

= Slip next 3 sts onto cn and hold in front; P2; K3 from cn

= Slip next 2 sts onto cn and hold in back; K3; P2 from cn

= Slip 3 sts onto cn #1 and hold in front; slip next st onto cn #2 and hold in back; K3; P1 from cn #2; K3 from cn #1

= K2tog

= SSK

= K3tog

= SSSK

MOTIF B
13 sts (inc to 19 sts)

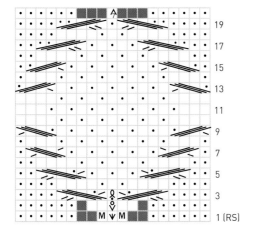

MOTIF C
13 sts (inc to 21 sts)

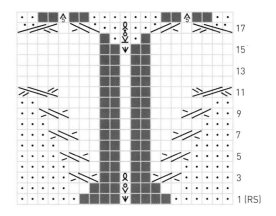

V = Central Double Increase = (Increases from 1 st to 3 sts) = K into back and then into front of indicated st and slip them off LH needle onto RH needle; insert point of LH needle behind the vertical strand that runs downward between the two sts just made and K *into the front of it*

ŏ = (Increases from 1 st to 3 sts) = (P1, yarn over, P1) into next st

= Slip 2 sts onto cn and hold in back; K3; (P1, K1) from cn

Ŷ = P *through back loop*

= Slip 3 sts onto cn and hold in front; (K1, P1) from cn; K3 from cn

= Slip next st onto cn and hold in back; K3; K1 from cn

= Slip 3 sts onto cn and hold in front; K1; K3 from cn

⋏ = (Decreases from 7 sts to 1 st) = Slip next 4 sts with yarn in back, drop yarn; *pass the second st on RH needle over the first st on RH needle; slip first st from RH needle back to LH needle; pass the second st on LH needle over the first st on LH needle; **slip first st from LH needle back to RH needle and repeat from * to ** twice more; pick up yarn and K remaining st

ŏ = (Increases from 1 st to 3 sts) = (K1, yarn over, K1) into next st

= Slip next st onto cn and hold in back; K2; K1 from cn

Ŷ = K *through back loop*

= Slip 2 sts onto cn and hold in front; K1; K2 from cn

= Slip 2 sts onto cn and hold in back; K2; K2 from cn

= Slip 2 sts onto cn and hold in front; K2; K2 from cn

= Slip 2 sts onto cn and hold in front; P2; K2 from cn

= Slip next st onto cn and hold in back; K2; P1 from cn

= Slip 2 sts onto cn and hold in front; P1; K2 from cn

= Slip 2 sts onto cn and hold in back; K2; P2 from cn

⋏₅ = (Decreases from 5 sts to 1 st) = Slip next 3 sts with yarn in back, drop yarn; *pass the second st on RH needle over the first st on RH needle; slip first st from RH needle back to LH needle; pass the second st on LH needle over the first st on LH needle; **slip first st from LH needle back to RH needle and repeat from * to ** once again; pick up yarn and K remaining st

Tweed Boyfriend Sweater

Graceful cable panels adorn this tweed sweater. Its horizontally knit neckband is as warm as it is beautiful. For a more conservative ribbed crewneck, just pick up and knit your favorite ribbing for 1" (2.5cm) instead.

SKILL LEVEL   Experienced

SIZES
Small (Medium, Large, Extra-Large, Extra-Extra Large). Instructions are for the smallest size, with changes for the other sizes noted in parentheses as necessary.

FINISHED MEASUREMENTS
Chest: 42 (47, 50, 53, 58)" [106.5 (119.5, 127, 134.5, 147.5)cm]
Total length: 26½" (67.5cm)

MATERIALS
- Westminster Fibers/Rowan *Yorkshire Tweed DK* (100% wool; each approximately 1¾ oz/50g and 123 yd/113m), 14 (15, 16, 17, 18) Balls in #343 Cheer, (**3**) light/DK
- One pair of size 4 (3.5mm) knitting needles
- One pair of size 6 (4mm) knitting needles or size needed to obtain gauge
- One cable needle
- Six stitch markers
- Blunt-end yarn needle

GAUGE
20 stitches and 28 rows = 4" (10cm) in Double Seed Stitch Pattern with larger needles. **To save time, take time to check gauge.**

STITCH PATTERNS
K1 P1 Rib Pattern (multiple of 2 stitches)
Patt Row: *K1, p1; repeat from * across.
Repeat Patt Row for pattern.
Double Seed Stitch Pattern (multiple of 2 + 1 stitches)
Row 1 (RS): *P1, k1; repeat from * across, ending row with p1.

Row 2: *K1, p1; repeat from * across, ending row with k1.
Row 3: Repeat Row 2.
Row 4: Repeat Row 1.
Repeat Rows 1–4 for pattern.
Panel A
See chart, page 110.
Panel B
See chart, page 110.
Panel C
See chart, page 110.
Panel D
See chart, page 111.
Panel E
See chart, page 111.
Panel F
See chart, page 111.
Stockinette Stitch Pattern (any number of stitches)
Row 1 (RS): Knit across.
Row 2: Purl across.
Repeat Rows 1 and 2 for pattern.

NOTE
- For sweater assembly, refer to the illustration for square indented saddle-shoulder construction on page 33.
- When decreasing stitches within the pattern, work k2tog or p2tog, depending on the stitch pattern.
- When increasing stitches within the pattern, use the M1 method.

BACK
With smaller needles, cast on 144 (156, 164, 184, 196) stitches.

Begin K1 P1 Rib Pattern, and work even until the piece measures approximately 3" (7.5cm) from the beginning, ending after a wrong-side row.

◇◇

Set Up Patterns

Next Row (RS): Change to larger needles, and work Row 1 of Double Seed Stitch Pattern over the first 3 (9, 13, 3, 9) stitches, place marker, work Row 1 of Panel A over the next 6 stitches, place marker, work Row 1 of Panel B over the next 40 (40, 40, 60, 60) stitches, place marker, work Row 1 of Panel C over the next 46 stitches, place marker, work Row 1 of Panel D over the next 40 (40, 40, 60, 60) stitches, place marker, work Row 1 of Panel E over the next 6 stitches, place marker, work Row 1 of Double Seed Stitch Pattern over the last 3 (9, 13, 3, 9) stitches.

Continue even in patterns as established until the piece measures approximately 16 (15½, 15, 14½, 14)" [40.5 (39.5, 38, 37, 35.5)cm] from the beginning, ending after a wrong-side row.

Shape Armholes

Bind off 21 (13, 17, 21, 27) stitches at the beginning of the next 2 rows.

Continue even until the piece measures approximately 23¼" (59cm) from the beginning, ending after Row 1 of pattern.

Shape Neck and Shoulders

Work across the first 28 (42, 42, 48, 48) stitches, join second ball of yarn and bind off the middle 46 stitches, work across to end of row.

Working both sides at once with separate balls of yarn, bind off 7 (10, 10, 12, 12) stitches at the beginning of the next 4 rows, then bind off 6 (10, 10, 11, 11) stitches at the beginning of the next 4 rows, and *at the same time*, decrease 1 stitch at each neck edge twice.

FRONT

Work as for the Back.

SLEEVES

With smaller needles, cast on 56 stitches.

Begin K1 P1 Rib Pattern, and work even until the piece measures approximately 3" (7.5cm) from the beginning, ending after a wrong-side row.

Set Up Patterns

Next Row (RS): Change to larger needles, and work Row 1 of Double Seed Stitch Pattern over the first 16 stitches, place marker, work Row 1 of Panel F over the next 24 stitches, place marker, work Row 1 of Double Seed Stitch Pattern over the next 16 stitches to end of row.

Continue patterns as established, and increase 1 stitch at each side every other row 0 (0, 0, 0, 4) times, every 4th row 0 (4, 14, 20, 22) times, every 6th row 12 (14, 7, 3, 0) times, then every 8th row 4 (0, 0, 0, 0) times, working new stitches in Double Seed Stitch Pattern as they accumulate—88 (92, 98, 102, 108) stitches.

Continue even until the Sleeve measures approximately 22½ (21, 21½, 21¾, 22¼)" [57 (53.5, 54.5, 55, 56.5)cm] from the beginning.

Shape Saddle

Bind off 31 (33, 36, 38, 41) stitches at the beginning of the next 2 rows—26 stitches remain.

Continue even in pattern as established, with one stitch at each side in Stockinette Stitch Pattern, until the saddle fits along the shoulder of the Front and Back.

Bind off.

Repeat for the second sleeve.

FINISHING

Neckband

With larger needles, cast on 27 stitches.

Set Up Patterns

Row 1 (RS): K1, work Row 1 of Panel F over the next 24 stitches, p2.
Row 2: K2, work Row 2 of Panel F over the next 24 stitches, k1.

Continue patterns as established until 9 repeats of Panel F have been completed in total.

Bind off.

Block the pieces to finished measurements.

Sew the saddles between Front and Back shoulders.

◇◇

Set in the Sleeves.

Sew the sleeve and side seams.

With the right sides facing and 2-stitch reverse stockinette stitch edge aligned with neck, beginning at center back neck, sew neckband to neck.

Sew the cast-on and bind-off edges of the neckband together.

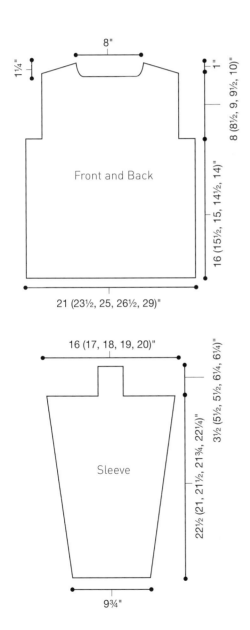

8"

1¼"

1"

8 (8½, 9, 9½, 10)"

Front and Back

16 (15½, 15, 14½, 14)"

21 (23½, 25, 26½, 29)"

16 (17, 18, 19, 20)"

3½ (5½, 5½, 6¼, 6¼)"

22½ (21, 21½, 21¾, 22¼)"

Sleeve

9¾"

PANEL A (6 sts)

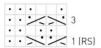

PANEL B (20 sts)

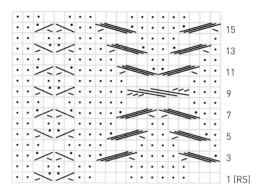

PANEL C
46 sts (inc to 58 sts)

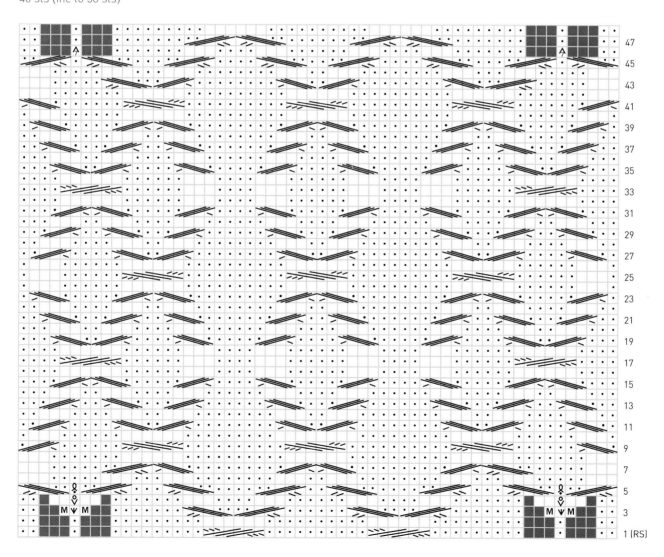

PANEL D (20 sts)

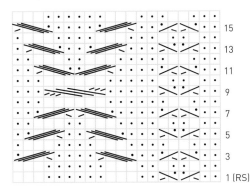

PANEL E (6 sts)

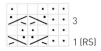

PANEL F (24 sts)

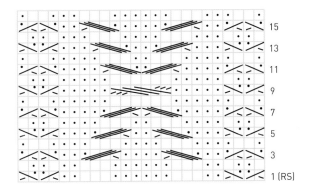

KEY

• = P on RS; K on WS	℘ = P *through back loop*
▪ = No stitch	⟋⟋⟍ = Slip next st onto cn and hold in back; K3; P1 from cn
⟍⟍⟋ = Slip 3 sts onto cn and hold in back; K3; K3 from cn	⟋⟋• = Slip 3 sts onto cn and hold in front; P1; K3 from cn
☐ = K on RS; P on WS	⟍⟍⟍ = Slip 3 sts onto cn and hold in front; K3; K3 from cn
M = M1 Knitwise = Insert LH needle under the horizontal strand between two sts from front to back and K it *through back loop*	⋏ = (Decreases from 7 sts to 1 st) = Slip next 4 sts with yarn in back, drop yarn; *pass the second st on RH needle over the first st on RH needle; slip first st from RH needle back to LH needle; pass the second st on LH needle over the first st on LH needle; **slip first st from LH needle back to RH needle and repeat from * to ** twice more; pick up yarn and K remaining st
⋎ = Central Double Increase = (Increases from 1 st to 3 sts) = K into back and then into front of indicated st and slip them off LH needle onto RH needle; insert point of LH needle behind the vertical strand that runs downward between the two sts just made and K *into the front of it*	
⟋⟋ = Slip 2 sts onto cn and hold in back; K3; P2 from cn	⟍ = Slip next st onto cn and hold in back; K1; P1 from cn
⟋⟋ = Slip 3 sts onto cn and hold in front; P2; K3 from cn	⟍• = Slip next st onto cn and hold in front; P1; K1 from cn
℧ = (Increases from 1 st to 3 sts) = (P1, yarn over, P1) into next st	

Child's Cables and Knots Pullover

This child's sweater showcases tons of texture on a small scale. Tiny knitted knots, garter ridges, and a beautiful Celtic-inspired cable panel make it special.

SKILL LEVEL   Intermediate

SIZES
Child's size 2 (4, 6, 8). Instructions are for the smallest size, with changes for the other sizes noted in parentheses as necessary.

FINISHED MEASUREMENTS
Chest: 26 (29, 32, 35)" [66 (74, 81, 89)cm]
Total length: 14½ (15¼, 16¼, 17¼)" [37 (38.5, 41.5, 44)cm]

MATERIALS
- Aurora Yarns/Ornaghi Filati *Merino Kind* (100% superwash wool; each approximately 1¾ oz/50g and 137 yd/125m), 7 (8, 9, 10) balls in #207 Rose Pink, **(3)** light/DK
- One pair of size 4 (3.5mm) knitting needles
- One pair of size 5 (3.75mm) knitting needles or size needed to obtain gauge
- Four stitch markers
- Two cable needles
- Blunt-end yarn needle

GAUGE
25 stitches and 35 rows = 4" (10cm) in Garter Ridge Stitch Pattern with larger needles. **To save time, take time to check gauge.**

STITCH PATTERNS
K1 P1 Rib Pattern
Patt Row (RS): *K1, p1; repeat from * across.
Repeat Patt Row for pattern.

Garter Ridge Stitch Pattern
Row 1 (RS): Knit across.
Row 2: Purl across.
Rows 3 and 4: Repeat Row 2.
Rows 5 and 6: Repeat Rows 1 and 2.
Repeat Rows 1–6 for pattern.
Panel A
See chart, page 116.
Panel B
See chart, page 116.
Panel C
See chart, page 116.

NOTE
- For sweater assembly, refer to the illustration for square indented saddle-shoulder construction on page 33.
- When decreasing stitches within the pattern, work k2tog or p2tog depending on the stitch pattern.
- When increasing stitches within the pattern, use the M1 method.

BACK
With smaller needles, cast on 108 (116, 128, 136) stitches.

Begin K1 P1 Rib Pattern, and work even until the piece measures approximately 1¼ (1¼, 1½, 2)" [3 (3, 3.8, 5)cm] from the beginning, ending after a wrong-side row.

Set Up Patterns
Next Row (RS): Change to larger needles, and work Row 1 of Garter Ridge Stitch Pattern over the first 4 (8, 14, 18) stitches, place marker, work Row 1 of Panel A over the next 39 stitches, place marker, work Row 1 of Panel B over the next 22 stitches, place marker, work Row 1 of Panel A over the next 39 stitches, place marker, work Row 1 of Garter Ridge Stitch Pattern across 4 (8, 14, 18) stitches to end of row.

Continue patterns as established until the piece measures approximately 8¾ (9¼, 9¾, 10¼)" [22 (23.5, 25, 26)cm] from the beginning, ending after a wrong-side row.

Shape Armholes
Bind off 4 (8, 8, 12) stitches at the beginning of the next 2 rows.

Continue even until the piece measures approximately 12¼ (13¼, 14¼, 15¼)" [31 (33.5, 36, 38.5)cm] from the beginning, ending after Row 24 (Row 8, Row 16, Row 20) of Panel B.

Bind off.

FRONT
Work as for the Back until the piece measures approximately 11½, (12¾, 13½, 14½)" [29 (32.5, 34.5, 37)cm] from the beginning, ending after Row 18 (Row 4, Row 10, Row 14) of Panel B.

Shape Neck
Next Row (RS): Work patterns as established across the first 29 (29, 34, 34) stitches, join second ball of yarn and bind off the middle 42 (50, 52, 52) stitches, work to end of row.

Work both sides at once with separate balls of yarn and decrease 1 stitch at each neck edge every row twice—27 (27, 32, 32) stitches remain on each side.

Continue even, if necessary, until the piece measures the same as the Back to the shoulders.

Bind off.

SLEEVES
With smaller needles, cast on 62 (62, 70, 70) stitches.

Begin K1 P1 Rib Pattern, and work even until the piece measures approximately 1¼ (1¼, 1½, 2)" [3 (3, 3.8, 5)cm] from the beginning, ending after a wrong-side row.

Set Up Patterns
Next Row (RS): Change to larger needles, and work Row 1 of Garter Ridge Stitch Pattern over the first 3 (3, 7, 7) stitches, place marker, work Row 1 of Panel C over the next 17 stitches, place marker, work Row 1 of Panel B over the next 22 stitches, place marker, work Row 1 of Panel C over the next 17 stitches, place marker, work Row 1 of Garter Ridge Stitch Pattern across 3 (3, 7, 7) stitches to end of row.

Continue patterns as established, and increase 1 stitch at each side every 4th row 0 (0, 1, 4) times, every 6th row 9 (14, 13, 13) times, then every 8th row 3 (1, 0, 0) times, working new stitches in Garter Ridge Stitch Pattern as they accumulate.

Continue even until the Sleeve measures approximately 11¼ (12¾, 12, 13¾)" [28.5 (32.5, 30.5, 35)cm] from the beginning, ending after a wrong-side row.

Shape Saddle

Bind off 27 (30, 33, 37) stitches at the beginning of the next 2 rows.

Continue even in pattern as established until the saddle fits along the shoulder of the Front and Back.

Bind off.

Repeat for the second sleeve.

FINISHING

Block the pieces to finished measurements.

Sew the left saddle between the Front and Back shoulders.

Sew the right saddle to the Front.

Neckband

With the right side facing and smaller needles, pick up and knit 120 (120, 124, 124) stitches evenly along the neckline.

Work K1 P1 Rib Pattern for 1" (2.5cm).

Bind off *loosely* in pattern.

Sew the right saddle to the Back.

Sew the side of the neckband.

Set in the Sleeves.

Sew the sleeve and side seams.

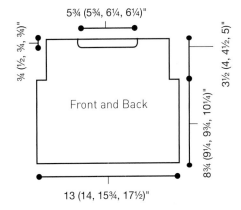

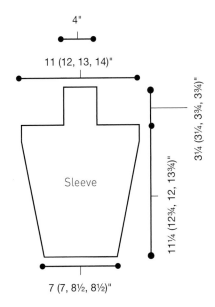

PANEL A (39 sts)

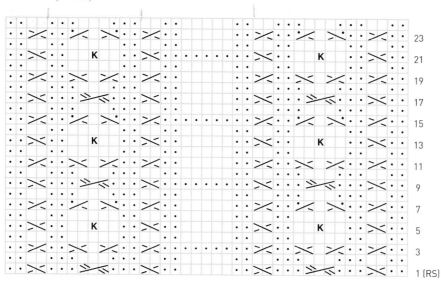

PANEL B

22 sts (inc to 30 sts)

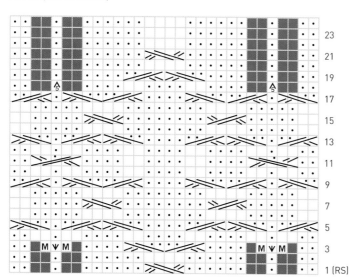

PANEL C (17 sts)

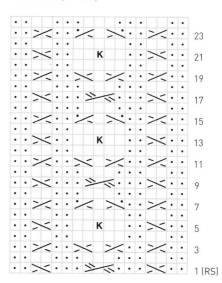

• = P on RS; K on WS

= Left Twist = Slip next st onto cn and hold in front; K1; K1 from cn OR skip first st and K next st in back loop; then K the skipped st; slip both sts off LH needle together

= Slip 2 sts onto cn and hold in back; K1; K2 from cn

= K on RS; P on WS

= No stitch

= Slip 2 sts onto cn and hold in front; K2; K2 from cn

= Right Twist = Slip next st onto cn and hold in back; K1; K1 from cn OR K2tog, leaving them on LH needle; insert point of RH needle between these 2 sts and K the first one again

M = M1 Knitwise = Insert LH needle under the horizontal strand between two sts from front to back and K it *through back loop*

v = Central Double Increase = (Increases from 1 st to 3 sts) = K into back and then into front of indicated st and slip them off LH needle onto RH needle; insert point of LH needle behind the vertical strand that runs downward between the two sts just made and K *into the front of it*

= Slip 2 sts onto cn and hold in back; K2; P2 from cn

= Slip 2 sts onto cn and hold in front; P2; K2 from cn

K = Knot = K into (front, back, front) of next st, turn; P3, turn; slip 2 sts at once knitwise, K1, p2sso

= Slip next st onto cn and hold in front; P1; K1 from cn

= Slip next st onto cn and hold in back; K1; P1 from cn

= Slip 2 sts onto cn and hold in back; K2; K2 from cn

= Slip 2 sts onto cn #1 and hold in front; slip next st onto cn #2 and hold in back; K2; P1 from cn #2; K2 from cn #1

= Slip 2 sts onto cn #1 and hold in back; slip next st onto cn #2 and hold in back; K2; P1 from cn #2; K2 from cn #1

 = (Decreases from 5 sts to 1 st) = Slip next 3 sts with yarn in back, drop yarn; *pass the second st on RH needle over the first st on RH needle; slip first st from RH needle back to LH needle; pass the second st on LH needle over the first st on LH needle; **slip first st from LH needle back to RH needle and repeat from * to ** once more; pick up yarn and K remaining st

Man's Entwined Circles Pullover

The pattern arrangement in this design is classic Aran style, although the individual cable patterns are anything but basic. Here, the main vertical panels are comprised of interlaced cables and circles.

SKILL LEVEL   Experienced

SIZES
Small (Medium, Large, Extra-Large, Extra-Extra Large). Instructions are for the smallest size, with changes for the other sizes noted in parentheses as necessary.

FINISHED MEASUREMENTS
Chest: 41½ (45½, 48½, 52, 55½)" [105.5 (115.5, 123, 132, 141)cm]
Total length: 26½" (67.5cm)

MATERIALS
- Classic Elite *Renaissance* (100% wool; each approximately 1¾ oz/50g and 110 yd/101m), 18 (19, 20, 21, 22) hanks in #7106 Sienna, **(3)** light/DK
- One pair of size 5 (3.75mm) knitting needles
- One pair of size 7 (4.5mm) knitting needles or size needed to obtain gauge
- Eight stitch markers
- Two cable needles
- Blunt-end yarn needle

GAUGE
20 stitches and 28 rows = 4" (10cm) in Box Stitch Pattern with larger needles. **To save time, take time to check gauge.**

STITCH PATTERNS
P2 K2 Rib Pattern (multiple of 4 + 2 stitches)
Row 1 (RS): *P2, k2; repeat from * across, ending row with p2.
Row 2: *K2, p2; repeat from * across, ending row with k2.
Repeat Rows 1 and 2 for pattern.

Box Stitch Pattern (multiple of 4 + 2 stitches)
Row 1 (RS): *K2, p2; repeat from * across, ending row with k2.
Row 2: *P2, k2; repeat from * across, ending row with p2.
Row 3: Repeat Row 2.
Row 4: Repeat Row 1.
Repeat Rows 1–4 for pattern.
Panel A
See chart, page 120.
Panel B
See chart, page 120.
Panel C
See chart, page 120.

NOTE
- For sweater assembly, refer to the illustration for square indented saddle-shoulder construction on page 33.
- When decreasing stitches within the pattern, work k2tog or p2tog depending on the stitch pattern.
- When increasing stitches within the pattern, use the M1 method.

BACK
With smaller needles, cast on 150 (158, 166, 174, 182) stitches.

Begin P2 K2 Rib Pattern, and work even until the piece

measures approximately 3" (7.5cm) from the beginning, ending after Row 1 of pattern.

Next Row (WS): Work P2 K2 Rib Pattern as established across the first 12 (16, 20, 24, 28) stitches, M1, k2, p2, k2, M1, (p2, k2) 3 times, p2, M1, (k2, p2) 4 times, M1, k2, p2, k2, M1, (p2, k2) 10 times, p2, M1, k2, p2, k2, M1, (p2, k2) 3 times, p2, M1, (k2, p2) 4 times, M1, k2, p2, k2, M1, (p2, k2) 3 (4, 5, 6, 7) times to end of row—160 (168, 176, 184, 192) stitches.

Set Up Patterns
Next Row (RS): Change to larger needles, and work Row 1 of Box Stitch Pattern over the first 6 (10, 14, 18, 22) stitches, place marker, work Row 1 of Panel A over the next 20 stitches, place marker, work Row 1 of Panel B over the next 19 stitches, place marker, work Row 1 of Panel A over the next 20 stitches, place marker, work Row 1 of Panel C over the next 30 stitches, place marker, work Row 1 of Panel A over the next 20 stitches, place marker, work Row 1 of Panel B over the next 19 stitches, place marker, work Row 1 of Panel A over the next 20 stitches, place marker, work Row 1 of Box Stitch Pattern across 6 (10, 14, 18, 22) stitches to end of row.

Continue patterns as established until the piece measures approximately 16½ (16, 15½, 15, 14½)" [42 (40.5, 39.5, 38, 37)cm] from the beginning, ending after a wrong-side row.

Shape Armholes
Bind off 5 (9, 12, 12, 16) stitches at the beginning of the next 2 rows.

Continue even until the piece measures approximately 24" (61cm) from the beginning, ending after Row 4 of Panel C.

Shape Shoulders
Bind off 13 (13, 13, 14, 14) stitches at the beginning of the next 6 rows, then bind off 13 (13, 14, 15, 15) stitches at the beginning of the next 2 rows—46 stitches remain.

Bind off all remaining stitches.

FRONT
Work as for the Back until the piece measures approximately 23" (58.5cm) from the beginning, ending after Row 20 of Panel C.

Shape Neck
Next Row (RS): Work patterns as established across the first 66 (66, 67, 71, 71) stitches, join second ball of yarn and bind off the middle 18 stitches, work to end of row.

Working both sides at once with separate balls of yarn, bind off 4 stitches at each neck edge once, bind off 2 stitches at each neck edge once, then decrease 1 stitch at each neck edge every row 4 times.

Shape Shoulders
Work as for the Back.

SLEEVES
With smaller needles, cast on 66 (66, 74, 74, 74) stitches.

Begin P2 K2 Rib Pattern, and work even until the piece measures approximately 3" (7.5cm) from the beginning, ending after Row 1 of pattern.

Next Row (WS): Work P2 K2 Rib Pattern as established across the first 12 (12, 16, 16, 16) stitches, M1, k2, p2, k2, M1, (p2, k2) 3 times, p2, M1, (k2, p2) 4 times, M1, k2, p2, k2, M1, (p2, k2) 3 (3, 4, 4, 4) times to end of row—71 (71, 79, 79, 79) stitches.

Set Up Patterns
Next Row (RS): Change to larger needles, and work Row 1 of Box Stitch Pattern over the first 6 (6, 10, 10, 10) stitches, place marker, work Row 1 of Panel A over the next 20 stitches, place marker, work Row 1 of Panel B over the next 19 stitches, place marker, work Row 1 of Panel A over the next 20 stitches, place marker, work Row 1 of Box Stitch Pattern across 6 (6, 10, 10, 10) stitches to end of row.

Continue patterns as established, and increase 1 stitch at each side every 4th row 0 (0, 0, 2, 9) times, every 6th row 2 (16, 9, 16, 11) times, then every 8th row 12 (1, 6, 0, 0) times, working new stitches in Box Stitch Pattern as they accumulate.

Continue even until the Sleeve measures approximately 20½ (21, 21¼, 21½, 22)" [52 (53.5, 54, 54.5, 56)cm] from the beginning, ending after a wrong-side row.

Shape Saddle
Bind off 37 (40, 42, 45, 47) stitches at the beginning of the next 2 rows.

Continue even in pattern as established, with one stitch at each side in Stockinette Stitch Pattern, until the saddle fits along the shoulder of the Front and Back.

Bind off.

Repeat for the second sleeve.

FINISHING
Block the pieces to finished measurements.

Sew the left saddle between the Front and Back shoulders.

Sew the right saddle to the Front.

Neckband
With the right side facing and smaller needles, pick up and knit 118 stitches evenly along the neckline.

Work P2 K2 Rib Pattern for 1" (2.5cm).

Bind off *loosely* in pattern.

Sew the right saddle to the Back.

Sew the side of the neckband.

Set in the Sleeves.

Sew the sleeve and side seams.

PANEL B
19 sts (dec to 15 sts)

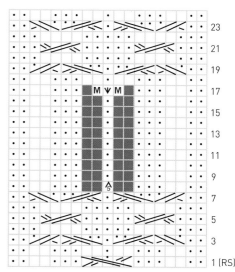

PANEL A
20 sts

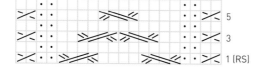

PANEL C
30 sts (inc to 38 sts)

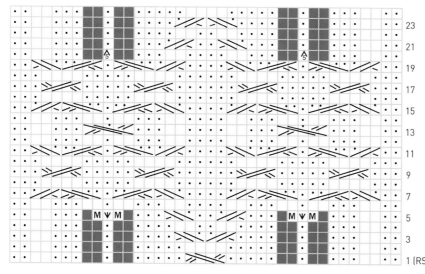

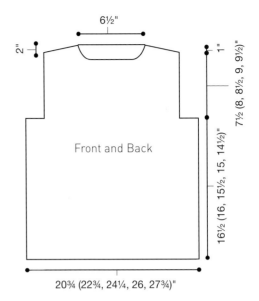

Front and Back

6½"

2"

1"

7½ (8, 8½, 9, 9½)"

16½ (16, 15½, 15, 14½)"

20¾ (22¾, 24¼, 26, 27¾)"

KEY

⤬ = Right Twist = Slip next st onto cn and hold in back; K1; K1 from cn OR K2tog, leaving them on LH needle; insert point of RH needle between these 2 sts and K the first one again

• = P on RS; K on WS

= Slip 2 sts onto cn and hold in front; K2; K2 from cn

= Slip 2 sts onto cn and hold in back; K2; K2 from cn

☐ = K on RS; P on WS

= Slip 2 sts onto cn #1 and hold in front; slip next st onto cn #2 and hold in back; K2; P1 from cn #2; K2 from cn #1

= Slip 2 sts onto cn and hold in front; P1; K2 from cn

= Slip 2 sts onto cn and hold in back; K2; P2 from cn

= Slip 2 sts onto cn and hold in front; P2; K2 from cn

= Slip next st onto cn and hold in back; K2; P1 from cn

⅄5 = (Decreases from 5 sts to 1 st) = Slip next 3 sts with yarn in back, drop yarn; *pass the second st on RH needle over the first st on RH needle; slip first st from RH needle back to LH needle; pass the second st on LH needle over the first st on LH needle; **slip first st from LH needle back to RH needle and repeat from * to ** once again; pick up yarn and K remaining st

◼ = No stitch

M = M1 Knitwise = Insert LH needle under the horizontal strand between two sts from front to back and K it *through back loop*

V = Central Double Increase = (Increases from 1 st to 3 sts) = K into back and then into front of indicated st and slip them off LH needle onto RH needle; insert point of LH needle behind the vertical strand that runs downward between the two sts just made and K *into the front of it*

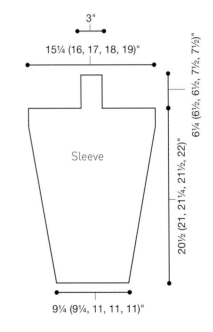

Sleeve

3"

15¼ (16, 17, 18, 19)"

6¼ (6½, 6½, 7½, 7½)"

20½ (21, 21¼, 21½, 22)"

9¼ (9¼, 11, 11, 11)"

Baby's Motif Pullover

Make this little sweater for your next baby shower gift. The back and sleeves are smooth, easy knitting, and the front has just enough technical interest to keep you engaged as you knit!

SKILL LEVEL   Intermediate

SIZES
Infant's Size 6 (12, 18) months. Instructions are for the smallest size, with changes for the other sizes noted in parentheses as necessary.

FINISHED MEASUREMENTS
Chest: 22 (24½, 27)" [56 (62, 68.5)cm]
Total length: 11 (12, 13)" [28 (30.5, 33)cm]

MATERIALS
- Cascade Yarn *Sierra* (80% pima cotton/20% wool; each approximately 3½ oz/100g and 191 yd/175m), 3 (3, 4) hanks in #47 Soft Turquoise, (**4**) medium/worsted
- One pair of size 4 (3.5mm) knitting needles
- One pair of size 6 (4mm) knitting needles or size needed to obtain gauge
- Two stitch holders
- Two cable needles
- Two stitch markers
- Four ½" (13mm) buttons

GAUGE
20 stitches and 28 rows = 4" (10cm) in Reverse Stockinette Stitch Pattern with larger needles. **To save time, take time to check gauge.**

STITCH PATTERNS
K3 P3 Popcorn Rib Pattern
See chart, page 125.
Reverse Stockinette Stitch Pattern (any number of stitches)
Row 1 (WS): Knit across.
Row 2: Knit across.
Repeat Rows 1 and 2 for pattern.

Cable Motif
See chart, page 125.

NOTES
- For ease in finishing, instructions include one selvedge stitch on each side; these stitches are not reflected in final measurements.
- To make bobble: Knit into (front, back, front) of the next stitch, turn; p1, (p1, yarn over, p1) all into next stitch, p1, turn; k5, turn; p2tog, p1, p2tog, turn; slip 2 stitches at once knitwise, k1, p2sso.
- For sweater assembly, refer to the illustration for square indented construction on page 33.
- When decreasing stitches within the pattern, work k2tog or p2tog depending on the stitch pattern.
- When increasing stitches within the pattern, use the M1 method.

BACK
With smaller needles, cast on 53 (59, 65) stitches.

Work Rows 1–5 of K3 P3 Popcorn Rib Pattern.

Next Row (WS): Change to larger needles, begin Reverse Stockinette Stitch Pattern, and increase 4 (4, 2) stitches evenly across—57 (63, 67) stitches.

Continue even until the piece measures approximately 11 (12, 13)" [28 (30.5, 33)cm] from the beginning, ending after a wrong-side row.

Next Row (RS): Work across the first 18 (21, 21) stitches and slip them onto holder, then bind off the remaining 39 (42, 46) stitches.

FRONT
Work as for the Back until the piece measures approximately 2 (3, 3½)" [5 (7.5, 9)cm] from the beginning, ending after a wrong-side row.

Set Up Patterns
Next Row (RS): Work across the first 15 (18, 20) stitches in pattern in Reverse Stockinette Stitch Pattern, work Row 1 of Cable Motif over the middle 27 stitches, work Reverse Stockinette Stitch Pattern to end of row.

Continue even in patterns as established until Row 46 of Cable Motif has been completed.

Continue even in Reverse Stockinette Stitch Pattern over all stitches until the piece measures approximately 9½ (10½, 11½)" [24 (26.5, 29)cm] from the beginning, ending after a wrong-side row.

Shape Neck
Next Row (RS): Work across the first 20 (23, 23) stitches; join second ball of yarn and bind off the middle 17 (17, 21) stitches, work to end of row.

Work both sides at once with separate balls of yarn, and decrease 1 stitch at each neck edge every row twice—18 (21, 21) stitches remain on each side.

Continue even, if necessary, until the piece measures 10¼ (11¼, 12¼)" [26 (28.5, 31)cm] from the beginning, ending after a wrong-side row.

Next Row (RS): Slip the first 18 (21, 21) stitches onto holder for buttonhole band; work across the remaining 18 (21, 21) stitches.

Continue even on this side until it measures approximately 11 (12, 13)" [28 (30.5, 33)cm] from the beginning.

Bind off.

SLEEVES
With smaller needles, cast on 35 stitches.

Work Rows 1–5 of K3 P3 Popcorn Rib Pattern.

Next Row (WS): Change to larger needles, begin Reverse Stockinette Stitch Pattern, and increase 0 (0, 2) stitches evenly across—35 (35, 37) stitches.

Increase 1 stitch at each side on the next row and then every 4th row 1 (3, 5) more times, then every 6th row 5 (4, 3) times—49 (51, 55) stitches.

Continue even until the piece measures approximately 6½ (7½, 8)" [16.5 (19, 20.5)cm] from the beginning.

Bind off.

Repeat for the second sleeve.

FINISHING
Block the pieces to finished measurements.

Sew the right shoulder seam.

Neckband
With the right side facing and smaller needles, pick up and knit 47 (47, 53) stitches along the neckline.

Next Row (WS): Work Row 2 of K3 P3 Popcorn Rib Pattern, then work Rows 1–5 of K3 P3 Popcorn Rib Pattern.

Next Row (WS): Bind off in pattern.

Buttonband

With the right side facing and smaller needles, pick up and knit 4 stitches along the side of the neckband, then slip 18 (21, 21) stitches from back buttonband holder onto the needle and work (p3, k3) 3 times, ending row p0 (p3, p3).

Knit the knit stitches and purl the purl stitches until the band measures approximately ¾" (2cm) from the beginning.

Bind off in pattern.

Place markers for 4 evenly-spaced buttons on the band, placing the first and last ¼" (6mm) from the side edges.

Buttonhole Band

With the right side facing and smaller needles, slip 18 (21, 21) stitches from the front buttonhole band holder onto the needle, work (p3, k3) 3 times, ending row with p0 (p3, p3), then pick up and knit 4 stitches along the side of the neckband—22 (25, 25) stitches.

Knit the knit stitches and purl the purl stitches until the band measures approximately ¼" (6mm) from the beginning, ending after a wrong-side row.

Next Row (RS): Continue in pattern as established, and make buttonholes opposite markers on buttonband by working (k2tog, yarn over) for buttonholes.

Continue even until the band measures approximately ¾" (2cm) from the beginning.

Bind off in pattern.

Overlap the buttonhole band over the buttonband, and sew the armhole ends together.

Place markers 4¾ (5, 5¼)" [12 (12.5, 13.5)cm] down from the shoulders.

Set in the Sleeves between markers.

Sew the sleeve and side seams.

Sew on the buttons.

KEY

- • = P on RS; K on WS

- ▩ = No stitch

- **M** = M1 Knitwise = Insert LH needle under the horizontal strand between two sts from front to back and K it *through back loop*

- **V** = Central Double Increase = (Increases from 1 st to 3 sts) = K into back and then into front of indicated st and slip them off LH needle onto RH needle; insert point of LH needle behind the vertical strand that runs downward between the two sts just made and K *into the front of it*

- ☐ = K on RS; P on WS

- ⱴ = (P1, yarn over, P1) into next st

- = Slip 2 sts onto cn and hold in back; K3; P2 from cn

- ⱷ = P *through back loop*

- = Slip 3 sts onto cn and hold in front; P2; K3 from cn

- = Slip next st onto cn and hold in back; K3; P1 from cn

- = Slip 3 sts onto cn and hold in front; P1; K3 from cn

- = Slip 3 sts onto cn and hold in back; K3; K3 from cn

- **B** = Bobble = K into (front, back, front) of next st, turn; P1, (P1, yarn over, P1) all into next st, P1, turn; K5, turn; P2tog, P1, P2tog, turn; slip 2 sts at once knitwise, K1, p2sso

- = Slip next 3 sts onto cn #1 and hold in front; slip next st onto cn #2 and hold in back; K3; P1 from cn #2; K3 from cn #1

- ⋏ = (Decreases from 7 sts to 1 st) = Slip next 4 sts with yarn in back, drop yarn; *pass the second st on RH needle over the first st on RH needle; slip first st from RH needle back to LH needle; pass the second st on LH needle over the first st on LH needle; **slip first st from LH needle back to RH needle and repeat from * to ** twice more; pick up yarn and K remaining st

CABLE MOTIF (27 sts, inc to 45 sts)

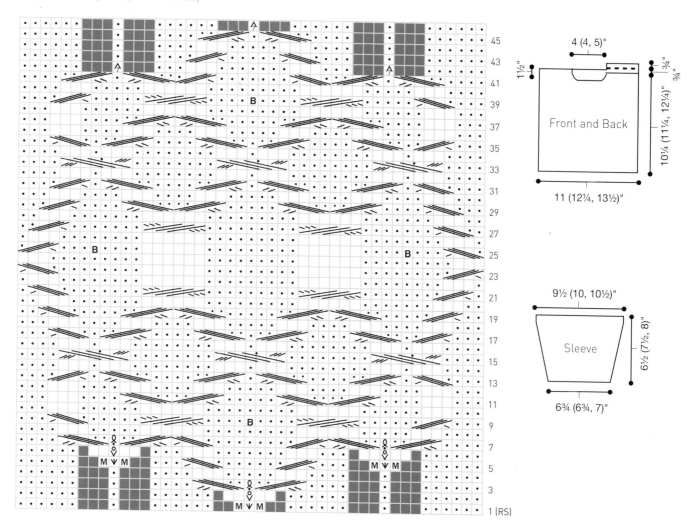

4 (4, 5)"

1½"

¾"

¾"

Front and Back

10¼ (11¼, 12¼)"

11 (12¼, 13½)"

9½ (10, 10½)"

Sleeve

6½ (7½, 8)"

6¾ (6¾, 7)"

K3 P3 Popcorn Rib Pattern
mult 6 + 5 sts

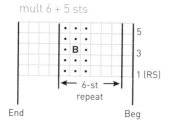

End

Beg

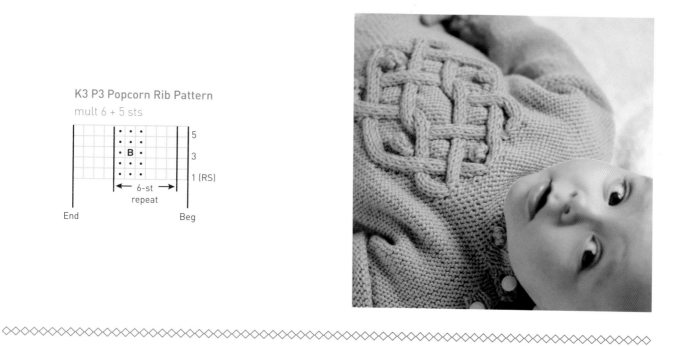

Celtic
Shoulder Bag

Want to try a Celtic panel on a small scale? Knit this cute bag. It's the perfect size and shape for daytime use!

SKILL LEVEL   Intermediate

SIZE
One size

FINISHED MEASUREMENTS
Approximately 10¼" (26cm) wide x 8" (20.5cm) deep

MATERIALS
- Brown Sheep Company *Naturespun Worsted* (100% wool; each approximately 3½ oz/100g and 245 yd/224m), 3 balls in #105 Bougainvillea, **4** medium/worsted
- One pair of size 7 (4.5mm) knitting needles or size needed to obtain gauge
- One cable needle
- One stitch marker
- Blunt-end yarn needle
- One size E/4 (3.5mm) crochet hook for edging
- Optional: coordinating fabric for lining

GAUGE
20 stitches and 28 rows = 4" (10cm) in Stockinette Stitch Pattern. **To save time, take time to check gauge.**

STITCH PATTERNS
Stockinette Stitch Pattern (any number of stitches)
Row 1 (RS): Knit across.
Row 2: Purl across.
Repeat Rows 1 and 2 for pattern.
Right Cable Pattern
See chart, page 128.
Center Cable Pattern
See chart, page 128.
Left Cable Pattern
See chart, page 128.

NOTE
Stockinette Stitch Pattern is used for knitting gauge swatch to determine correct needle size; it is not used in this design.

BACK
Cast on 80 stitches.

Work Row 1 of Right Cable Pattern over the first 22 stitches; place marker; work Row 1 of Center Cable Pattern over the next 36 stitches; place marker; work Row 1 of Left Cable Pattern over the next 22 stitches to end of row.

Work even in patterns as established until the piece measures approximately 17½" (44.5cm) from the beginning, ending after Row 1 of pattern.

Bind off in pattern.

FRONT
Same as for the Back until the piece measures approximately 8" (20.5cm) from the beginning, ending after Row 1 of pattern.

Bind off in pattern.

FINISHING
Strap/Gusset
Cast on 21 stitches.

Row 1 (RS): P1, *p1 *through the back loop*, k1 *through the back loop*; repeat from * across, ending row with p1 *through the back loop*, p1.

Row 2: K1, *knit next stitch *through the back loop*, purl next stitch *through the back loop*; repeat from * across, ending row with knit next stitch *through the back loop*, k1.

Repeat Rows 1 and 2 until the Strap/Gusset measures approximately 66½" (169cm) from the beginning.

Bind off in pattern.

Block the pieces to measurements.

With the right side facing, sew together the cast-on and bind-off edges of the Strap/Gusset.

With the right sides facing and centering the Strap/Gusset seam at the center bottom of the Front, sew one side of the Strap/Gusset to the Front. Sew the other side of the Strap/Gusset to the Back, leaving 9½" (24cm) unsewn for the top flap.

Optional: Cut lining to fit bag, including flap. Sew lining into place, folding ¼" (6mm) hems to the wrong side.

Edging
With the right side facing, attach yarn with a slip stitch to the edge of the top flap and ch 1. Work 52 sc evenly spaced along the edge of the flap. Ch 1. Do not turn.

Next Row: *Working from left to right,* work one row of reverse single crochet along edge of flap.

Fasten off.

Work edging along the top edge of the front as for the flap.

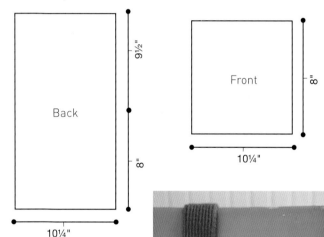

◇◇

LEFT CABLE PATTERN (22 sts)

RIGHT CABLE PATTERN (22 sts)

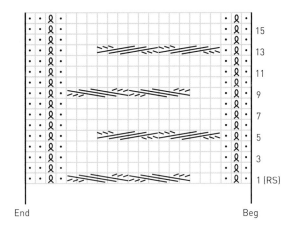

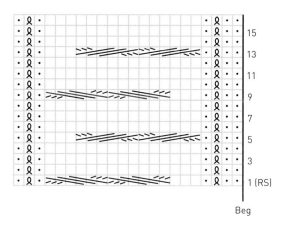

End   Beg   Beg

CENTER CABLE PATTERN
36 sts (inc to 44 sts)

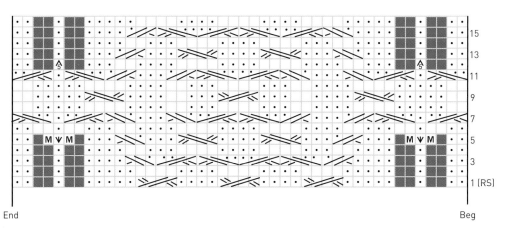

End   Beg

◇◇◇◇◇◇◇◇◇◇◇◇◇◇◇◇◇◇◇◇◇◇◇◇◇◇◇◇◇◇◇◇ KEY ◇◇◇◇◇◇◇◇◇◇◇◇◇◇◇◇◇◇◇◇◇◇◇◇◇◇◇◇◇◇◇◇

• = P on RS; K on WS

Ջ = K through back loop on RS; P through back loop on WS

☐ = K on RS; P on WS

= Slip 3 sts onto cn and hold in front; K3; K3 from cn

■ = No stitch

= Slip 2 sts onto cn and hold in back; K2; K2 from cn

= Slip next st onto cn and hold in back; K2; P1 from cn

= Slip 2 sts onto cn and hold in front; P2; K2 from cn

= Slip 2 sts onto cn and hold in back; K2; P2 from cn

= Slip 2 sts onto cn and hold in front; P1; K2 from cn

= Slip 3 sts onto cn and hold in back; K3; K3 from cn

M = M1 Knitwise = Insert LH needle under the horizontal strand between two sts from front to back and K it through back loop

Ⅴ = Central Double Increase = (Increases from 1 st to 3 sts) = K into back and then into front of indicated st and slip them off LH needle onto RH needle; insert point of LH needle behind the vertical strand that runs downward between the two sts just made and K into the front of it

= Slip 2 sts onto cn and hold in front; K2; K2 from cn

= (Decreases from 5 sts to 1 st) = Slip next 3 sts with yarn in back, drop yarn; *pass the second st on RH needle over the first st on RH needle; slip first st from RH needle back to LH needle; pass the second st on LH needle over the first st on LH needle; **slip first st from LH needle back to RH needle and repeat from * to ** once more; pick up yarn and K remaining st

◇◇

Stitch Dictionary

Working on this collection of closed-ring cables was truly a designer's dream come true for me. I hope you will find it fun, useful, and inspiring!

ORGANIZATION

This closed-ring cable stitch pattern dictionary consists of three parts: Panels, Motifs, and Horizontal Bands.

Panels

Cable panels are vertical cable designs typically placed on a plain background. Each panel is beautiful alone and also works well in combination with others.

Motifs

The closed-ring motifs are stand-alone designs that are meant to be isolated on knitted fabric. My inspiration for many of these patterns came from Celtic art and knotwork.

Horizontal Bands

These patterns appear as cable panels turned on their side. They're particularly effective as borders.

USING THE CABLE STITCH PATTERNS

To incorporate one of these stitch patterns into a project, first knit up a swatch.

For the Panels, cast on the required number of stitches for Row 1 of the chart (usually the number of stitches prior to the increases necessary for the closed rings) plus several stitches on each side for the background. Work the center stitches according to the chart, with the side stitches in reverse stockinette until you've repeated the cable pattern at least twice length-wise. Then, wash and block your swatch. Finally, measure the width of the cabled section.

For the Motifs, cast on the number of stitches required for Row 1 of the chart (usually the number of stitches prior to the increases necessary for the closed rings) plus several stitches on each side for the background. Work a few inches of reverse stockinette stitch, then set up the patterns as follows: Work the center stitches according to the chart with the side stitches in reverse stockinette. When the chart has been completed, continue in reverse stockinette stitch for a couple more inches, then bind off. Then, measure the width of the cabled section.

For the Horizontal Bands, cast on enough stitches for least two repeats of Row 1 of the chart (usually the number of stitches prior to the increases necessary for the closed rings), plus any balancing stitches outside the repeats and several stitches on each side for the background. Work a few inches of reverse stockinette stitch, then set up the patterns as follows: Work the center stitches according to the chart with the side stitches in reverse stockinette. When the chart has been completed, continue in reverse stockinette stitch for a couple more inches, then bind off. Then, measure your gauge.

CABLING UP CLOSE

You might find it helpful to place markers on your knitting needles to separate the reverse stockinette background stitches from the charted cable stitches.

If you plan to wash and block your project pieces, it's important to take the time to treat your gauge swatch in the same manner before measuring it. Yarn often behaves differently after washing. Some fibers become limp while others bloom; some will contract lengthwise or widthwise. Consider your gauge swatch the perfect opportunity to preview a tiny piece of your completed project.

To check the gauge of a swatch of Horizontal Band 4, for example, cast on 41 stitches, and work a few inches of reverse stockinette stitch (purl across right-side rows and knit across wrong-side rows). Then, set up the patterns as follows: Work reverse stockinette stitch over the first 10 stitches, place a marker, begin Row 1 of the chart where indicated, and work Row 1 over the next 21 stitches, place another marker, work reverse stockinette stitch over the remaining 10 stitches to end the row. Work all rows of the chart, with reverse stockinette at the sides. Finish your swatch with a few more inches of reverse stockinette stitch, and then bind off.

Lay your swatch flat and measure the width of the three 7-stitch repeats. If, for example, that measurement is 6", then your stitch gauge would be 21 stitches divided by 6", or 3½ stitches to the inch. Do not round this number—fractional stitches add up when factored over an entire piece of fabric!

If, on the other hand, you're using thicker yarn, the width of those same 21 stitches might be 10½", so your stitch gauge would be 21 stitches divided by 10½", or two stitches to the inch.

If you're using several panels or stitch patterns within a single project, knit a separate gauge swatch for each of the panels or stitch patterns, including your background fabric. Draw a rough sketch of your project, including the location of each cabled component. Figure out how many stitches you'll need for each section to achieve your desired width.

Happy designing!

CABLING UP CLOSE
Since staring at a blank sheet of paper can be rather intimidating, use the shape and measurements of schematic illustrations such as those found in this book as a starting point for designing your own projects.

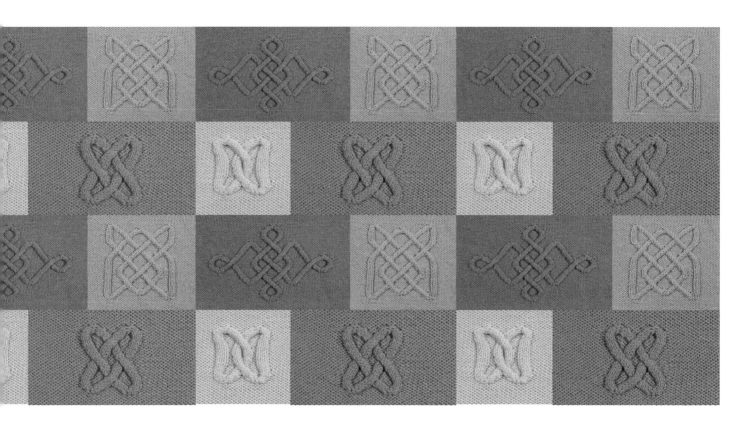

PANEL 1
27 sts (inc to 33 sts)

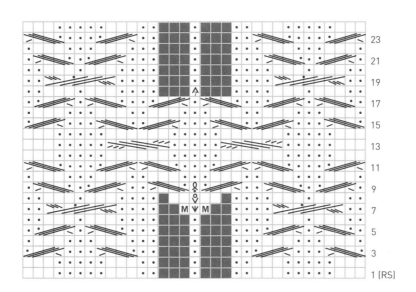

23
21
19
17
15
13
11
9
7
5
3
1 (RS)

• = P on RS; K on WS

⬛ = No stitch

☐ = K on RS; P on WS

M = M1 Knitwise = Insert LH needle under the horizontal strand between two sts from front to back and K it *through back loop*

V = Central Double Increase = (Increases from 1 st to 3 sts) = K into back and then into front of indicated st and slip them off LH needle onto RH needle; insert point of LH needle behind the vertical strand that runs downward between the two sts just made and K *into the front* of it

V = (P1, yarn over, P1) into next st

 = Slip next st onto cn and hold in back; K3; P1 from cn

Q = P *through back loop*

 = Slip 3 sts onto cn and hold in front; P1; K3 from cn

= Slip 3 sts onto cn #1 and hold in back; slip next st onto cn #2 and hold in back; K3; P1 from cn #2; K3 from cn #1

A = (Decreases from 7 sts to 1 st) = Slip next 4 sts with yarn in back, drop yarn; *pass the second st on RH needle over the first st on RH needle; slip first st from RH needle back to LH needle; pass the second st on LH needle over the first st on LH needle; **slip first st from LH needle back to RH needle and repeat from * to ** twice more; pick up yarn and K remaining st

 = Slip 3 sts onto cn and hold in front; K3; K3 from cn

◇◇

PANEL 2
13 sts (inc to 17 sts)

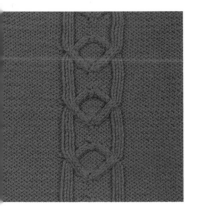

PANEL 3
15 sts (inc to 25 sts)

PANEL 4
17 sts (inc to 21 sts)

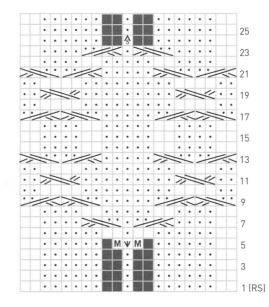

□ = K on RS; P on WS

• = P on RS; K on WS

⬛ = No stitch

M = M1 Knitwise = Insert LH needle under the horizontal strand between two sts from front to back and K it *through back loop*

⌄ = Central Double Increase = (Increases from 1 st to 3 sts) = K into back and then into front of indicated st and slip them off LH needle onto RH needle; insert point of LH needle behind the vertical strand that runs downward between the two sts just made and K *into the front of it*

⟋⟍ = Slip 2 sts onto cn and hold in back; K2; P2 from cn

⟋⟍ = Slip 2 sts onto cn and hold in front; P2; K2 from cn

⟋⟍ = Slip 2 sts onto cn and hold in back K2; K2 from cn

⟋⟍ = Slip 2 sts onto cn and hold in front; K2; K2 from cn

⬆5 = (Decreases from 5 sts to 1 st) = Slip next 3 sts with yarn in back, drop yarn; *pass the second st on RH needle over the first st on RH needle; slip first st from RH needle back to LH needle; pass the second st on LH needle over the first st on LH needle; **slip first st from LH needle back to RH needle and repeat from * to ** once again; pick up yarn and K remaining st

⌄ = (P1, yarn over, P1) into next st

⟋ = Slip next st onto cn and hold in back; K3; P1 from cn

Ȣ = P *through back loop*

⟋ = Slip 3 sts onto cn and hold in front; P1; K3 from cn

⟋⟍ = Slip 3 sts onto cn #1 and hold in back; slip next st onto cn #2 and hold in back; K3; P1 from cn #2; K3 from cn #1

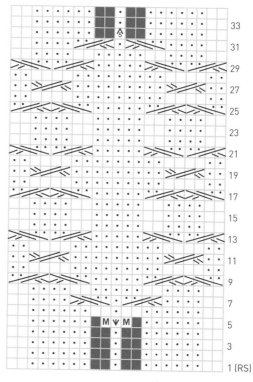

33
31
29
27
25
23
21
19
17
15
13
11
9
7
5
3
1 (RS)

⬆7 = (Decreases from 7 sts to 1 st) = Slip next 4 sts with yarn in back, drop yarn; *pass the second st on RH needle over the first st on RH needle; slip first st from RH needle back to LH needle; pass the second st on LH needle over the first st on LH needle; **slip first st from LH needle back to RH needle and repeat from * to ** twice more; pick up yarn and K remaining st

⟋⟍ = Slip 3 sts onto cn #1 and hold in front; slip next st onto cn #2 and hold in back; K3; P1 from cn #2; K3 from cn #1

⟋⟍ = Slip 3 sts onto cn and hold in front; K3; K3 from cn

PANEL 6
20 sts (inc to 26 sts)

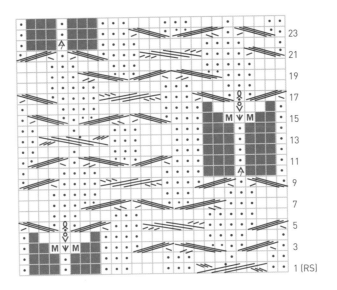

PANEL 7
20 sts (inc to 26 sts)

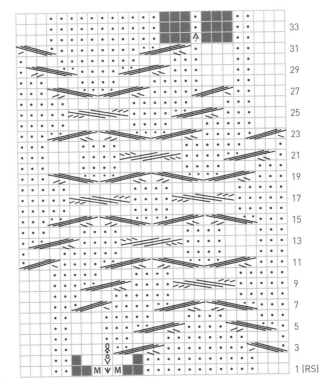

PANEL 8
19 sts (inc to 25 sts)

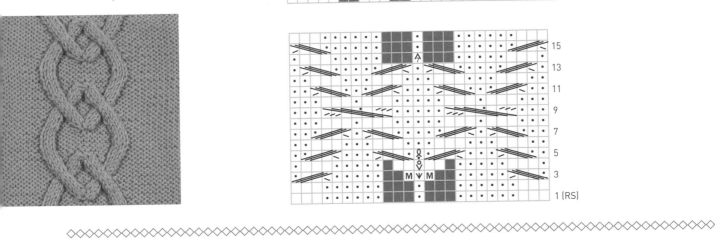

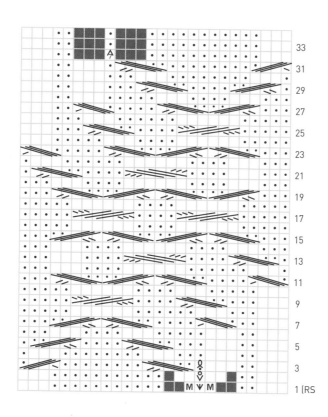

33
31
29
27
25
23
21
19
17
15
13
11
9
7
5
3
1 (RS

M M

• = P on RS; K on WS

 = Slip 3 sts onto cn #1 and hold in back; slip next st onto cn #2 and hold in back; K3; P1 from cn #2; K3 from cn #1

☐ = K on RS; P on WS

■ = No stitch

= Slip next st onto cn and hold in back; K3; P1 from cn

= Slip 3 sts onto cn and hold in front; P2; K3 from cn

M = M1 Knitwise = Insert LH needle under the horizontal strand between two sts from front to back and K it *through back loop*

V = Central Double Increase = (Increases from 1 st to 3 sts) = K into back and then into front of indicated st and slip them off LH needle onto RH needle; insert point of LH needle behind the vertical strand that runs downward between the two sts just made and K *into the front of it*

⦶ = (P1, yarn over, P1) into next st

 = Slip 3 sts onto cn and hold in front; K3; K3 from cn

Ȣ = P *through back loop*

= Slip 3 sts onto cn and hold in front; P1; K3 from cn

= Slip 2 sts onto cn and hold in back; K3; P2 from cn

= Slip 3 sts onto cn and hold in back; K3; K3 from cn

⋏ = (Decreases from 7 sts to 1 st) = Slip next 4 sts with yarn in back, drop yarn; *pass the second st on RH needle over the first st on RH needle; slip first st from RH needle back to LH needle; pass the second st on LH needle over the first st on LH needle; **slip first st from LH needle back to RH needle and repeat from * to ** twice more; pick up yarn and K remaining st

= Slip 3 sts onto cn #1 and hold in front; slip next st onto cn #2 and hold in back; K3; P1 from cn #2; K3 from cn #1

PANEL 10
33 sts (inc to 37 sts)

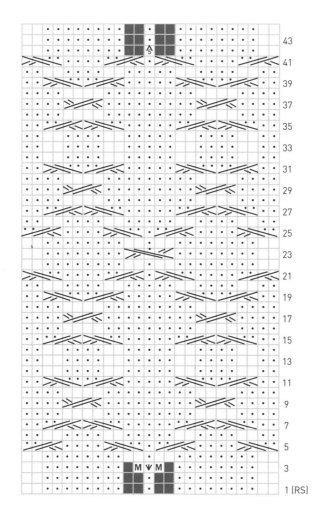

PANEL 11
21 sts (inc to 25 sts)

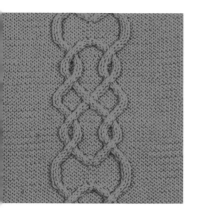

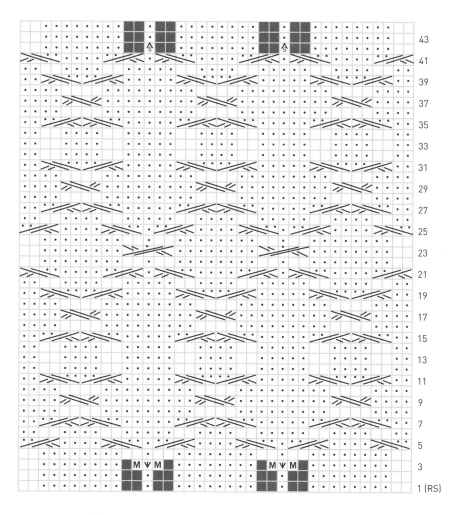

Chart row numbers (right side, odd): 43, 41, 39, 37, 35, 33, 31, 29, 27, 25, 23, 21, 19, 17, 15, 13, 11, 9, 7, 5, 3, 1 (RS)

PANEL 12
30 sts (inc to 38 sts)

□ = K on RS; P on WS

• = P on RS; K on WS

= Slip 2 sts onto cn and hold in front; K2; K2 from cn

■ = No stitch

= Slip 2 sts onto cn and hold in front; P2; K2 from cn

= Slip 2 sts onto cn and hold in back; K2; P2 from cn

M = M1 Knitwise = Insert LH needle under the horizontal strand between two sts from front to back and K it *through back loop*

V = Central Double Increase = (Increases from 1 st to 3 sts) = K into back and then into front of indicated st and slip them off LH needle onto RH needle; insert point of LH needle behind the vertical strand that runs downward between

the two sts just made and K *into the front of it*

= Slip 2 sts onto cn and hold in back; K2; K2 from cn

= Slip 2 sts onto cn #1 and hold in front; slip next st onto cn #2 and hold in back; K2; P1 from cn #2; K2 from cn #1

⚤₅ = (Decreases from 5 sts to 1 st) = Slip next 3 sts with yarn in back, drop yarn; *pass the second st on RH needle over the first st on RH needle; slip first st from RH needle back to LH needle; pass the second st on LH needle over the first st on LH needle; **slip first st from LH needle back to RH needle and repeat from * to ** once again; pick up yarn and K remaining st

= Slip 2 sts onto cn #1 and hold in back; slip next st onto cn #2 and hold in back; K2; P1 from cn #2; K2 from cn #1

PANEL 13
17 sts (inc to 21 sts)

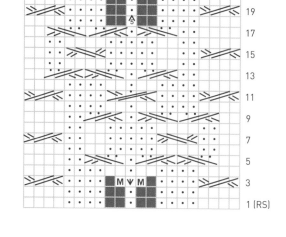

PANEL 14
30 sts (inc to 38 sts)

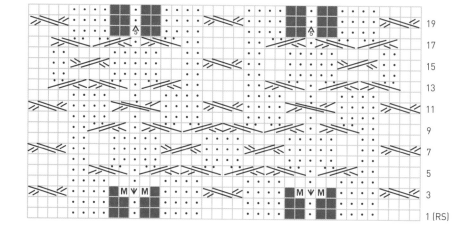

PANEL 15
26 sts (inc to 34 sts)

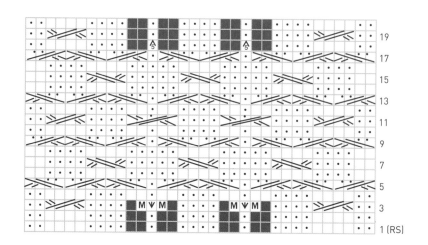

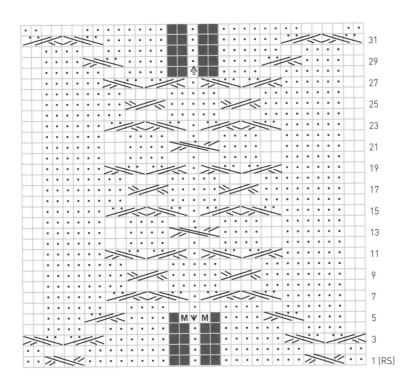

□ = K on RS; P on WS

• = P on RS; K on WS

■ = No stitch

 = Slip 2 sts onto cn and hold in back; K2; K2 from cn

M = M1 Knitwise = Insert LH needle under the horizontal strand between two sts from front to back and K it *through back loop*

Ψ = Central Double Increase = (Increases from 1 st to 3 sts) = K into back and then into front of indicated st and slip them off LH needle onto RH needle; insert point of LH needle behind the vertical strand that runs downward between the two sts just made and K *into the front of it*

 = Slip 2 sts onto cn and hold in front; P2; K2 from cn

 = Slip 2 sts onto cn and hold in back; K2; P2 from cn

= Slip 2 sts onto cn and hold in front; K2; K2 from cn

⚠5 = (Decreases from 5 sts to 1 st) = Slip next 3 sts with yarn in back, drop yarn; *pass the second st on RH needle over the first st on RH needle; slip first st from RH needle back to LH needle; pass the second st on LH needle over the first st on LH needle; **slip first st from LH needle back to RH needle and repeat from * to ** once again; pick up yarn and K remaining st

PANEL 17
26 sts (inc to 34 sts)

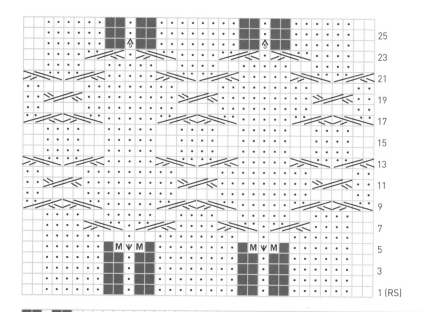

PANEL 18
31 sts (inc to 39 sts)

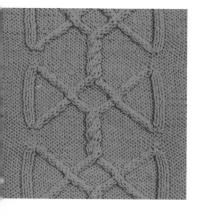

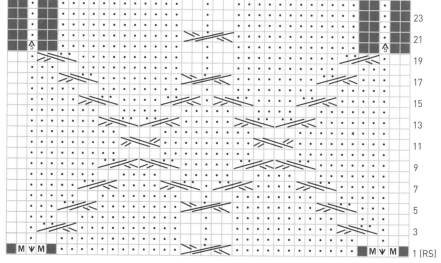

PANEL 19
18 sts (inc to 26 sts)

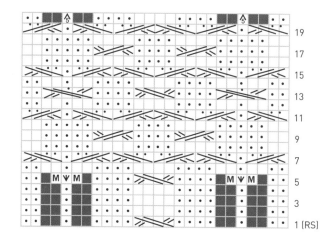

◇◇◇

☐ = K on RS; P on WS

• = P on RS; K on WS

■ = No stitch

M = M1 Knitwise = Insert LH needle under the horizontal strand between two sts from front to back and K it *through back loop*

⋎ = Central Double Increase = (Increases from 1 st to 3 sts) = K into back and then into front of indicated st and slip them off LH needle onto RH needle; insert point of LH needle behind the vertical strand that runs downward between the two sts just made and K *into the front of it*

= Slip 2 sts onto cn and hold in back; K2; P2 from cn

= Slip 2 sts onto cn and hold in front; P2; K2 from cn

= Slip 2 sts onto cn and hold in back; K2; K2 from cn

= (Decreases from 5 sts to 1 st) = Slip next 3 sts with yarn in back, drop yarn; *pass the second st on RH needle over the first st on RH needle; slip first st from RH needle back to LH needle; pass the second st on LH needle over the first st on LH needle; **slip first st from LH needle back to RH needle and repeat from * to ** once again; pick up yarn and K remaining st

= Slip 2 sts onto cn and hold in front; K2; K2 from cn

= Slip 2 sts onto cn #1 and hold in back; slip next st onto cn #2 and hold in back; K2; P1 from cn #2; K2 from cn #1

= Slip 2 sts onto cn #1 and hold in front; slip next st onto cn #2 and hold in back; K2; P1 from cn #2; K2 from cn #1

PANEL 20
33 sts (inc to 49 sts)

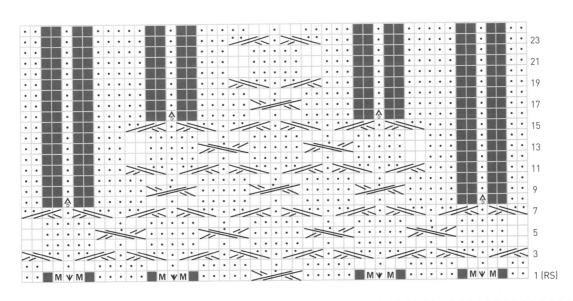

◇◇◇

◇◇◇

PANEL 21
38 sts (inc to 62 sts)

• = P on RS; K on WS

■ = No stitch

☐ = K on RS; P on WS

M = M1 Knitwise = Insert LH needle under the horizontal strand between two sts from front to back and K it *through back loop*

V = Central Double Increase = (Increases from 1 st to 3 sts) = K into back and then into front of indicated st and slip them off LH needle onto RH needle; insert point of LH needle behind the vertical strand that runs downward between the two sts just made and K *into the front of it*

Ÿ = (Increases from 1 st to 3 sts) = (P1, yarn over, P1) into next st

 = Slip 3 sts onto cn and hold in front; P2; K3 from cn

 = Slip 2 sts onto cn and hold in back; K3; P2 from cn

Ω = P *through back loop*

 = Slip 3 sts onto cn and hold in front; K3; K3 from cn

 = Slip next st onto cn and hold in back; K3; P1 from cn

 = Slip 3 sts onto cn and hold in front; P1; K3 from cn

 = Slip 3 sts onto cn and hold in back; K3; K3 from cn

 = Slip 3 sts onto cn #1 and hold in back; slip next st onto cn #2 and hold in back; K3; P1 from cn #2; K3 from cn #1

Ⱥ = (Decreases from 7 sts to 1 st) = Slip next 4 sts with yarn in back, drop yarn; *pass the second st on RH needle over the first st on RH needle; slip first st from RH needle back to LH needle; pass the second st on LH needle over the first st on LH needle; **slip first st from LH needle back to RH needle and repeat from * to ** twice more; pick up yarn and K remaining st

B = Bobble = K into (front, back, front) of next st, turn; P1, (P1, yarn over, P1) all into next st, P1, turn; K5, turn; P2tog, P1, P2tog, turn; slip 2 sts at once knitwise, K1, p2sso

 = Slip 3 sts onto cn #1 and hold in front; slip next st onto cn #2 and hold in back; K3; P1 from cn #2; K3 from cn #1

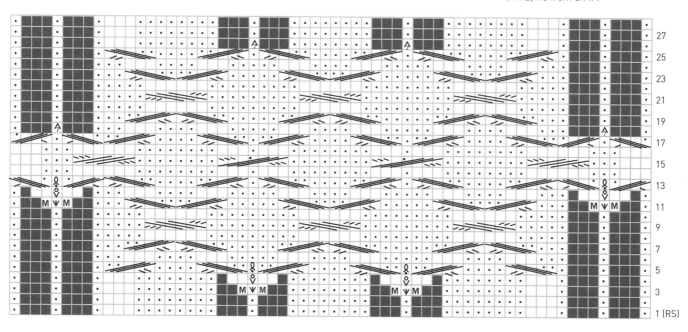

◇◇◇

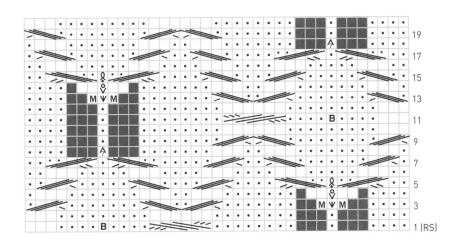

19
17
15
13
11
9
7
5
3
1 (RS)

PANEL 22
31 sts (inc to 37 sts)

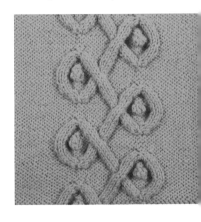

PANEL 23
32 sts (inc to 44 sts)

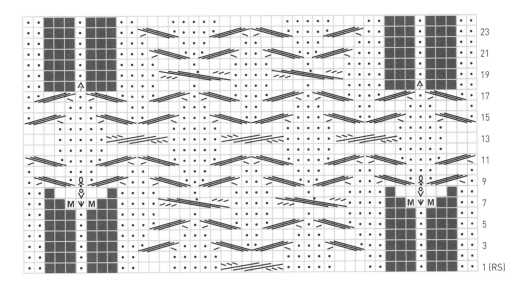

23
21
19
17
15
13
11
9
7
5
3
1 (RS)

PANEL 24
31 sts (inc to 43 sts)

PANEL 25
40 sts (inc to 52 sts)

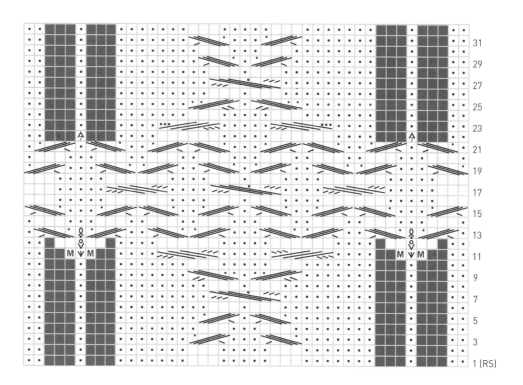

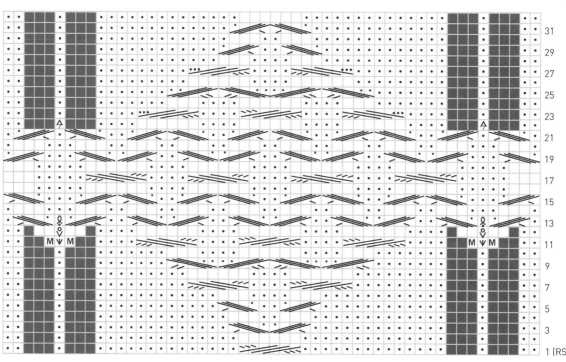

PANEL 26
32 sts (inc to 44 sts)

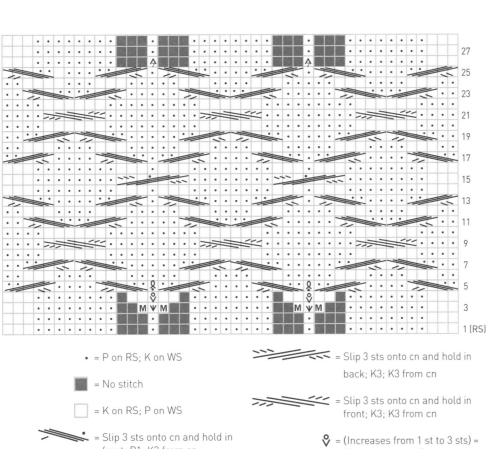

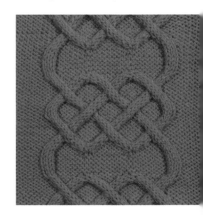

27
25
23
21
19
17
15
13
11
9
7
5
3
1 (RS)

• = P on RS; K on WS

= No stitch

= K on RS; P on WS

= Slip 3 sts onto cn and hold in front; P1; K3 from cn

= Slip next st onto cn and hold in back; K3; P1 from cn

= Slip 3 sts onto cn #1 and hold in front; slip next st onto cn #2 and hold in back; K3; P1 from cn #2; K3 from cn #1

= Slip 2 sts onto cn and hold in back; K3; P2 from cn

= Slip 3 sts onto cn and hold in front; P2; K3 from cn

M = M1 Knitwise = Insert LH needle under the horizontal strand between two sts from front to back and K it *through back loop*

V = Central Double Increase = (Increases from 1 st to 3 sts) = K into back and then into front of indicated st and slip them off LH needle onto RH needle; insert point of LH needle behind the vertical strand that runs downward between the two sts just made and K *into the front of it*

= Slip 3 sts onto cn and hold in back; K3; K3 from cn

= Slip 3 sts onto cn and hold in front; K3; K3 from cn

= (Increases from 1 st to 3 sts) = (P1, yarn over, P1) into next st

= P *through back loop*

= (Decreases from 7 sts to 1 st) = Slip next 4 sts with yarn in back, drop yarn; *pass the second st on RH needle over the first st on RH needle; slip first st from RH needle back to LH needle; pass the second st on LH needle over the first st on LH needle; **slip first st from LH needle back to RH needle and repeat from * to ** twice more; pick up yarn and K remaining st

= Slip 3 sts onto cn and hold in front; P3; K3 from cn

= Slip 3 sts onto cn and hold in back; K3; P3 from cn

= Slip 3 sts onto cn #1 and hold in back; slip next st onto cn #2 and hold in back; K3; P1 from cn #2; K3 from cn #1

PANEL 27
21 sts (inc to 33 sts)

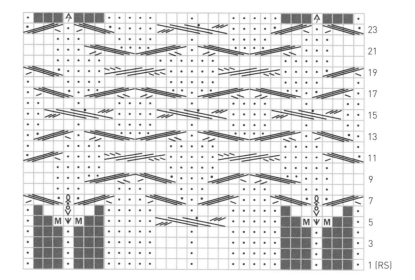

PANEL 28
22 sts (inc to 34 sts)

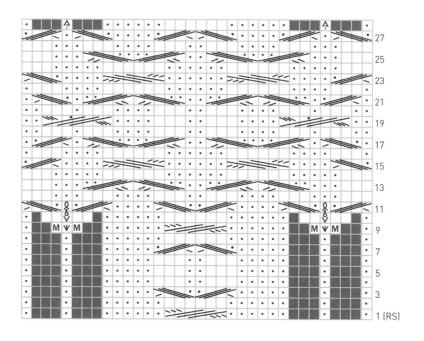

27

25

23

21

19

17

15

13

11

9

7

5

3

1 (RS)

• = P on RS; K on WS

⬛ = No stitch

⬜ = K on RS; P on WS

M = M1 Knitwise = Insert LH needle under the horizontal strand between two sts from front to back and K it *through back loop*

V = Central Double Increase = (Increases from 1 st to 3 sts) = K into back and then into front of indicated st and slip them off LH needle onto RH needle; insert point of LH needle behind the vertical strand that runs downward between the two sts just made and K *into the front of it*

= Slip next 3 sts onto cn #1 and hold in front; slip next st onto cn #2 and hold in back; K3; P1 from cn #2; K3 from cn #1

= (P1, yarn over, P1) into next st

= Slip next st onto cn and hold in back; K3; P1 from cn

Q = P *through back loop*

= Slip next 3 sts onto cn and hold in front; P1; K3 from cn

= Slip next 3 sts onto cn and hold in front; P2; K3 from cn

= Slip next 2 sts onto cn and hold in back; K3; P2 from cn

= Slip next 3 sts onto cn and hold in back; K3; K3 from cn

= (Decreases from 7 sts to 1 st) = Slip next 4 sts with yarn in back, drop yarn; *pass the second st on RH needle over the first st on RH needle; slip first st from RH needle back to LH needle; pass the second st on LH needle over the first st on LH needle; **slip first st from LH needle back to RH needle and repeat from * to ** twice more; pick up yarn and K remaining st

= Slip 3 sts onto cn #1 and hold in back; slip next st onto cn #2 and hold in back; K3; P1 from cn #2; K3 from cn #1

PANEL 30
39 sts (inc to 45 sts)

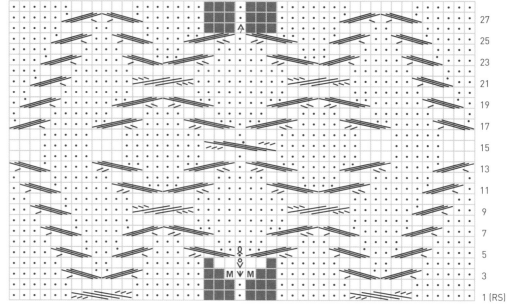

PANEL 31
41 sts (inc to 59 sts)

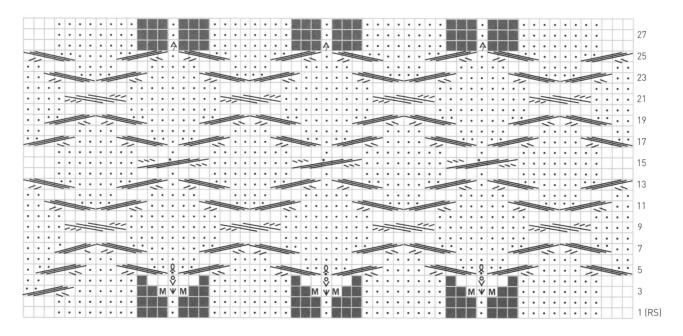

• = P on RS; K on WS

 = Slip 3 sts onto cn and hold in front; K3; K3 from cn

 = No stitch

 = K on RS; P on WS

 = Slip next st onto cn and hold in back; K3; P1 from cn

= Slip 3 sts onto cn and hold in front; P1; K3 from cn

M = M1 Knitwise = Insert LH needle under the horizontal strand between two sts from front to back and K it *through back loop*

V = Central Double Increase = (Increases from 1 st to 3 sts) = K into back and then into front of indicated st and slip them off LH needle onto RH needle; insert point of LH needle behind the vertical strand that runs downward between the two sts just made and K *into the front of it*

 = (Increases from 1 st to 3 sts) = (P1, yarn over, P1) into next st

 = Slip 2 sts onto cn and hold in back; K3; P2 from cn

 = P *through back loop*

 = Slip 3 sts onto cn and hold in front; P2; K3 from cn

= Slip 3 sts onto cn and hold in back; K3; K3 from cn

 = Slip 3 sts onto cn #1 and hold in front; slip next st onto cn #2 and hold in back; K3; P1 from cn #2; K3 from cn #1

= (Decreases from 7 sts to 1 st) = Slip next 4 sts with yarn in back, drop yarn; *pass the second st on RH needle over the first st on RH needle; slip first st from RH needle back to LH needle; pass the second st on LH needle over the first st on LH needle; **slip first st from LH needle back to RH needle and repeat from * to ** twice more; pick up yarn and K remaining st

PANEL 32
40 sts (inc to 52 sts)

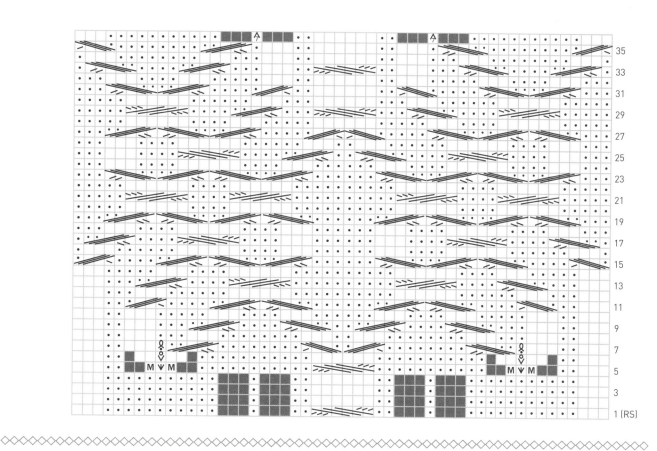

PANEL 33
46 sts (inc to 54 sts)

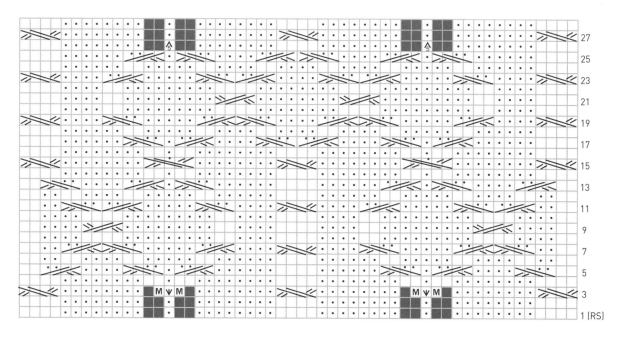

☐ = K on RS; P on WS

• = P on RS; K on WS

■ = No stitch

= Slip 2 sts onto cn #1 and hold in front;
slip next st onto cn #2 and hold in back; K2; P1
from cn #2; K2 from cn #1

= Slip 2 sts onto cn and hold in front;
P2; K2 from cn

M = M1 Knitwise = Insert LH needle under the
horizontal strand between two sts from front to
back and K it *through back loop*

PANEL 34
33 sts (inc to 51 sts)

43
41
39
37
35
33
31
29
27
25
23
21
19
17
15
13
11
9
7
5
3
1 (RS)

✛ = Central Double Increase = (Increases from 1 st to 3 sts) = K into back and then into front of indicated st and slip them off LH needle onto RH needle; insert point of LH needle behind the vertical strand that runs downward between the two sts just made and K *into the front of it*

⩕ = (Decreases from 5 sts to 1 st) = Slip next 3 sts with yarn in back, drop yarn; *pass the second st on RH needle over the first st on RH needle; slip first st from RH needle back to LH needle; pass the second st on LH needle over the first st on LH needle; **slip first st from LH needle back to RH needle and repeat from * to ** once again; pick up yarn and K remaining st

= Slip 2 sts onto cn and hold in back; K2; P2 from cn

= Slip 2 sts onto cn and hold in front; P1; K2 from cn

= Slip next st onto cn and hold in back; K2; P1 from cn

= Slip 2 sts onto cn and hold in back; K2; K2 from cn

= Slip 2 sts onto cn and hold in front; K2; K2 from cn

◇◇◇

PANEL 35
11 sts (inc to 17 sts)

PANEL 36
26 sts (inc to 38 sts)

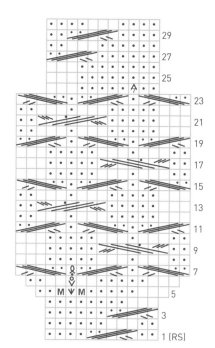

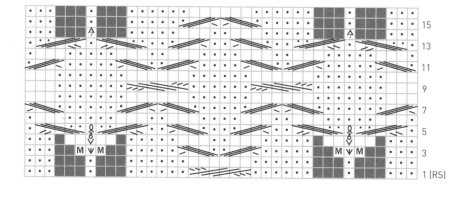

PANEL 37
9 sts (inc to 15 sts)

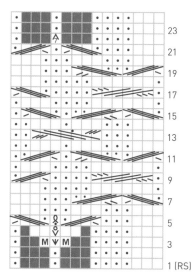

◇◇◇

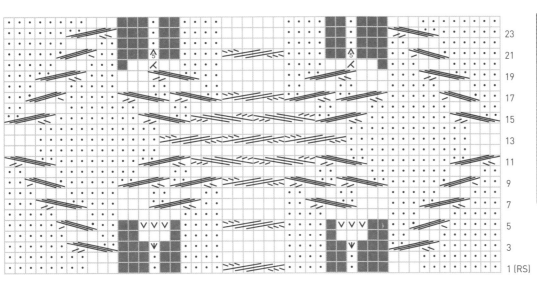

23
21
19
17
15
13
11
9
7
5
3
1 (RS)

☐ = K on RS; P on WS

• = P on RS; K on WS

■ = No stitch

⬥ = Slip 3 sts onto cn and hold in front; P1; K3 from cn

M = M1 Knitwise = Insert LH needle under the horizontal strand between two sts from front to back and K it *through back loop*

V = Central Double Increase = (Increases from 1 st to 3 sts) = K into back and then into front of indicated st and slip them off LH needle onto RH needle; insert point of LH needle behind the vertical strand that runs downward between the two sts just made and K *into the front of it*

⬥ = Slip next st onto cn and hold in back; K3; P1 from cn

⬥ = (P1, yarn over, P1) into next st

⬥ = Slip 2 sts onto cn and hold in back; K3; P2 from cn

⚶ = P *through back loop*

⬥ = Slip 3 sts onto cn and hold in front; P2; K3 from cn

⬥ = Slip 3 sts onto cn and hold in back; K3; K3 from cn

⋏ = (Decreases from 7 sts to 1 st) = Slip next 4 sts with yarn in back, drop yarn; *pass the second st on RH needle over the first st on RH needle; slip first st from RH needle back to LH needle; pass the second st on LH needle over the first st on LH needle; **slip first st from LH needle back to RH needle and repeat from * to ** twice more; pick up yarn and K remaining st

⬥ = Slip 3 sts onto cn and hold in front; K3; K3 from cn

V = Increase 1 st = K into front and then into back of st

⋏ = P2tog on WS

⋏ = (Decreases from 5 sts to 1 st) = Slip next 3 sts with yarn in back, drop yarn; *pass the second st on RH needle over the first st on RH needle; slip first st from RH needle back to LH needle; pass the second st on LH needle over the first st on LH needle; **slip first st from LH needle back to RH needle and repeat from * to ** once more; pick up yarn and P remaining st

⬥ = Slip 3 sts onto cn #1 and hold in back; slip next st onto cn #2 and hold in back; K3; P1 from cn #2; K3 from cn #1

⬥ = Slip 3 sts onto cn #1 and hold in front; slip next st onto cn #2 and hold in back; K3; P1 from cn #2; K3 from cn #1

= No stitch

• = P on RS; K on WS

 = K on RS; P on WS

 = Slip 2 sts onto cn and hold in front; P2; K2 from cn

= Slip 2 sts onto cn and hold in back; K2; P2 from cn

M = M1 Knitwise = Insert LH needle under the horizontal strand between two sts from front to back and K it *through back loop*

Ψ = Central Double Increase = (Increases from 1 st to 3 sts) = K into back and then into

front of indicated st and slip them off LH needle onto RH needle; insert point of LH needle behind the vertical strand that runs downward between the two sts just made and K *into the front of it*

 = Slip 2 sts onto cn #1 and hold in back; slip next st onto cn #2 and hold in back; K2; P1 from cn #2; K2 from cn #1

 = Slip 2 sts onto cn and hold in front; K2; K2 from cn

= Slip 2 sts onto cn and hold in front; P1; K2 from cn

 = Slip next st onto cn and hold in back; K2; P1 from cn

 = Slip 2 sts onto cn and hold in back; K2; K2 from cn

⬆ = (Decreases from 7 sts to 1 st) = Slip next 4 sts with yarn in back, drop yarn; *pass the second st on RH needle over the first st on RH needle; slip first st from RH needle back to LH needle; pass the second st on LH needle over the first st on LH needle; **slip first st from LH needle back to RH needle and repeat from * to ** twice more; pick up yarn and K remaining st

PANEL 39
27 sts (inc to 35 sts)

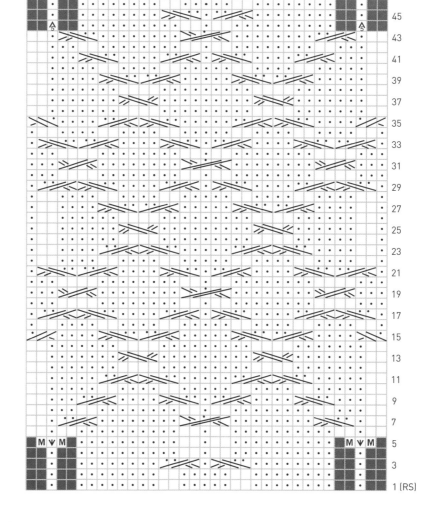

= Slip 3 sts onto cn and hold in front; P1; K3 from cn

 = Slip 3 sts onto cn #1 and hold in back; slip next st onto cn #2 and hold in back; K3; P1 from cn #2; K3 from cn #1

 = Slip next st onto cn and hold in back; K3; P1 from cn

= (Increases from 1 st to 3 sts) = (P1, yarn over, P1) into next st

 = Slip 2 sts onto cn and hold in back; K3; P2 from cn

= P through back loop

 = Slip 3 sts onto cn and hold in front; P2; K3 from cn

 = Slip 3 sts onto cn and hold in front; K3; K3 from cn

= (Decreases from 7 sts to 1 st) = Slip next 4 sts with yarn in back, drop yarn; *pass the second st on RH needle over the first st on RH needle; slip first st from RH needle back to LH needle; pass the second st on LH needle over the first st on LH needle; **slip first st from LH needle back to RH needle and repeat from * to ** twice more; pick up yarn and K remaining st

PANEL 40
49 sts (inc to 61 sts)

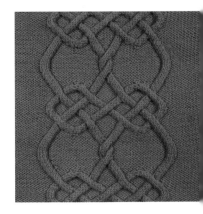

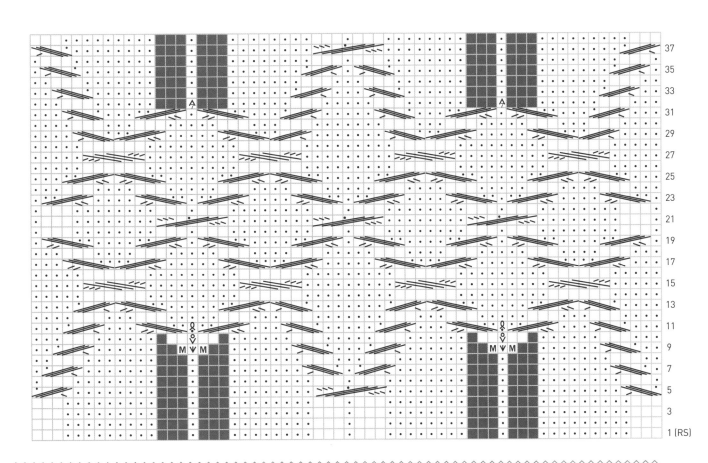

PANEL 41
29 sts (inc to 35 sts)

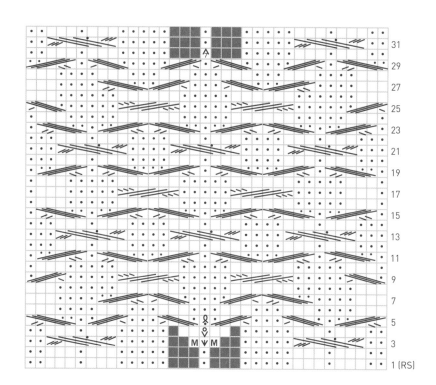

31
29
27
25
23
21
19
17
15
13
11
9
7
5
3
1 (RS)

• = P on RS; K on WS

☐ = K on RS; P on WS

■ = No stitch

 = Slip 3 sts onto cn #1 and hold in front; slip next st onto cn #2 and hold in back; K3; P1 from cn #2; K3 from cn #1

M = M1 Knitwise = Insert LH needle under the horizontal strand between two sts from front to back and K it *through back loop*

Ѱ = Central Double Increase = (Increases from 1 st to 3 sts) = K into back and then into front of indicated st and slip them off LH needle onto RH needle; insert point of LH needle behind the vertical strand that runs downward between the two sts just made and K *into the front of it*

Ѽ = (Increases from 1 st to 3 sts) = (P1, yarn over, P1) into next st

 = Slip 2 sts onto cn and hold in back; K3; P2 from cn

= Slip 3 sts onto cn and hold in front; P1; K3 from cn

= Slip next st onto cn and hold in back; K3; P1 from cn

Ƣ = P *through back loop*

= Slip 3 sts onto cn and hold in front; P2; K3 from cn

= Slip 3 sts onto cn and hold in back; K3; K3 from cn

↑ = (Decreases from 7 sts to 1 st) = Slip next 4 sts with yarn in back, drop yarn; *pass the second st on RH needle over the first st on RH needle; slip first st from RH needle back to LH needle; pass the second st on LH needle over the first st on LH needle; **slip first st from LH needle back to RH needle and repeat from * to ** twice more; pick up yarn and K remaining st

= Slip 2 sts onto cn and hold in front; K2; K2 from cn

= Slip 2 sts onto cn and hold in front; P2; K2 from cn

= Slip 2 sts onto cn and hold in back; K2; P2 from cn

= Slip 2 sts onto cn and hold in back; K2; K2 from cn

= Slip 2 sts onto cn #1 and hold in front; slip next st onto cn #2 and hold in back; K2; P1 from cn #2; K2 from cn #1

↑₅ = (Decreases from 5 sts to 1 st) = Slip next 3 sts with yarn in back, drop yarn; *pass the second st on RH needle over the first st on RH needle; slip first st from RH needle back to LH needle; pass the second st on LH needle over the first st on LH needle; **slip first st from LH needle back to RH needle and repeat from * to ** once again; pick up yarn and K remaining st

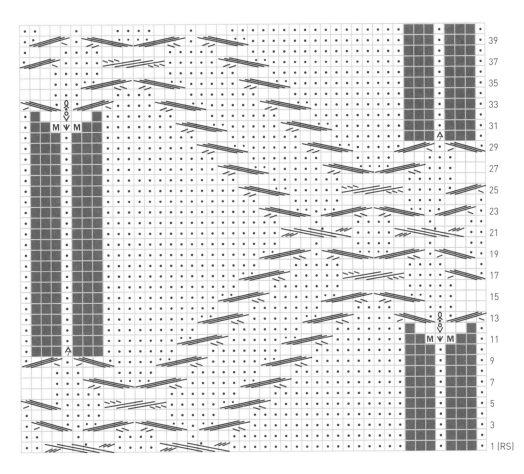

39
37
35
33
31
29
27
25
23
21
19
17
15
13
11
9
7
5
3
1 (RS)

PANEL 42
39 sts (dec to 33 sts)

PANEL 43
25 sts (inc to 29 sts)

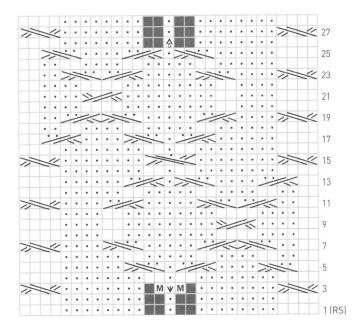

27
25
23
21
19
17
15
13
11
9
7
5
3
1 (RS)

MOTIF 1
7 sts (inc to 13 sts)

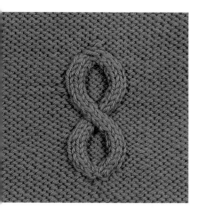

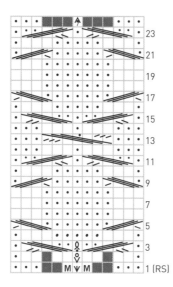

23
21
19
17
15
13
11
9
7
5
3
1 (RS)

MOTIF 2
9 sts (inc to 21 sts)

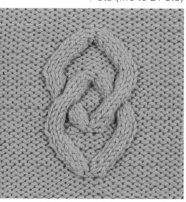

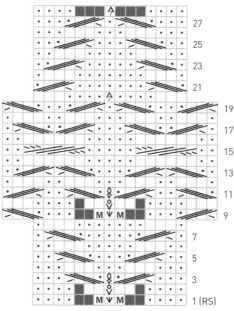

27
25
23
21
19
17
15
13
11
9
7
5
3
1 (RS)

• = P on RS; K on WS

■ = No stitch

M = M1 Knitwise = Insert LH needle under the horizontal strand between two sts from front to back and K it *through back loop*

V = Central Double Increase = (Increases from 1 st to 3 sts) = K into back and then into front of indicated st and slip them off LH needle onto RH needle; insert point of LH needle behind the vertical strand that runs downward between the two sts just made and K *into the front of it*

□ = K on RS; P on WS

Q = (Increases from 1 st to 3 sts) = (P1, yarn over, P1) into next st

= Slip 2 sts onto cn and hold in back; K3; P2 from cn

Q = P *through back loop*

= Slip 3 sts onto cn and hold in front; P2; K3 from cn

= Slip next st onto cn and hold in back; K3; P1 from cn

= Slip 3 sts onto cn and hold in front; P1; K3 from cn

= Slip 3 sts onto cn #1 and hold in front; slip next st onto cn #2 and hold in back; K3; P1 from cn #2; K3 from cn #1

= (Decreases from 7 sts to 1 st) = Slip next 4 sts with yarn in back, drop yarn; *pass the second st on RH needle over the first st on RH needle; slip first st from RH needle back to LH needle; pass the second st on LH needle over the first st on LH needle; **slip first st from LH needle back to RH needle and repeat from * to ** twice more; pick up yarn and K remaining st

= Slip 3 sts onto cn and hold in back; K3; K3 from cn

= Slip next 3 sts onto cn and hold in front; K3; K3 from cn

= Slip next 3 sts onto cn #1 and hold in back; slip next st onto cn #2 and hold in back; K3; P1 from cn #2; K3 from cn #1

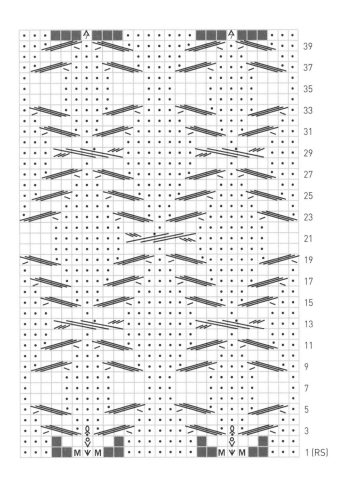

39
37
35
33
31
29
27
25
23
21
19
17
15
13
11
9
7
5
3
1 (RS)

MOTIF 3
15 sts (inc to 27 sts)

MOTIF 4
19 sts (inc to 37 sts)

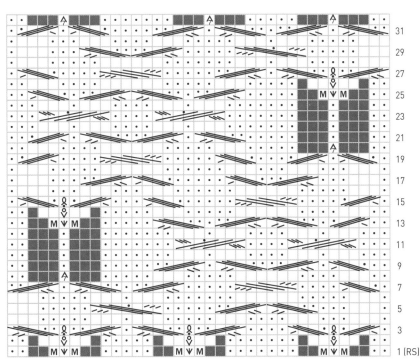

31
29
27
25
23
21
19
17
15
13
11
9
7
5
3
1 (RS)

MOTIF 5
10 sts (inc to 22 sts)

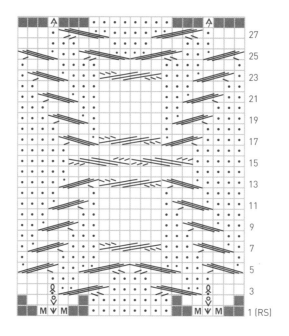

MOTIF 6
12 sts (inc to 24 sts)

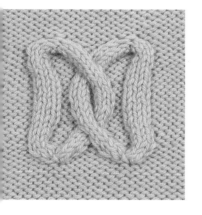

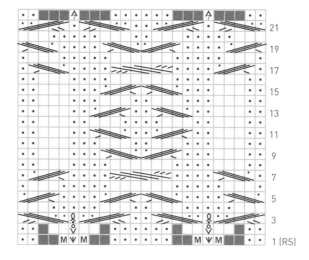

MOTIF 7
14 sts (inc to 26 sts)

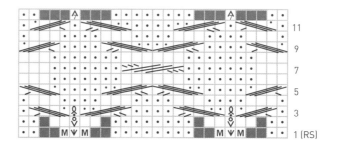

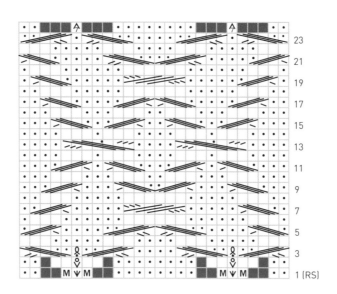

• = P on RS; K on WS

■ = No stitch

M = M1 Knitwise= Insert LH needle under the horizontal strand between two sts from front to back and K it *through back loop*

V = Central Double Increase = (Increases from 1 st to 3 sts) = K into back and then into front of indicated st and slip them off LH needle onto RH needle; insert point of LH needle behind the vertical strand that runs downward between the two sts just made and K *into the front of it*

□ = K on RS; P on WS

Ŏ = (P1, yarn over, P1) into next st

 = Slip next st onto cn and hold in back; K3; P1 from cn

Ŏ = P *through back loop*

 = Slip next 3 sts onto cn and hold in front; P2; K3 from cn

 = Slip next 3 sts onto cn and hold in front; P1; K3 from cn

 = Slip next 2 sts onto cn and hold in back; K3; P2 from cn

 = Slip next 3 sts onto cn and hold in front; K3; K3 from cn

= Slip next 3 sts onto cn #1 and hold in back; slip next st onto cn #2 and hold in back; K3; P1 from cn #2; K3 from cn #1

Ⱥ = Slip next 4 sts with yarn in back, drop yarn; *pass the second st on RH needle over the first st on RH needle; slip first st from RH needle back to LH needle; pass the second st on LH needle over the first st on LH needle; **slip first st from LH needle back to RH needle and repeat from * to ** twice more; pick up yarn and K remaining st

= Slip 3 sts onto cn and hold in back; K3; K3 from cn

= Slip 3 sts onto cn #1 and hold in front; slip next st onto cn #2 and hold in back; K3; P1 from cn #2; K3 from cn #1

MOTIF 9
11 sts (inc to 19 sts)

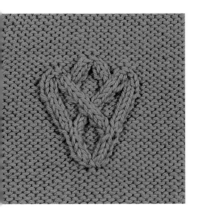

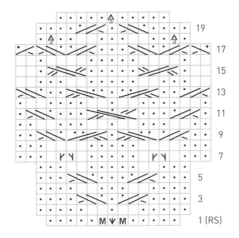

MOTIF 10
23 sts (inc to 31 sts)

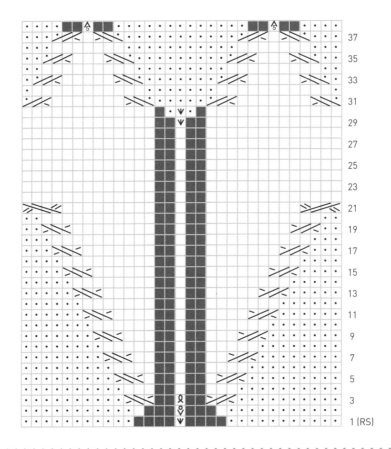

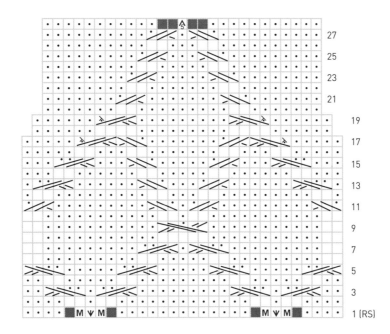

MOTIF 11
23 sts (inc to 31 sts)

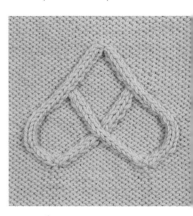

• = P on RS; K on WS

■ = No stitch

M = M1 Knitwise= Insert LH needle under the horizontal strand between two sts from front to back and K it *through back loop*

Ѵ = Central Double Increase = (Increases from 1 st to 3 sts) = K into back and then into front of indicated st and slip them off LH needle onto RH needle; insert point of LH needle behind the vertical strand that runs downward between the two sts just made and K *into the front of it*

☐ = K on RS; P on WS

⟋⟍ = Slip next st onto cn and hold in back; K2; P1 from cn

⟍⟋ = Slip 2 sts onto cn and hold in front; P1; K2 from cn

Ⅴ = Left-slanting lifted increase

Ⅴ = Right-slanting lifted increase

⟋⟍ = Slip 2 sts onto cn and hold in front; P2; K2 from cn

⟍⟋ = Slip 2 sts onto cn and hold in back; K2; P2 from cn

⟋⟍ = Slip 2 sts onto cn #1 and hold in front; slip next st onto cn #2 and hold in back; K2; P1 from cn #2; K2 from cn #1

⟍⟋ = Slip 2 sts onto cn and hold in back; K2; K2 from cn

⟋⟍ = Slip 2 sts onto cn and hold in front; K2; K2 from cn

⟍⟍• = Slip next st onto cn and hold in front; P1; K1 from cn

•⟋⟋ = Slip next st onto cn and hold in back; K1; P1 from cn

⅄₃ = (Decreases from 3 sts to 1 st) = Slip next 2 sts with yarn in back, drop yarn; *pass the second st on RH needle over the first st on RH needle; slip first st from RH needle back to LH needle; pass the second st on LH needle over the first st on LH needle; pick up yarn and K remaining st

⅄₅ = (Decreases from 5 sts to 1 st) = Slip next 3 sts with yarn in back, drop yarn; *pass the second st on RH needle over the first st on RH needle; slip first st from RH needle back to LH needle; pass the second st on LH needle over the first st on LH needle; **slip first st from LH needle back to RH needle and repeat from * to ** once more; pick up yarn and K remaining st

ᴼ̌ = (Increases from 1 st to 3 sts) = (P1, yarn over, P1) into next st

⟍⟋ = Slip next st onto cn and hold in back; K2; K1 from cn

Ω = K *through back loop*

⟍⟋ = Slip next 2 sts onto cn and hold in front; K1; K2 from cn

⟋⟍ = Slip 2 sts onto cn and hold in front; P2tog; K2 from cn

⟍⟋ = Slip next 2 sts onto cn and hold in back; K2; P2tog from cn

MOTIF 12

15 sts (inc to 33 sts)

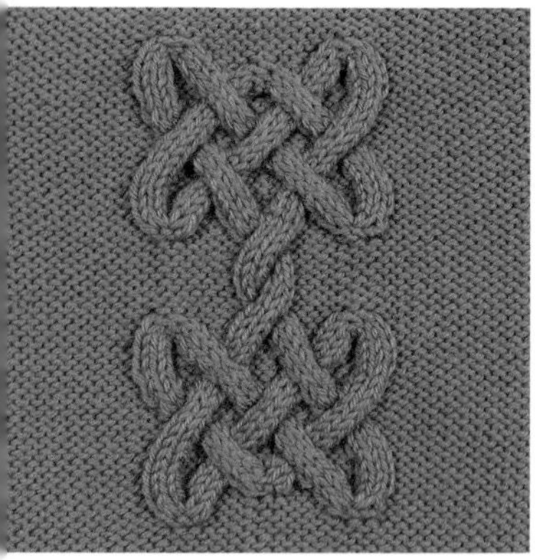

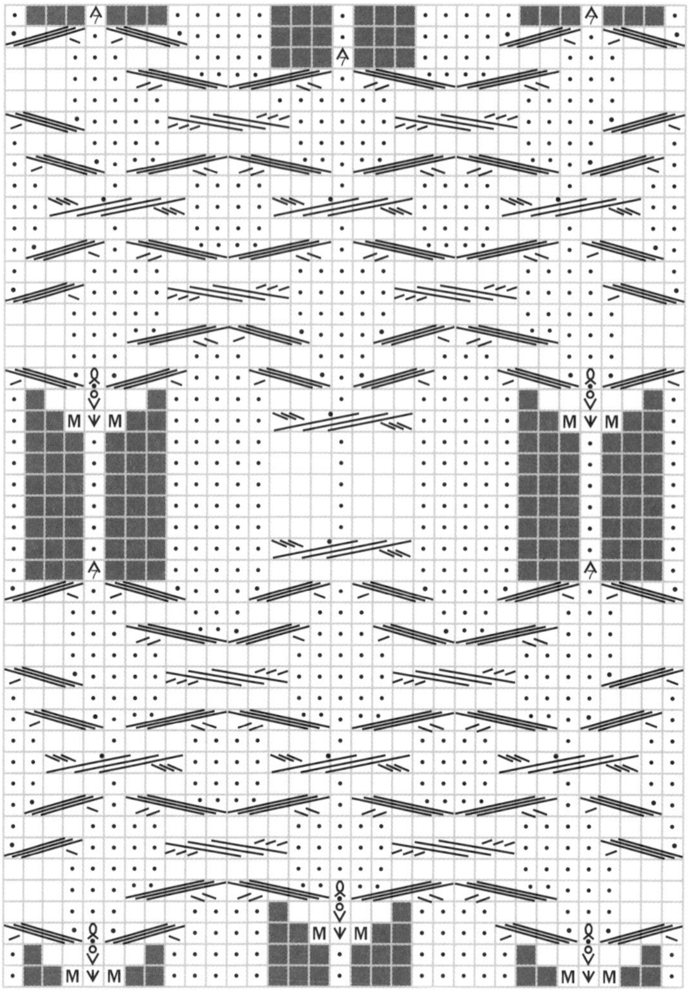

• = P on RS; K on WS

= No stitch

M = M1 Knitwise = Insert LH needle under the horizontal strand between two sts from front to back and K it *through back loop*

= Central Double Increase = (Increases from 1 st to 3 sts) = K into back and then into front of indicated st and slip them off LH needle onto RH needle; insert point of LH needle behind the vertical strand that runs downward between the two sts just made and K *into the front of it*

= K on RS; P on WS

= (P1, yarn over, P1) into next st

= Slip next st onto cn and hold in back; K3; P1 from cn

= P *through back loop*

= Slip next 3 sts onto cn and hold in front; P1; K3 from cn

= Slip next 3 sts onto cn and hold in front; P2; K3 from cn

= Slip next 2 sts onto cn and hold in back; K3; P2 from cn

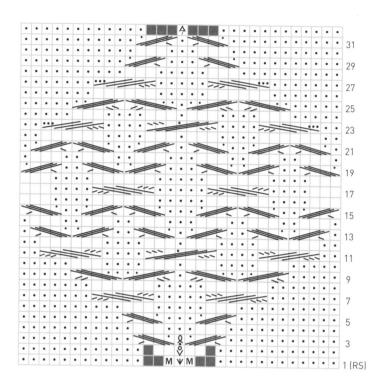

31
29
27
25
23
21
19
17
15
13
11
9
7
5
3
1 (RS)

 = Slip next 3 sts onto cn and hold in front; K3; K3 from cn

 = Slip 3 sts onto cn and hold in back; K3; K3 from cn

 = Slip next 3 sts onto cn #1 and hold in back; slip next st onto cn #2 and hold in back; K3; P1 from cn #2; K3 from cn #1

 = Slip 3 sts onto cn and hold in front; P3; K3 from cn

 = (Decreases from 7 sts to 1 st) = Slip next 4 sts with yarn in back, drop yarn; *pass the second st on RH needle over the first st on RH needle; slip first st from RH needle back to LH needle; pass the second st on LH needle over the first st on LH needle; **slip first st from LH needle back to RH needle and repeat from * to ** twice more; pick up yarn and K remaining st

 = Slip 3 sts onto cn and hold in back; K3; P3 from cn

MOTIF 14
16 sts (inc to 28 sts)

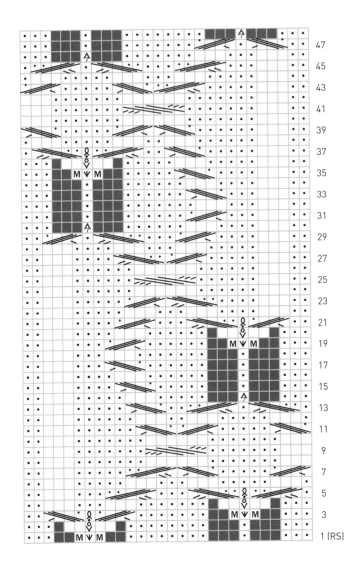

• = P on RS; K on WS

■ = No stitch

M = M1 Knitwise = Insert LH needle under the horizontal strand between two sts from front to back and K it *through back loop*

Ѵ = Central Double Increase = (Increases from 1 st to 3 sts) = K into back and then into front of indicated st and slip them off LH needle onto RH needle; insert point of LH needle behind the vertical strand that runs downward between the two sts just made and K *into the front of it*

☐ = K on RS; P on WS

♀ = (P1, yarn over, P1) into next st

= Slip next st onto cn and hold in back; K3; P1 from cn

☿ = P *through back loop*

= Slip next 3 sts onto cn and hold in front; P1; K3 from cn

= Slip next 3 sts onto cn and hold in front; P2; K3 from cn

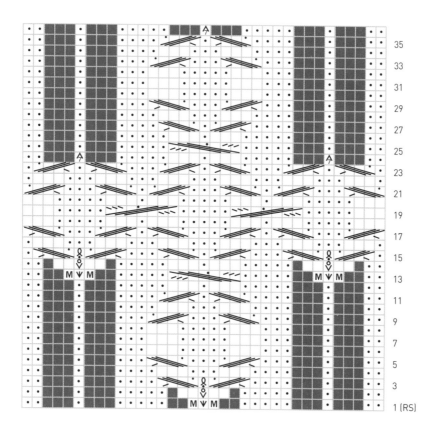

35
33
31
29
27
25
23
21
19
17
15
13
11
9
7
5
3
1 (RS)

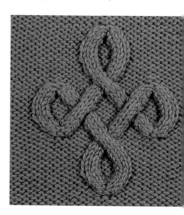

 = Slip next 2 sts onto cn and hold in back; K3; P2 from cn

 = Slip next 3 sts onto cn and hold in front; K3; K3 from cn

 = Slip next 3 sts onto cn #1 and hold in back; slip next st onto cn #2 and hold in back; K3; P1 from cn #2; K3 from cn #1

 = Slip 3 sts onto cn #1 and hold in front; slip next st onto cn #2 and hold in back; K3; P1 from cn #2; K3 from cn #1

⋏ = (Decreases from 7 sts to 1 st) = Slip next 4 sts with yarn in back, drop yarn; *pass the second st on RH needle over the first st on RH needle; slip first st from RH needle back to LH needle; pass the second st on LH needle over the first st on LH needle; **slip first st from LH needle back to RH needle and repeat from * to ** twice more; pick up yarn and K remaining st

MOTIF 16
14 sts (inc to 22 sts)

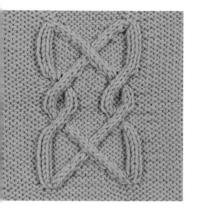

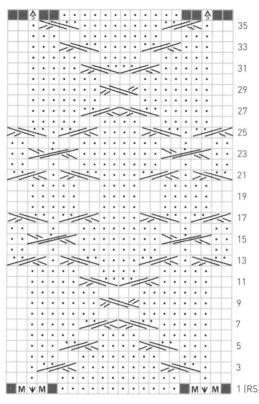

 = No stitch

M = M1 Knitwise= Insert LH needle under the horizontal strand between two sts from front to back and K it *through back loop*

Ψ = Central Double Increase = (Increases from 1 st to 3 sts) = K into back and then into front of indicated st and slip them off LH needle onto RH needle; insert point of LH needle behind the vertical strand that runs downward between the two sts just made and K *into the front of it*

• = P on RS; K on WS

☐ = K on RS; P on WS

= Slip 2 sts onto cn and hold in front; P2; K2 from cn

= Slip 2 sts onto cn and hold in back; K2; P2 from cn

= Slip 2 sts onto cn and hold in front; K2; K2 from cn

MOTIF 17
23 sts (inc to 35 sts)

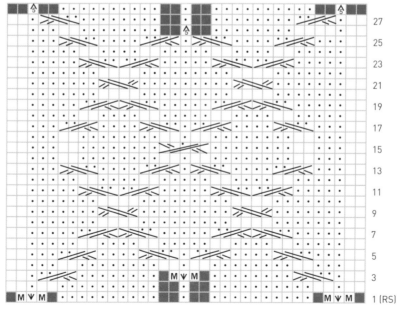

= Slip 2 sts onto cn #1 and hold in back; slip next st onto cn #2 and hold in back; K2; P1 from cn #2; K2 from cn #1

 = Slip 2 sts onto cn and hold in front; P1; K2 from cn

 = Slip next st onto cn and hold in back; K2; P1 from cn

 = Slip 2 sts onto cn and hold in back; K2; K2 from cn

$\overset{\wedge}{5}$ = (Decreases from 5 sts to 1 st) = Slip next 3 sts with yarn in back, drop yarn; *pass the second st on RH needle over the first st on RH needle; slip first st from RH needle back to LH needle; pass the second st on LH needle over the first st on LH needle; **slip first st from LH needle back to RH needle and repeat from * to ** once more; pick up yarn and K remaining st

MOTIF 18
21 sts (inc to 29 sts)

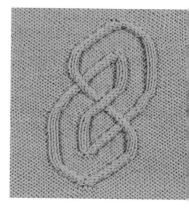

51
49
47
45
43
41
39
37
35
33
31
29
27
25
23
21
19
17
15
13
11
9
7
5
3
1 (RS)

MOTIF 19
18 sts (inc to 27 sts)

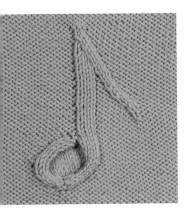

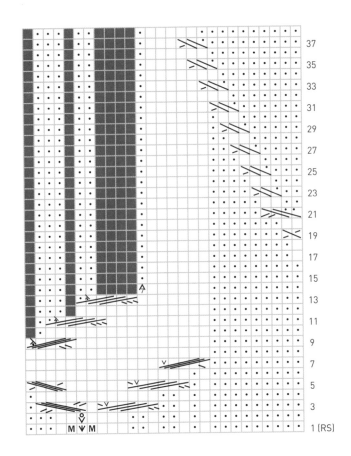

• = P on RS; K on WS

■ = No stitch

M = M1 Knitwise = Insert LH needle under the horizontal strand between two sts from front to back and K it *through back loop*

⩔ = Central Double Increase = (Increases from 1 st to 3 sts) = K into back and then into front of indicated st and slip them off LH needle onto RH needle; insert point of LH needle behind the vertical strand that runs downward between the two sts just made and K into the front of it

☐ = K on RS; P on WS

⥁ = (P1, yarn over, P1) into next st

= Slip next st onto cn and hold in back; K3; K1 from cn

δ = P *through back loop*

= Slip next 3 sts onto cn and hold in front; K1; K3 from cn

= Slip next 2 sts onto cn and hold in back; K3; P2 from cn

= Slip next 3 sts onto cn and hold in front; P2; K3 from cn

= Slip next st onto cn and hold in back; K3; P1 from cn

= Slip next 3 sts onto cn and hold in front; P1; K3 from cn

= Slip next st onto cn and hold in front; P1; K1 from cn

= Slip next st onto cn and hold in back; K1; P1 from cn

✗ = P2tog on WS

B = Bobble = K into (front, back, front) of next st, turn; P1, (P1, yarn over, P1) all into next st P1, turn; K5, turn; P2tog, P1, P2tog, turn; slip 2 sts at once knitwise, K1, p2sso

= Left Twist = Slip next st onto cn and hold in front; K1; K1 from cn OR skip first st and K next st *in back loop*; then K the skipped st; slip both sts off LH needle together

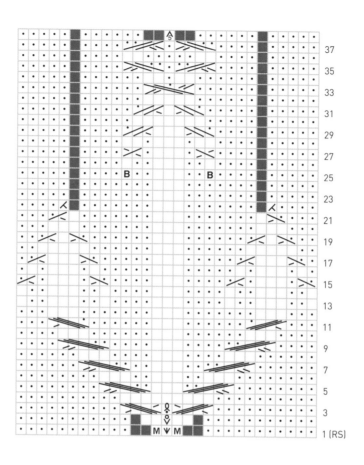

37
35
33
31
29
27
25
23
21
19
17
15
13
11
9
7
5
3
1 (RS)

>< = Right Twist = Slip next st onto cn and hold in back; K1; K1 from cn OR K2tog, leaving them on LH needle; insert point of RH needle between these 2 sts and K the first one again

= Slip next 2 sts onto cn and hold in front; P1; K2 from cn

= Slip next st onto cn and hold in back; K2; P1 from cn

= Slip next 2 sts onto cn #1 and hold in front; slip next st onto cn #2 and hold in back; K2; P1 from cn #2; K2 from cn #1

= Slip next 2 sts onto cn and hold in back; K2; P2 from cn

= Slip next 2 sts onto cn and hold in front; P2; K2 from cn

= (Decreases from 5 sts to 1 st) = Slip next 3 sts with yarn in back, drop yarn; *pass the second st on RH needle over the first st on RH needle; slip first st from RH needle back to LH needle; pass the second st on LH needle over the first st on LH needle; **slip

first st from LH needle back to RH needle and repeat from * to ** once more; pick up yarn and K remaining st

= Slip next 2 sts to cn and hold in back; K3; K st from cn through both back and front loops; K second st from cn

= Slip next 3 sts onto cn and hold in front; K2; K3 from cn

= Slip next st to cn and hold in back; K3; K st from cn through back loop; K same st on cn the regular way

= Slip next 2 sts to cn and hold in back; K3; P2tog sts from cn

= Slip next 3 sts to cn and hold in back; K3; P2tog the first 2 sts from cn; P1 the remaining st from cn

= (Decreases from 7 sts to 1 st) = Slip next 4 sts with yarn in back, drop yarn; *pass the second st on RH needle over the first st on RH needle; slip first st from RH needle back to LH needle; pass the second st on LH needle over the first st on LH needle; **slip first st from LH needle back to RH needle and repeat from * to ** twice more; pick up yarn and K remaining st

MOTIF 21
23 sts (inc to 35 sts)

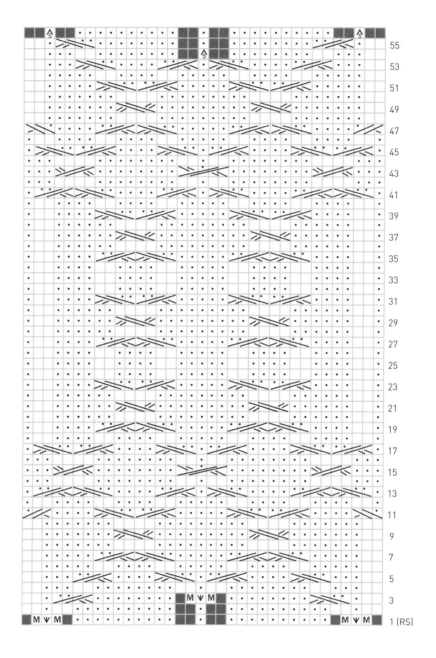

MOTIF 22
23 sts (inc to 35 sts)

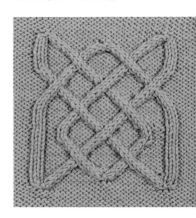

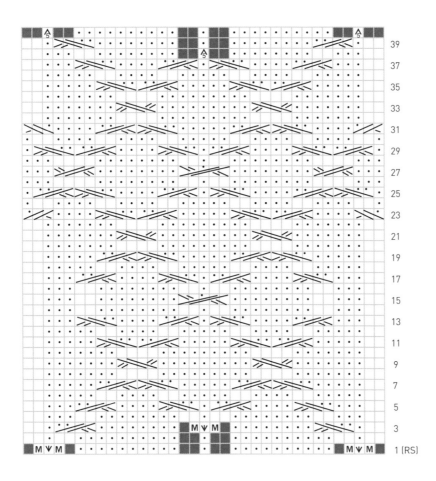

39
37
35
33
31
29
27
25
23
21
19
17
15
13
11
9
7
5
3
1 (RS)

■ = No stitch

M = M1 Knitwise = Insert LH needle under the horizontal strand between two sts from front to back and K it *through back loop*

Ⅴ = Central Double Increase = (Increases from 1 st to 3 sts) = K into back and then into front of indicated st and slip them off LH needle onto RH needle; insert point of LH needle behind the vertical strand that runs downward between the two sts just made and K *into the front of it*

• = P on RS; K on WS

□ = K on RS; P on WS

 = Slip 2 sts onto cn and hold in front; P2; K2 from cn

 = Slip 2 sts onto cn and hold in back; K2; P2 from cn

 = Slip 2 sts onto cn and hold in front; K2; K2 from cn

= Slip 2 sts onto cn and hold in front; P1; K2 from cn

= Slip next st onto cn and hold in back; K2; P1 from cn

 = Slip 2 sts onto cn and hold in back; K2; K2 from cn

 = Slip 2 sts onto cn #1 and hold in back; slip next st onto cn #2 and hold in back; K2; P1 from cn #2; K2 from cn #1

⋀₅ = (Decreases from 5 sts to 1 st) = Slip next 3 sts with yarn in back, drop yarn; *pass the second st on RH needle over the first st on RH needle; slip first st from RH needle back to LH needle; pass the second st on LH needle over the first st on LH needle; **slip first st from LH needle back to RH needle and repeat from * to ** once more; pick up yarn and K remaining st

MOTIF 23
27 sts (inc to 39 sts)

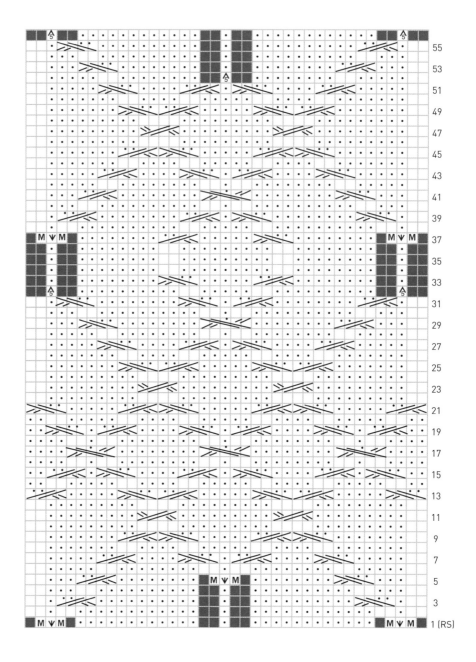

Chart rows (right side, bottom to top): 1 (RS), 3, 5, 7, 9, 11, 13, 15, 17, 19

■ = No stitch

M = M1 Knitwise= Insert LH needle under the horizontal strand between two sts from front to back and K it *through back loop*

V = Central Double Increase = (Increases from 1 st to 3 sts) = K into back and then into front of indicated st and slip them off LH needle onto RH needle; insert point of LH needle behind the vertical strand that runs downward between the two sts just made and K *into the front of it*

• = P on RS; K on WS

☐ = K on RS; P on WS

= Slip 2 sts onto cn and hold in front; P2; K2 from cn

= Slip 2 sts onto cn and hold in back; K2; P2 from cn

= Slip 2 sts onto cn and hold in back; K2; K2 from cn

= Slip 2 sts onto cn #1 and hold in front; slip next st onto cn #2 and hold in back; K2; P1 from cn #2; K2 from cn #1

= (Decreases from 5 sts to 1 st) = Slip next 3 sts with yarn in back, drop yarn; *pass the second st on RH needle over the first st on RH needle; slip first st from RH needle back to LH needle; pass the second st on LH needle over the first st on LH needle; **slip first st from LH needle back to RH needle and repeat from * to ** once more; pick up yarn and K remaining st

⚲ = (Increases from 1 st to 3 sts) = (P1, yarn over, P1) into next st

= Slip 2 sts onto cn and hold in back; K3; P2 from cn

⚯ = P through back loop

= Slip 3 sts onto cn and hold in front; P2; K3 from cn

= Slip next st onto cn and hold in back; K3; P1 from cn

= Slip 3 sts onto cn and hold in front; P1; K3 from cn

= (Decreases from 7 sts to 1 st) = Slip next 4 sts with yarn in back, drop yarn; *pass the second st on RH needle over the first st on RH needle; slip first st from RH needle back to LH needle; pass the second st on LH needle over the first st on LH needle; **slip first st from LH needle back to RH needle and repeat from * to ** twice more; pick up yarn and K remaining st

= Slip next 3 sts onto cn and hold in front; K3; K3 from cn

= Slip next 3 sts onto cn #1 and hold in back; slip next st onto cn #2 and hold in back; K3; P1 from cn #2; K3 from cn #1

MOTIF 25
29 sts (inc to 53 sts)

• = P on RS; K on WS

▓ = No stitch

M = M1 Knitwise= Insert LH needle under the horizontal strand between two sts from front to back and K it *through back loop*

⋎ = Central Double Increase = (Increases from 1 st to 3 sts) = K into back and then into front of indicated st and slip them off LH needle onto RH needle; insert point of LH needle behind the vertical strand that runs downward between the two sts just made and K *into the front of it*

☐ = K on RS; P on WS

⋏ = (Decreases from 7 sts to 1 st) = Slip next 4 sts with yarn in back, drop yarn; *pass the second st on RH needle over the first st on RH needle; slip first st from RH needle back to LH needle; pass the second st on LH needle over the first st on LH needle; **slip first st from LH needle back to RH needle and repeat from * to ** twice more; pick up yarn and K remaining st

 = Slip next 3 sts onto cn and hold in front; P2; K3 from cn

 = Slip next 2 sts onto cn and hold in back; K3; P2 from cn

 = Slip next 3 sts onto cn #1 and hold in back; slip next st onto cn #2 and hold in back; K3; P1 from cn #2; K3 from cn #1

 = Slip 3 sts onto cn #1 and hold in front; slip next st onto cn #2 and hold in back; K3; P1 from cn #2; K3 from cn #1

⋎ = (Increases from 1 st to 3 sts) = (P1, yarn over, P1) into next st

 = Slip next st onto cn and hold in back; K3; P1 from cn

ȣ = P through back loop

 = Slip next 3 sts onto cn and hold in front; P1; K3 from cn

 = Slip next 3 sts onto cn and hold in front; K3; K3 from cn

= Slip 3 sts onto cn and hold in back; K3; K3 from cn

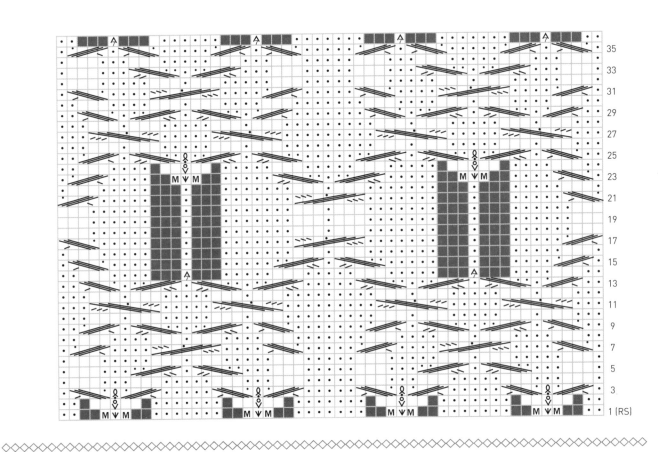

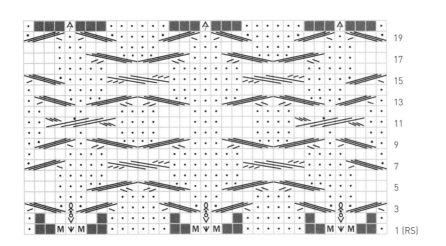

19
17
15
13
11
9
7
5
3
1 (RS)

MOTIF 26
15 sts (inc to 27 sts)

35
33
31
29
27
25
23
21
19
17
15
13
11
9
7
5
3
1 (RS)

MOTIF 27
10 sts (inc to 22 sts)

MOTIF 28
28 sts (inc to 32 sts)

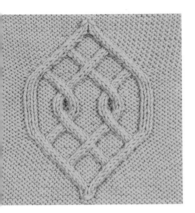

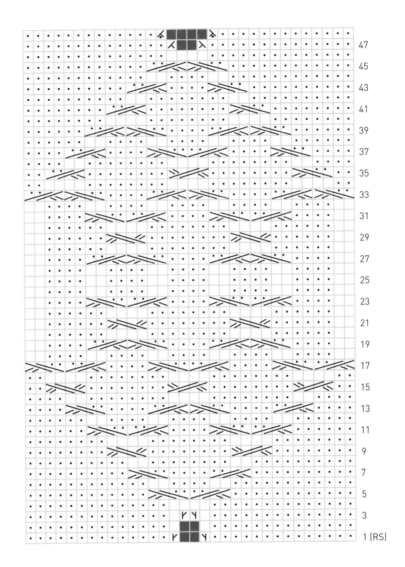

• = P on RS; K on WS

Y = Left lifted increase

■ = No stitch

ⴐ = Right lifted increase

☐ = K on RS; P on WS

 = Slip 2 sts onto cn and hold in back; K2; P2 from cn

= Slip 2 sts onto cn and hold in front; P2; K2 from cn

= Slip 2 sts onto cn and hold in back; K2; K2 from cn

= Slip 2 sts onto cn and hold in front; K2; K2 from cn

⅄ = SSK on RS

⅄ = K2tog on RS

⅄ = K2tog on WS

⅄ = SSK on WS

MOTIF 29
39 sts (inc to 51 sts)

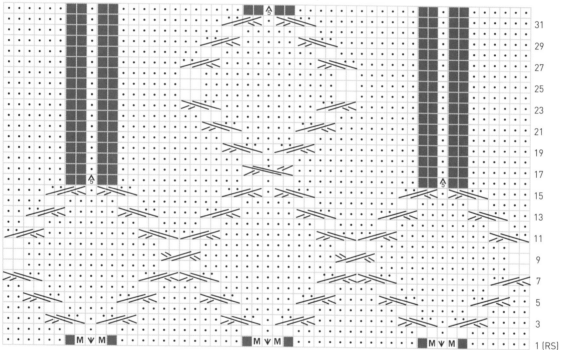

31
29
27
25
23
21
19
17
15
13
11
9
7
5
3
1 (RS)

M = M1 Knitwise = Insert LH needle under the horizontal strand between two sts from front to back and K it *through back loop*

V = Central Double Increase = (Increases from 1 st to 3 sts) = K into back and then into front of indicated st and slip them off LH needle onto RH needle; insert point of LH needle behind the vertical strand that runs downward between the two sts just made and K *into the front of it*

$\underset{5}{\wedge}$ = (Decreases from 5 sts to 1 st) = Slip next 3 sts with yarn in back, drop yarn; *pass the second st on RH needle over the first st on RH needle; slip first st from RH needle back to LH needle;pass the second st on LH needle over the first st on LH needle; **slip first st from LH needle back to RH needle and repeat from * to ** once more; pick up yarn and K remaining st

 = Slip 2 sts onto cn #1 and hold in front; slip next st onto cn #2 and hold in back; K2; P1 from cn #2; K2 from cn #1

MOTIF 30
49 sts (inc to 79 sts)

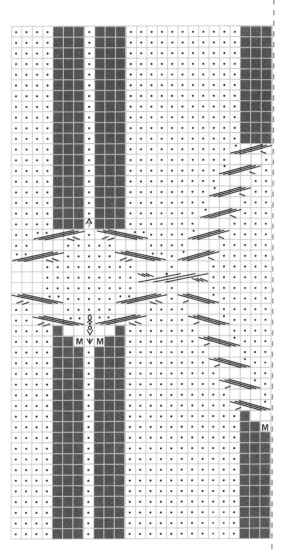

Note: Right-hand side of this chart appears on opposite page on other side of dotted line.

• = P on RS; K on WS

☐ = K on RS; P on WS

■ = No stitch

Ⴘ = (Increases from 1 st to 3 sts) = (P1, yarn over, P1) into next st

M = M1 Knitwise = Insert LH needle under the horizontal strand between two sts from front to back and K it through back loop

= Slip 2 sts onto cn and hold in back; K3; P2 from cn

Ⴘ = P through back loop

V = Central Double Increase = (Increases from 1 st to 3 sts) = K into back and then into front of indicated st and slip them off LH needle onto RH needle; insert point of LH needle behind the vertical strand that runs downward between the two sts just made and K into the front of it

= Slip 3 sts onto cn and hold in front; P2; K3 from cn

= Slip next st onto cn and hold in back; K3; P1 from cn

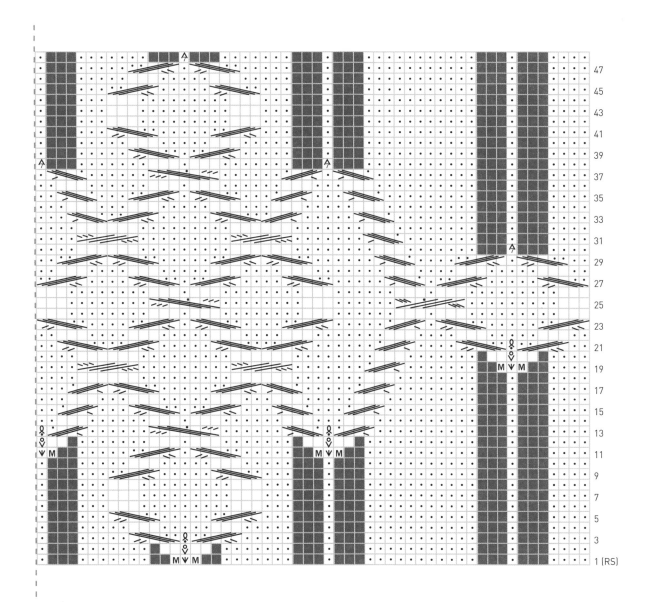

47
45
43
41
39
37
35
33
31
29
27
25
23
21
19
17
15
13
11
9
7
5
3
1 (RS)

 • = Slip next 3 sts onto cn and hold in front; P1; K3 from cn

 = Slip 3 sts onto cn #1 and hold in front; slip next st onto cn #2 and hold in back; K3; P1 from cn #2; K3 from cn #1

 = Slip 3 sts onto cn and hold in back; K3; K3 from cn

 = Slip 3 sts onto cn #1 and hold in back; slip next st onto cn #2 and hold in back; K3; P1 from cn #2; K3 from cn #1

↟ = (Decreases from 7 sts to 1 st) = Slip next 4 sts with yarn in back, drop yarn; *pass the second st on RH needle over the first st on RH needle; slip first st from RH needle back to LH needle; pass the second st on LH needle over the first st on LH needle; **slip first st from LH needle back to RH needle and repeat from * to ** twice more; pick up yarn and K remaining st

MOTIF 31
17 sts (inc to 29 sts)

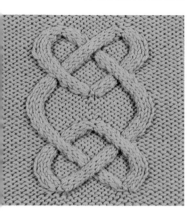

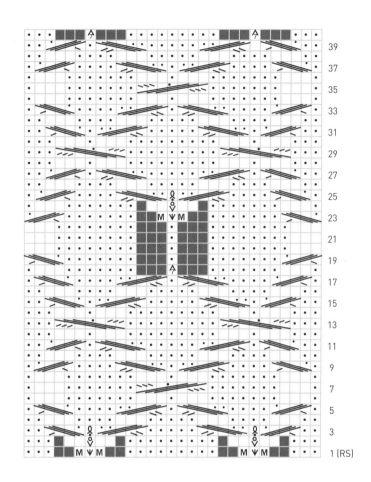

• = P on RS; K on WS

■ = No stitch

M = M1 Knitwise= Insert LH needle under the horizontal strand between two sts from front to back and K it *through back loop*

V = Central Double Increase = (Increases from 1 st to 3 sts) = K into back and then into front of indicated st and slip them off LH needle onto RH needle; insert point of LH needle behind the vertical strand that runs downward between the two sts just made and K *into the front of it*

☐ = K on RS; P on WS

ᛦ = (Increases from 1 st to 3 sts) = (P1, yarn over, P1) into next st

= Slip next st onto cn and hold in back; K3; P1 from cn

ᛩ = P *through back loop*

= Slip next 3 sts onto cn and hold in front; P2; K3 from cn

= Slip next 2 sts onto cn and hold in back; K3; P2 from cn

= Slip next 3 sts onto cn and hold in front; P1; K3 from cn

= Slip next 3 sts onto cn #1 and hold in back; slip next st onto cn #2 and hold in back; K3; P1 from cn #2; K3 from cn #1

= Slip 3 sts onto cn #1 and hold in front; slip next st onto cn #2 and hold in back; K3; P1 from cn #2; K3 from cn #1

ᛘ = (Decreases from 7 sts to 1 st) = Slip next 4 sts with yarn in back, drop yarn; *pass the second st on RH needle over the first st on RH needle; slip first st from RH needle back to LH needle; pass the second st on LH needle over the first st on LH needle; **slip first st from LH needle back to RH needle and repeat from * to ** twice more; pick up yarn and K remaining st

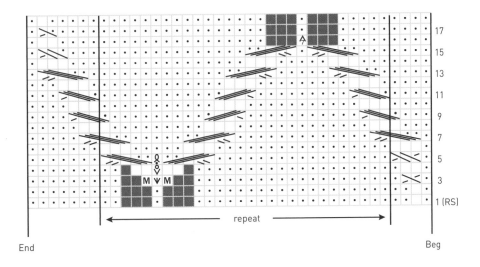

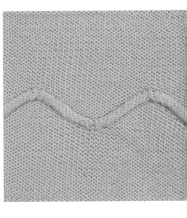

HORIZONTAL BAND 1
mult 22 + 11 sts
(inc to mult 28 + 11 sts)

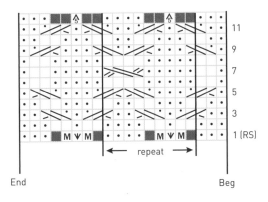

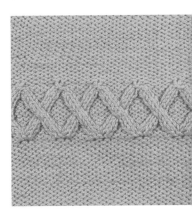

HORIZONTAL BAND 2
mult 5 + 7 sts
(inc to mult 9 + 11 sts)

⟩⟨ = Left Twist = Slip next st onto cn and hold in front; K1; K1 from cn **OR** skip first st and K next st in back loop; then K the skipped st; slip both sts off LH needle together

⟩⟨ = Slip next 2 sts onto cn and hold in front; K1; K2 from cn

⟩⟨• = Slip next 2 sts onto cn and hold in front; P1; K2 from cn

⟩⟨• = Slip next sts onto cn and hold in front; P1; K1 from cn

•⟋⟋ = Slip next st onto cn and hold in back; K2; P1 from cn

⟋⟋⟋ = Slip next 2 sts onto cn and hold in front; K2; K2 from cn

⩜₅ = (Decreases from 5 sts to 1 st) = Slip next 3 sts with yarn in back, drop yarn; *pass the second st on RH needle over the first st on RH needle; slip first st from RH needle back to LH needle; pass the second st on LH needle over the first st on LH needle; **slip first st from LH needle back to RH needle and repeat from * to ** once more; pick up yarn and K remaining st

HORIZONTAL BAND 3
mult 10 + 12 sts
(inc to mult 14 + 16 sts)

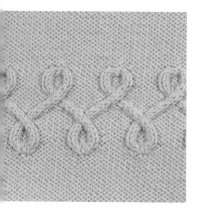

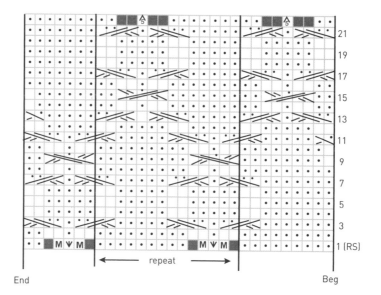

HORIZONTAL BAND 4
mult 10 + 5 sts
(inc to mult 18 + 9 sts)

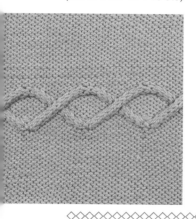

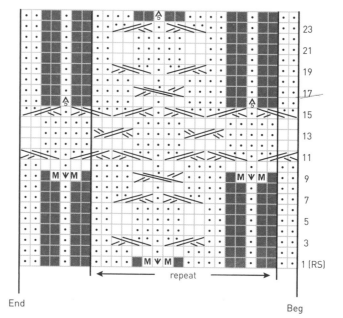

HORIZONTAL BAND 5
mult 10 + 9 sts
(inc to mult 14 + 13 sts)

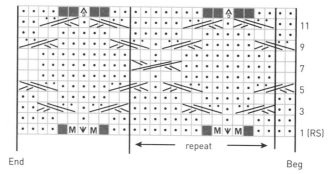

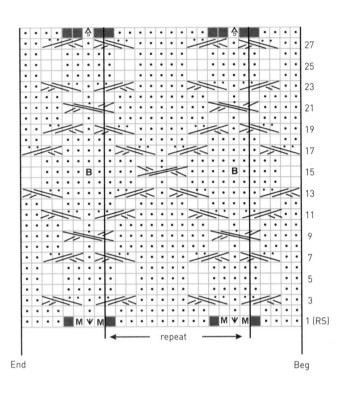

• = P on RS; K on WS

■ = No stitch

M = M1 Knitwise = Insert LH needle under the horizontal strand between two sts from front to back and K it *through back loop*

Ψ = Central Double Increase = (Increases from 1 st to 3 sts) = K into back and then into front of indicated st and slip them off LH needle onto RH needle; insert point of LH needle behind the vertical strand that runs downward between the two sts just made and K *into the front of it*

☐ = K on RS; P on WS

= Slip next 2 sts onto cn and hold in back; K2; P2 from cn

= Slip next 2 sts onto cn and hold in front; P2; K2 from cn

= Slip 2 sts onto cn #1 and hold in front; slip next st onto cn #2 and hold in back; K2; P1 from cn #2; K2 from cn #1

= Slip next st onto cn and hold in front; P1; K1 from cn

= Slip next 2 sts onto cn #1 and hold in back; slip next st onto cn #2 and hold in back; K2; P1 from cn #2; K2 from cn #1

⚠₅ = (Decreases from 5 sts to 1 st) = Slip next 3 sts with yarn in back, drop yarn; *pass the second st on RH needle over the first st on RH needle; slip first st from RH needle back to LH needle; pass the second st on LH needle over the first st on LH needle; **slip first st from LH needle back to RH needle and repeat from * to ** once more; pick up yarn and K remaining st

= Slip 2 sts onto cn and hold in back; K2; K2 from cn

B = Bobble = K into (front, back, front) of next st, turn; P1, (P1, yarn over, P1) all into next st, P1, turn; K5, turn; P2tog, P1, P2tog, turn; slip 2 sts at once knitwise, K1, p2sso

◇◇

HORIZONTAL BAND 7
mult 7 + 9 sts
(inc to mult 11 + 13 sts)

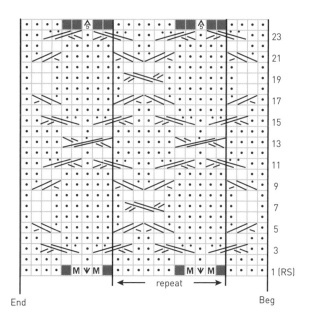

repeat

End   Beg

• = P on RS; K on WS

■ = No stitch

M = M1 Knitwise = Insert LH needle under the horizontal strand between two sts from front to back and K it through back loop

Ⅴ = Central Double Increase = (Increases from 1 st to 3 sts) = K into back and then into front of indicated st and slip them off LH needle onto RH needle; insert point of LH needle behind the vertical strand that runs downward between the two sts just made and K into the front of it

☐ = K on RS; P on WS

= Slip next 2 sts onto cn and hold in back; K2; P2 from cn

= Slip next 2 sts onto cn and hold in front; P2; K2 from cn

= Slip next st onto cn and hold in back; K2; P1 from cn

= Slip next 2 sts onto cn and hold in front; P1; K2 from cn

= Slip next 2 sts onto cn and hold in front; K2; K2 from cn

= Slip next 2 sts onto cn #1 and hold in back; slip next st onto cn #2 and hold in back; K2; P1 from cn #2; K2 from cn #1

⚊ = (Decreases from 5 sts to 1 st) = Slip next 3 sts with yarn in back, drop yarn; *pass the second st on RH needle over the first st on RH needle; slip first st from RH needle back to LH needle; pass the second st on LH needle over the first st on LH needle; **slip first st from LH needle back to RH needle and repeat from * to ** once more; pick up yarn and K remaining st

Ⴤ = Left-slanting lifted increase

Ⴤ = Right-slanting lifted increase

= Slip 2 sts onto cn and hold in back; K2; K2 from cn

⋋ = SSK on RS

⋌ = K2tog on RS

⋋ = K2tog on WS

⋌ = SSK on WS

= Slip 2 sts onto cn #1 and hold in front; slip next st onto cn #2 and hold in back; K2; P1 from cn #2; K2 from cn #1

◇◇

mult 7 + 7 sts
(inc to mult 11 + 11 sts)

35
33
31
29
27
25
23
21
19
17
15
13
11
9
7
5
3
1 (RS)

← repeat →

End   Beg

HORIZONTAL BAND 9
mult 4 + 8 sts
(inc to mult 11 + 13 sts)

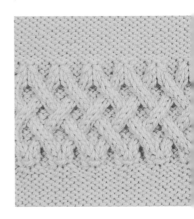

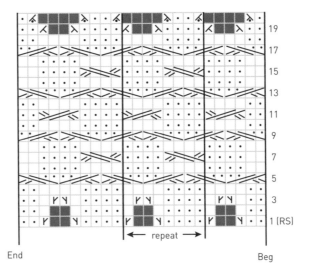

19
17
15
13
11
9
7
5
3
1 (RS)

← repeat →

End   Beg

◇◇

HORIZONTAL BAND 10
mult 12 + 11 sts
(inc to mult 18 + 17 sts)

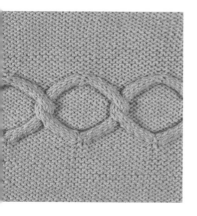

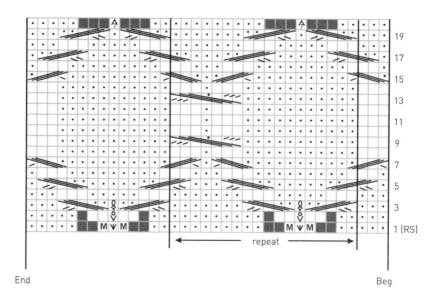

HORIZONTAL BAND 11
mult 11 + 16 sts
(inc to mult 15 + 16 sts)

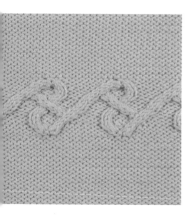

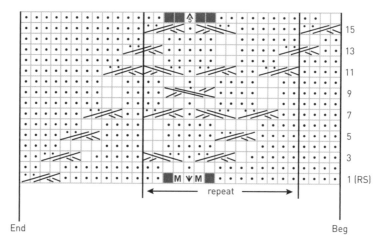

• = P on RS; K on WS

■ = No stitch

M = M1 Knitwise = Insert LH needle under the horizontal strand between two sts from front to back and K it *through back loop*

Ψ = Central Double Increase = (Increases from 1 st to 3 sts) = K into back and then into front of indicated st and slip them off LH needle onto RH needle; insert point of LH needle behind the vertical strand that runs downward between the two sts just made and K *into the front of it*

☐ = K on RS; P on WS

⟍⟍⟋ = Slip 2 sts onto cn and hold in back; K2; P2 from cn

⟍⟍⟋ = Slip 2 sts onto cn and hold in front; P2; K2 from cn

⟍⟍⟋ = Slip 2 sts onto cn and hold in front; K2; K2 from cn

⟍⟍⟋ = Slip 2 sts onto cn #1 and hold in back; slip next st onto cn #2 and hold in back; K2; P1 from cn #2; K2 from cn #1

⟁₅ = (Decreases from 5 sts to 1 st) = Slip next 3 sts with yarn in back, drop yarn; *pass the second st on RH needle over the first st on RH needle; slip first st from RH needle back to LH needle; pass the second st on LH needle over the first st on LH needle;**slip first st from LH needle back to RH needle and repeat from * to ** once more; pick up yarn and K remaining st

⟂ = (Increases from 1 st to 3 sts) = (P1, yarn over, P1) into next st

⟍⟍⟋ = Slip 2 sts onto cn and hold in back; K3; P2 from cn

◇◇

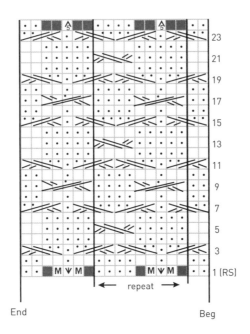

23
21
19
17
15
13
11
9
7
5
3
1 (RS)

repeat

End

Beg

HORIZONTAL BAND 12
mult 5 + 5 sts
(inc to mult 9 + 9 sts)

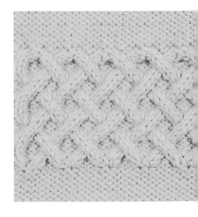

HORIZONTAL BAND 13
mult 14 + 17 sts
(inc to mult 22 + 21 sts)

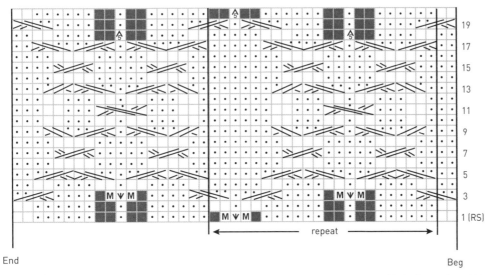

19
17
15
13
11
9
7
5
3
1 (RS)

repeat

End

Beg

 = P *through back loop* on RS; K *through back loop* on WS

 = Slip 3 sts onto cn and hold in front; P2; K3 from cn

 = Slip next st onto cn and hold in back; K3; P1 from cn

 = Slip next 3 sts onto cn and hold in front; P1; K3 from cn

= (Decreases from 7 sts to 1 st) = Slip next 4 sts with yarn in back, drop yarn; *pass the second st on RH needle over the first st on RH needle; slip first st from RH needle back to LH needle; pass the second st on LH needle over the first st on LH needle;

**slip first st from LH needle back to RH needle and repeat from * to ** twice more; pick up yarn and K remaining st

 = Slip 3 sts onto cn #1 and hold in front; slip next st onto cn #2 and hold in back; K3; P1 from cn #2; K3 from cn #1

 = Slip next st onto cn and hold in back; K2; P1 from cn

 = Slip next 2 sts onto cn and hold in front; P1; K2 from cn

 = Slip 2 sts onto cn #1 and hold in front; slip next st onto cn #2 and hold in back; K2; P1 from cn #2; K2 from cn #1

 = Slip 2 sts onto cn and hold in back; K2; K2 from cn

Resources

Here's information on resources and materials, including yarn choice and substitution, materials suppliers, and an index.

YARN CHOICE AND SUBSTITUTION

Each project in this book was designed for a specific yarn. Different yarns possess their own characteristics, which will affect the way they appear and behave when knitted. In order to duplicate the sweaters as photographed, I suggest that you use the designated yarns.

However, if you would like to make a yarn substitution, be sure to choose one of similar weight to the one called for in the pattern. Yarn sizes and weights are usually located on the label, but for an accurate test, knit a swatch of stockinette stitch pattern using the recommended needle size, making it at least 4" (10cm) square.

Count the number of stitches over 4" (10cm) and refer to the table below to determine its weight.

YARN SIZE AND WEIGHT	DESCRIPTION	STITCHES PER 4" (10CM) IN STOCKINETTE STITCH
1 Super Fine	Fingering weight	27 or more
2 Fine	Sport weight	23–26 stitches
3 Light	DK weight	21–24 stitches
4 Medium	Worsted weight	16–20 stitches
5 Bulky	Bulky weight	12–15 stitches
6 Super Bulky	Super Bulky weight	11 or fewer

MATERIAL RESOURCES

Manufacturers

The yarns used in this book are widely available at fine yarn stores everywhere. Use this list of manufacturers and their websites to locate a store in your area.

Aurora Yarns
PO Box 3068
Moss Beach, CA 94038
(650) 728-2730

Brown Sheep Company
100662 County Road 16
Mitchell, NE 69357
(308) 635-2198
www.brownsheep.com

Cascade Yarns
1224 Andover Park E
Tukwila, WA 98188
(206) 574-0440
www.cascadeyarns.com

Classic Elite Yarns
122 Western Avenue
Lowell, MA 01851
(978) 453-2837
www.classiceliteyarns.com

Dale of Norway
4750 Shelburne Road
Shelburne, VT 05482
www.daleofnorway.com

Fiber Trends, Inc.
315 Colorado Park Place
PO Box 7266
E. Wenatchee, WA 98802
www.fibertrends.com

GGH
(see Muench Yarns)

JCA, Inc.
35 Scales Lane
Townsend, MA 01469
(978) 597-8794
www.jcacrafts.com

JHB International, Inc.
1955 South Quince Street
Denver, CO 80231
(303) 751-8100
www.buttons.com

Kolláge Yarns
3591 Cahaba Beach Road, Suite 101
Birmingham, AL 35242
www.kollageyarns.com

Malabrigo Yarn
Gaboto 1277
Montevideo 11200
Uruguay
www.malabrigoyarn.com

Muench Yarns
1323 Scott Street
Petaluma, CA 94954
(707) 763-9377
www.muenchyarns.com

Naturally Yarns
(see Fiber Trends, Inc.)

Ornaghi Filati
(see Aurora Yarns)

Plymouth Yarn Company
500 Lafayette Street
PO Box 28
Bristol, PA 19007
(215) 788-0459
www.plymouthyarn.com

Reynolds Yarn
(see JCA, Inc.)

Rowan Yarns
(see Westminster Fibers)

Tahki/Stacy Charles
70-30 80th Street
Ridgewood, NY 11385
(718) 326-4433
www.tahkistacycharles.com

Westminster Fibers
18 Celina Avenue #17
Nashua, NH 03063
(603) 886-5041
www.westminsterfibers.com

Mail Order and Internet Yarn Source

I always recommend purchasing supplies at your local yarn shop. If there isn't one in your area, try the following:

Patternworks
Route 25
PO Box 1618
Center Harbor, NH 03226
(800) 438-5464
www.patternworks.com

The Knitting Guild Association

To meet other knitters and to learn more about the craft, contact:

The Knitting Guild Association
PO Box 3388
Zanesville, OH 43702-3388
(877) 852-9190
tkga@tkga.com
www.tkga.com

INDEX